Ethics in Higher Education

Values-driven Leaders for the Future

Ethics in Higher Education

Values-driven Leaders for the Future

Divya Singh / Christoph Stückelberger (Eds.)

Globethics.net Education Ethics No. 1

Globethics.net Education Ethics
Series Editors: Divya Singh, Director of Globethics.net Southern Africa.
Vice Principal University of South Africa, South Africa.
Christoph Stueckelberger, President and Founder of Globethics.net, Executive
Director of Geneva Agape Foundation GAF, Professor of Ethics in
Moscow/Russia, Enugu/Nigeria, Beijing/China.
Director: Obiora Ike, Executive Director of Globethics.net in Geneva
and Professor of Ethics at the Godfrey Okoye University Enugu/Nigeria.

Globethics.net Education Ethics 1
Divya Singh / Christoph Stückelberger (Eds.), *Ethics in Higher Education
Values-driven Leaders for the Future*
Geneva: Globethics.net, 2017
ISBN 978-2-88931-164-4 (online version)
ISBN 978-2-88931-165-1 (print version)
© 2017 Globethics.net
Acknowledgements to Unisa for permitting the 2015 ICDE World Conference
logo to be used on the front cover of the book.

Managing Editor: Ignace Haaz
Assistant Editor: Samuel Davies

Globethics.net International Secretariat
150 route de Ferney
1211 Geneva 2, Switzerland
Website: *www.globethics.net/publications*
Email: *publications@globethics.net*

All web links in this text have been verified as of January 2017.

TABLE OF CONTENTS

Introduction 13

SECTION 1: Values in Higher Education

1 Ethics in Higher Education as a Tool for Discovering Our Ultimate Destiny 17
Obiora Ike

    1.1 Introduction 17
    1.2 Ethics Matters 20
    1.3 Defining Education in Context 22
    1.4 Change Process that Leads to Transformation 24
    1.5 Quality and Management of Ethics Education in Higher and Secondary Learning 27
    1.6 Conclusion – The Normative Values of Ethics 28

2 The Significant Role of Higher Education in Developing a Global Ethical Culture 31
Christoph Stückelberger

    2.1 Scandals Destroy Reputation and Capital 31
    2.2 The Decline of Trust: Tasks for Leadership and Governance in Higher Education 32
    2.3 Why a Global and Contextual Ethical Culture is Needed 34
    2.4 Why a Specific Role for Higher Education? 35
    2.5 Reasons for and the Effects of Ethical Challenges in Higher Education 37
    2.6 Which are the Values for a Global Ethical Culture? 39
    2.7 Which Virtues for a Global Ethical Culture? 41

2.8 Strengthening the Ethical Culture of Higher Education:
Eight Recommendations 42

2.9 Conclusion 51

3 Harmony as the Horizon of Higher Education **53**

Paulachan Kochappilly

3.1 Introduction 53

3.2 Discussion 54

3.3 Conclusion 62

**4 The Relationship between the Sustainable Development
Goals and the Role of Higher Education Institutions:
A South African Perspective** **65**

Avani Singh

4.1 Introduction 65

4.2 The Legal Framework for the Right to Higher Education 69

4.3 The Role of Higher Education Institutions 73

4.4 A Transformative Agenda 77

**5 Universities, Cultural Diversity and Global Ethics:
Opportunities for Moral Leadership** **79**

Martin Prozesky

5.1 Introduction 79

5.2 The Global Ethics Movement 80

5.3 Universities, Cultural Diversity and Inclusivity 84

5.4 Practical Considerations for Universities 86

5.5 Chapter References 89

**6 Infusing Ethics into Everyday Practice
in Higher Education** 91

EM Lemmer

6.1 Introduction 91

6.2 Ethics in the Current Context of the University 92

6.3 Ethics and the University: the Educator's Multiple Roles 95

6.4 Concluding Comments 96

6.5 Chapter References.. 97

SECTION 2: Responsible Leadership

**7 Responding to the Challenges of Gendered Career
Aspirations: Responsible Academic Leadership in Support
of the Golden Triad of Access, Equity and Justice** 103

Divya Singh

7.1 Introduction 103

7.2 The Research Survey 105

7.3 Discussion 109

7.4 Recommendations 115

7.5 Conclusion... 120

7.6 Chapter References.. 120

**8 Change Leadership, Ethics and the Future
of Higher Education** 123

Maxim Jean-Louis

8.1 Introduction 123

8.2 The Ethics of Change Leadership................................. 125

8.3 Managing Change... 128

8.4 Conclusion... 130

8.5 Chapter References.. 131

**9 Leadership and Ethics in Higher Education:
Some Perspectives from Experience** **133**

N. Barney Pityana

9.1 Introduction 133
9.2 Discussion 134
9.3 Conclusion... 160

**10 Leadership and Epistemological Responsibility
in African Universities in the 21st Century**............................**163**

Catherine A. Odora-Hoppers

10.1 Introduction: Eurocentric Thought and "Otherness"........... 163
10.2 Inwards to Outwards: What has this Meant
for Strategies for Leadership in Africa? 165
10.3 Implications for Policy and Institutions for the IKS
Initiative in South Africa.. 171
10.4 What this Effort Enables in Scholarly Terms..................... 174
10.5 Facing the Public Policy and the Academic System 175
10.6 Confronting the Epistemological Irresponsibility 178
10.7 Conclusion.. 181
10.8 Chapter References.. 183

**11 Ethical Leadership in Higher Education
in the Era of Complexity**..**187**

Narend Baijnath

11.1 Introduction 187
11.2 A Context of Perpetual Change............................... 191
11.3 University Leadership in the Era of Complexity 197
11.4 Ethical Leadership in the Era of Complexity 200
11.5 Conclusion.. 203
11.6 Chapter References.. 204

SECTION 3: Ethical Topics in Higher Education

12 Governance for Sustainability in Higher Education 217

Heather Davis and Leo Goedegebuure

12.1 Discussion 217

12.2 Case Study: Testing a Corporate Sustainability
Development Model (CSDM) in Australian Universities 221

12.3 Conclusion 225

12.4 Chapter References 227

**13 Building up a Research Ethics System:
Experience of a Teaching University** 231

Kam Cheong Li and Billy T. M. Wong

13.1 Overview 231

13.2 Research Capacity Development of a Teaching University 232

13.3 Building up a Research Ethics System 233

13.4 Tackling Emerging Challenges 237

13.5 Summary 239

13.6 Chapter References 240

**14 Nowhere to Hide? Ethical Social Media Use in Higher
Education Institutions** 245

Jeanette C. Botha

14.1 The Social Media Context in South Africa 245

14.2 The Higher Education Response 251

14.3 Looking Ahead: The Ethical Use of Social Media 254

14.4 Conclusion 256

14.5 Chapter References 257

**15 Universities in Transformation: The Ethics
of Preparing Graduates for Global Citizenship**....................**261**

Mandla Makhanya

    15.1 Introduction 261

    15.2 Discussion 262

    15.3 Conclusion... 266

    15.4 Chapter References... 267

SECTION 4: Open and Distance Education

**16 Some Exploratory Thoughts on *Openness*
and an Ethics of Care**..**273**

Elizabeth Archer & Paul Prinsloo

    16.1 Introduction 273

    16.2 Ethics, Responsibility and Care............................ 274

    16.3 *Openness* in Distance Education 276

    16.4 Openness in OER 277

    16.6 *Openness* in MOOCs.. 278

    16.7 The Fallacy of *Openness* (Moving Beyond Binaries) 280

    16.8 Conclusion... 282

    16.9 Chapter References... 283

17 Open Educational Practice: Caveat Emptor....................**287**

Som Naidu

    17.1 Introduction 287

    17.2 The Case for Open Educational Resources 288

    17.3 The Case for Massive Open Online Courses (MOOCs)...... 291

    17.4 The Case for Open Educational Practices 293

    17.5 Assuring Quality of Educational Provision 295

    17.6 Assuring Quality in the Adoption of OER 297

    17.7 Assuring Quality in the Adoption of MOOCs.................... 299

17.8 Integrity and Duty of Care of Students and Staff 302

17.9 Concluding Remarks 304

17.10 Chapter References 305

18 Universitas Terbuka Indonesia Open Policy: Securing the Rights to Knowledge and Higher Education 311

Daryono & Sri Sedyainingsih

18.1 Background 311

18.2 Introduction 312

18.3 Democratisation of Higher Education 313

18.4 Eradicating the Knowledge Divide...................... 319

18.5 OER Integration into UT Online-Learning........... 322

18.6 Conclusion... 324

18.7 Chapter References.. 324

19 The Advantages of Distance Learning 327

Brad Huddleston

19.1 Creative Engineering to Expand the Internet....... 328

19.2 Unintended Consequences................................. 329

19.3 Neuroscience and Ethics................................... 331

19.4 I No Longer Feel Anything - Anhedonia.............. 332

19.5 The Addictive Process...................................... 333

19.6 Multitasking Is a Myth 334

19.7 Multitasking, Depression and Anger 335

19.8 Digital Education Content Causes the Same Reaction
in the Brain 337

19.9 The Ramifications for Distance Learning............. 338

19.10 Solutions.. 339

19.11 It All Begins at Home..................................... 339

19.12 Remove All Technology from Bedrooms and Sleep 341

19.13 Work Sequentially 342

19.14 Combine Analog When Possible 343

19.15 Dramatically Reduce Screen Time 344

19.16 What We Would NOT Say to a Cocaine Addict 346

Contributing Authors...349

INTRODUCTION

Higher education is leadership education. The values and virtues practised in universities heavily influence the future leaders. Many institutions of higher education show excellence not only in academic subjects, as green campuses, with manifold ethics curricula and in their community engagement, but also in the value-orientation of the Board and teaching staff as well as students. But, additionally, in many universities and schools around the world, fundamental values and virtues are violated: cheating, plagiarism, unethical research, nepotism in staff recruitment, corruption in exams, sexual harassment or simply the lack of ethics curricula give then the signal to the future leaders that 'this is how the world functions' and only with unethical behaviour can one achieve professional success.

This book is a fascinating compilation of 19 articles written by authors from eight countries and five continents. The articles are grouped in four sections: (1) Values in higher education, (2) Responsible Leadership, (3) Education Topics and (4) Open and Distance Education. This fourth topic, and the fact that a part of the authors come from South Africa, specifically shows the origin of this book: it is the fruit of the 26th ICDE World Conference, organised by the International Council for Open and Distance Education ICDE with the University of South Africa UNISA in Johannesburg, held in Sun City in South Africa from 14-16 October 2015 under the theme "Growing Capacities for sustainable Distance E-learning Provision".

The ethics dimension popped up in several contributions, among other also at the Presidents' Summit of almost 100 Presidents of Open and Distance Learning Universities across the globe, but the book is now focused only on this cross-sectoral topic of values. The authors bring a truly international perspective on topics which are similar in many countries, but also rooted in their respective societies and experiences.

The Globethics.net Foundation, a global network on ethics based in Geneva, Switzerland, home to the world's largest free online library on ethics with over 4.5 million books and documents and 176,000 registered participants from 200 countries, decided in its strategy 2016-2020 to make "Ethics in Higher Education" the strategic priority! Globethics.net as publisher of this book is proud to announce that this book is the first volume of a new Series "Education Ethics", in which other volumes will soon follow. We invite authors and organisations around the world to propose and submit manuscripts as single authors or collection of articles around ethics in (higher) education. We together want to contribute to values-driven leaders for the future which our societies so urgently need.

Johannesburg/Geneva, January 2017

Prof. Dr. Divya Singh, Vice-Prinicpal and Ethics Office,
University of South Africa

Prof. Dr. Dr. h.c. Christoph Stückelberger,
President Globethics.net

SECTION 1

Values in Higher Education

1

ETHICS IN HIGHER EDUCATION AS A TOOL FOR DISCOVERING OUR ULTIMATE DESTINY

Obiora Ike

1.1 Introduction

The topic of Ethics, though ancient in its origins, has in our time and clime become a novel and compelling subject, both in its theoretical and practical engagements. Globally, issues of ethics are legion. In the media reporting on local and international cases of scandals around the themes of corruption, bad governance, abuse of public trust, value-less lifestyles, unethical behaviour, conflicts of interest and insider dealings, nepotism and mediocrity, it makes common sense to accept the fact that there is a better way to conduct the affairs of men and women, namely: The Ethical Way. This conclusion leads the agenda of stakeholders in Education to seriously promote Ethics in citadels of learning and in higher Education.

Education is at the center of every human settlement. It is necessary for character formation for the young. Through education, the realization of meaning and purpose in society is enabled and beneficiaries are empowered to gain more access to opportunities, resources and power. Education if acquired continues to increase the value chain of any nation. This explains why the agenda for Education Reform remains priority for almost every country in the world. Under such transformational situations, there is urgency to adapt the world's educational systems to consciously evolve and transform themselves in order to support the critical swifts and transitions happening around the globe. The educational sector is challenged to proffer practical solutions for the challenges that face mankind at this time.

In the ongoing search for 'Promoting Leadership in Thought that leads to Action', the CADMUS Journal on its editorial commentary carried in Volume 2, Issue 5 of October 2015 makes a compelling point which bears repetition in this context. "There is need for multi-dimensional shift in higher education from an over-emphasis on information in an age of information glut to greater emphasis on understanding and organizing principles and relationships between phenomena. There is need to move education from memorization of facts to creative thinking; from passive to active learning; from fragmented to contextual knowledge. There is need to move education from mechanistic to organic or ecological conceptions; from abstract to life-centric studies; from discipline-specific to trans-disciplinary perspectives. Finally, there is need to move education from abstract principles to spiritual values and from subject to person-centered and personality-centered education".

The conclusion of this paper is the fundamental idea that education does not happen in isolation but is carried out through societal, environmental and human channels. Through education, the young and future generations receive knowledge and traditions that help them enter into the totality of reality. Therefore, a primary concern of society essentially is to teach the young. Society can only successfully rebuild itself through the younger generation. This is the opposite of what currently happens. But what do we teach the young? Can the teacher give to students what the teacher does not possess? How do we educate ourselves? How does education take place? Is education anything, nothing or something? Does this something stand for a system that educates what is human in humankind, especially the young, leading to recognition of the needs of humanity through all ages by pointing to their source, origin and end?

This realization helps the dialogue around the topic of education generally, and Ethics in Higher Education in particular. Although expressed in different ways in each individual, culture, custom and forms of diversity, the human heart is one and the same for it reflects the same substance.

The education of the heart of man in its originality as creation made it is one that calls for a genuine concern. Unfortunately, the opposite is the case as many modern societies through education destroy the human heart and innocence. This is where the debate must begin, namely, to distinguish the proper aim of Higher education from that which it is not. It is the ethical dimension for ethics after all is the establishment of right and wrong, founded on reason and what is ought, a category of good conscience, sound moral judgment and the free choice of a rational mind.

A university exists to provide multi-disciplinary and multi-dimensional services to the community. As an autonomous institution at the heart of societies differently organized, the Magna Charta Universitatum states that a university "produces, examines, appraises and hands down culture through research and teaching'. To hand down culture is to transmit traditions and adaptable ways of life. Culture in itself is not static but constantly dynamic, containing values, wisdom and knowledge tested over generation. One major component from the above definition is to state that a university is Knowledge and value Provider. It stands or fails in its ability or inability to deliver on these criteria. Properly stated, education conveys learning and character. If it provides only one aspect, it lacks in wholeness, leading to the failures which many institutions operate and humanity suffers. The point is gradually clear. University teachers produce the global leaders of tomorrow. Fact is that the teachers are leaders of future leaders because they train the young. Teachers therefore bear a grave responsibility in their institutions, alongside parents, the government and the Media with the traditional institutions amongst others, to encourage value-driven leadership through the content, curriculum and methods of training professionals.

1.2 Ethics Matters

Worldwide, information is multiplying at a phenomenal rate. Globalization has increased the social space, leading to borderless boundaries on the financial, economic, social, ecological, political and cultural dimensions of traditional societies. The world is changing with unprecedented speed and this is observed in virtually all sectors including within the university walls. Following the financial crisis of 2008 and the collapse of institutions and even governments, a phenomenon that started in the United States of America in year 2008, people lost jobs, investments and retirement funds. An example of the crisis was the collapse of a world class company ENRON, alongside others and many wondered how this could be possible. The deeper meaning in the fall of this company is the fact that any system or governing structure is only as good as the people who administer it. In the case of ENRON, the need for morally informed corporate governance, founded on solid ethical principles, has been quite obvious. Abdicating such leadership in attempting to cover up poor management decisions is something that cannot stand if our society is to be free and virtuous. Writing in the New York Times in his January 18 Editorial, Paul Krugman made the point that the "Enron debacle was not just the story of a company that failed. It is the story of a system that failed. And the system did not fail through carelessness. It was corrupted".

Yet, teachers in Business schools and educational institutions who had over the years turned out first class students and highly successful professionals and excellent specialists wondered at how this could happen with their bright students acting in freedom as 'moral crooks' but lacking in responsibility and virtue! Educational institutions produced them. These institutions are challenged to revisit their educational content, the school curricula and their overall systems which produce bright managers lacking in integrity and engage in teaching, training and research that links the heart and the mind of the human person in wholeness.

The few and simple questions to ask for the purposes of this paper include the following but is not necessarily exhausted or even in order of priority, namely:

1. What does education consist of, and how does it take place?
2. How can parents, teachers in schools, the responsible agents in the educational system and institutions within the larger society assist the education of youth and leaders of tomorrow with school curricula that contains Ethics and promotes freedom, truth, responsibility, skills, knowledge and virtue?
3. Is there a link between Ethics and Technology and how do we balance technological innovation with social and organizational motivation?
4. Does diversity and difference in contextually independent realities make a unity on global values and virtues impossible?
5. What possibilities exist to strengthen classroom curricula of studies that enhance both character and learning?
6. Is it possible to combine distance-learning education with formation of character in the ongoing available platforms of distance education?
7. How can societies and responsible agents systematically strengthen an ethical culture of integrity?

8. If young students are confronted with corrupt employers in a permissive and corrupt society, what mechanisms of support exist to promote values-driven education of students in their professional life especially in the early years?

At this period of world history, much of humanity stand in trepidation on the crossroads of insecurity, dissatisfaction, anxiety, wars, corruption, meaninglessness, discontent, unhappiness, economic and social upheavals. On the other hand however, the challenges of the present creates great opportunities, chances and hope for humanity on the threshold, using the tools of Education to promote responsible leaders who govern nations and institutions across cultures and borders. Such leaders shall be driven by universal values that sustain life and development for all and lead to the much expected paradigm shift on international discourse towards a world for everybody that is peaceful and sustainable.

1.3 Defining Education in Context

It does seem that many have an opinion about education and for that very fact divergent views that are predicated on personal experience. Several definitions depict varied understandings and points of view around the topic of Education. The English word 'Education' itself is borrowed from the old Latin word 'duco' which root means 'to Lead', to guide. Education which is abbreviated from the Latin roots of 'duco' and 'vocation', namely 'educo - educare- educavi- educatum' give vent to wider meanings and understandings which include aspects of: 'leadership, cultured; knowledgeable and learned. To lead others implies ability to lead with requisite knowledge, methods and ends. In considering the term therefore, the dimension of reasoning and acting emerge in the open discourse concerning the dual but integrated role of educational institutions in preparing the citizenry to become enlightened and civic –minded persons.

From the viewpoint of looking at things from their essence, purpose, last end and primary goals, to educate means to help the human soul to enter into the totality of the real. This gift and ability of humans to think and reason, described as rationality was considered by the Greek philosopher Aristotle over two thousand years ago as unique to humankind. Integral Education makes possible the emergence of all-round persons, equipped upon completion of studies to transform society and positively. This is the business of a university in the current times. In defining education in the context of society in the twenty first century, 'true education' must be an 'education in criticism'. It is the exercise to question things from their origin, allowing doubt and examination of the problem to come to a balanced conclusion and position. Therefore, 'krinein', 'krisis' which is the original Greek word for 'critique' means to 'take hold of things' and explore their content. This exploration of the content, such as the received 'tradition' is compared with the other realities including the 'longings of the heart'. To criticize helps the inquirer to arrive at the need for the true, the ultimate, the beautiful and the inner standard of judgment which is identical for all humans. It is the search for the Good.

Ethics in Higher education seeks exactly to become a vehicle to make people original and whole in thought and belief. In order to educate, we need to present the past in a suitable form. If young people are not taught about the past and tradition, they shall have a future without guide and may grow up either unbalanced or skeptical. In educating the youth, the past is presented within the context of life where experience speaks for itself. For the purposes of emphasis therefore, education must be critical. The young student must be exposed to the past through the experience that can propose that past and justify it through life experience. This is what ethics in higher education seeks to achieve.

1.4 Change Process that Leads to Transformation

The challenges facing humanity at this time are many. The questions for humankind in virtually every country revolve often around the contradictions and issues of meaning and meaninglessness, truth and relativity, poverty and wealth, governance and insecurity, economic stability and greed occasioning harm, the crisis of leadership and insurrection in many places challenged by rising radicalism and the use of terror. Other major challenges are ecological as we face diminishing resources, climate change and environmental degradation unknown in millennia of the existence of humanity. There are overall threats to legacies inherited as tradition as well as value orientation and questions of life byu a new generation of young people, eager to live well and move on, but not knowing how. How can value-orientation and value-driven leadership emerge with the right solutions to the many problems? The answer given by those who know is that Education is the key. It gives a new way especially such education that has foundations on knowledge and character.

Outlines for educational re-orientation mention the urgent need for a new vision for education. Such a new vision is radical in its nature because the topic of education especially for the teacher is referred to as a vocation and not a job. This new vision understands a shift from knowledge to practice and is aimed at self-reliance and sustainable education. This approach conveys the values of responsibility and transformation which prepare students for the position of global citizenship. With such shift, education protects and promotes the dignity of the human person and strives to create equal access to many.

Yet, required performance has barely improved in decades. Mckinsey (2007) in his report on "How the World's best performing school system come out on top" establishes many different ways for the improvement of the school system despite all complexity. He identifies three factors that make schools succeed and excel above others namely: a) getting the right people to become teachers: b) developing the teachers into effective instructors; c) ensuring that the system is able to deliver the best possible instruction for every child.

According to Fullan (2012) the deliberate attempt to use 'change knowledge' to bring about whole-system reform in schools is barely fifteen years old. By change knowledge, he was referring to ideas and strategies that cause the system to move forward in performance, especially when it comes to raising the bar and closing the gap for all students. This model is particularly interesting to study because of the multiple strategies selected by school systems to ensure that they accomplish holistic change. Eight steps are proposed, based on the work of John Kotter (2011) that assist and guide the education for change approach and the process that leads to transformation in the sector with ethical challenges.

i.   Establish a sense of urgency: This implies an urgent examination of the current realities of the education system. Without Ethics in higher institutions, students with much knowledge emerge but often lacking in character, lack in meaning and solid foundations. It is therefore necessary to build a compelling story using data and align it to economic indicators that reflect national development and quality of life. It must be compelling enough to reflect current and potential crises that can come from in-action. It also grants major opportunities inherent in the current situation of interdisciplinary models of education.

ii. Form a powerful guiding coalition: This is the role of the ICDE and other stakeholders in the education sector to lead the change agenda in Higher education for ethical orientation of students and future leaders.

iii.   Create a vision for all stakeholders: the questions to ask include the following: How do we help create a vision that will direct the change effort? What strategies can we develop to achieve our vision for educational progress and systems?

iv.   Communicating the vision: These include the strategies for implementation, the monitoring framework and networking. Questions to ask include: What impression does a new teacher bring concerning our educational institution? How shall this impression change after a period of 6 to 12 months serving the institution?

v.   Empower others to act on the vision: The Leadership has potential to identify real and imaginary obstacles to the agenda of transformation and works to find solutions. People at the decision levels can take risks and think outside of the conventional approaches if delegated to do so.

vi.   Planning for and creating short term wins: The basic question towards a successful transformation plan is to ask 'How can we measure performance in a visible or verifiable manner?' The next step would be to identify improvements and strategies ranging from interventions in teacher quality, teachers assessment model, students literacy and numeracy gaps, conducive school environment gaps, and gaps in instructional leadership understanding and modeling. Finally we should always seek for ways to reward performance.

vii.   Consolidating improvements and producing more change: Here, one builds on the credibility of successes recorded. A framework is established to consider the methodology of moving away from public service longevity model where promotions come based on group mentality and not on personal achievement and professional effort. Benchmarks for rewards shall be established with the change action plan.

viii. Institutionalizing new approaches: How do we overcome the fad mentality as we plan to change and transform the education system? How do we institutionalize the changes and successes we have accomplished so it reflects at all levels of our educational system and processes? How do we recruit the best minds and encourage them to stay within our schools system? How do we create a wow effect at our most rural schools as a measure of our institutional quality? How do we ensure leadership development and succession? These form part of the thinking in the initial and mid-level assessment of performance.

1.5 Quality and Management of Ethics Education in Higher and Secondary Learning

The key factors that may lead to success in this endeavour to establish quality education and proper management of Ethics in institutions of higher learning and even in secondary schools include some of the following factors:

i. Forming and strengthening at the international level, an advocacy think-tank such as the ICDE, the Globethics.net and others that among other education reform thinking shall lobby at all levels of government and educational regulatory institutions for an education model that establishes a curriculum framework that is different from the current smorgasbord approach.

ii. Build a structured collaboration with teacher education systems for hiring new teachers and re-training existing teachers in line with the vision for a result-oriented student centered school system in ethics matters.

iii.   Create a mentor teacher support structure for supporting new teachers in the first three years of joining the profession. This structure will also serve as a peer review and support team for experienced teachers not meeting performance expectation based on their student achievement.

iv.   Empowering the heads of ethics departments with   resources necessary to deal with the obstacles that hinder the change process

v.   Build an assessment structure that will measure student overall achievement outside traditional frameworks and review indicators for measuring teacher overall efficacy – using student performance and professional development hours as some indicators. This assessment structure will not be used solely for measuring student or teacher rankings but for making decisions that improve whole school systems.

vi.   Continually review curriculum in subjects of Ethics to give room for topics that relate to freedom and responsibility.

vii.   Ensure that the students of universities already in early years in the university are made to attend the lectures on an obligatory level as General studies

viii.   Ensure methods of reward and punishment by awarding prizes and aiding endowments and scholarships on Ethics Studies

1.6 Conclusion – The Normative Values of Ethics

In conclusion, it is important to state that the normative value of ethics in life explores what is our origin as human beings. It takes into consideration the fact 'the unexamined life is not worth living;' to quote the ancient sage, Socrates. Without the fundamental factors of self-critique, of the ethical questioning and practical engagement, of the fundamental factors of tradition – something lived out in the present that proposes and gives its reasons – the youth would remain fragile, doubtful and sceptical. Exposure to life's experiences which is achieved beyond the classroom is risky. But it helps the student to become authentic, standing on one's own feet and daring the current. This is not the domain of Ethics in Higher education but the normative value of ethics and life. It is confrontation with man's real identity and the questions of contradictions of life, yet tackled beyond doubt.

In this quest for the establishment of the value of life for education, higher learning institutions integrate ethics and ecology in their programs. The context of a new vision for education which calls for mindset shift from reading and writing to skills acquisition with relevance for daily life and society becomes imperative. Ethics education is opportunity for a new value orientation. Such education ensures the training of both the teacher and the student, develops new technologies and conclusively allows a new vision, a new policy, a new market, new resources and a new system. The normative value of this kind of education is the emergence of a new humanity of responsible leaders driven by values and virtues and knowledgeable enough to transform their environment and serve entire humanity in a new society yearning for ethical and fair minded leaders.

2

THE SIGNIFICANT ROLE OF HIGHER EDUCATION IN DEVELOPING A GLOBAL ETHICAL CULTURE[1]

Christoph Stückelberger

2.1 Scandals Destroy Reputation and Capital

Integrity is the most important capital of a person and of an institution. It is an ethical capital which is also closely linked to financial capital! Three recent cases in 2015 show this clearly: Volkswagen, a world leader in the automobile industry, lost as a result of the scandal over the manipulation of diesel emissions readings over 25 billion euros in stock value in two weeks, which is more than the market capitalisation of global companies such as the largest reinsurer Allianz. In addition, billions of dollars and euros will have to be paid in penalties. Some analysts say that it is not sure that the company can survive this crisis.[2] And last, the President and Vice President of the world football federation FIFA (with its headquarters in Zurich, only a

---

[1] The article is based on the keynote speech at the President's Summit of the International Council for Open and Distance Education ICDE, hosted by UNISA, South Africa, 14-15 Oct 2015.

[2] "Kosten für Abgasskandal könnten VW zerstören", Handelszeitung 23 Sept 2015. http://www.handelszeitung.ch/unternehmen/kosten-fuer-abgas-skandal-koennten-vw-zerstoeren-867449

few kilometres from where I live), have been suspended for suspected illegal transfers. FIFA, after years of corruption scandals, has lost its reputation.[3] Switzerland's largest newspaper, the Tages-Anzeiger, on its front page last week, stated that the main quality of the next President of FIFA must be integrity![4] There are other examples of the importance of integrity in the field of higher education. Who could have imagined that in Germany, with its good reputation for quality education, the Minister of Defence Ursula von der Leyen, has been accused of plagiarism in her doctoral thesis. And two other ministers of the German Government, Schawan and zu Guttenberg, have already lost their positions in government for the same reason.

2.2 The Decline of Trust: Tasks for Leadership and Governance in Higher Education

Such scandals lead to a decrease in trust in individuals and in institutions worldwide. The Global Edelman Trust Barometer, published annually since 2001, in its latest report for 2015 shows the decline of trust in NGOs from 66% to 63%, in business from 59% to 57% and in the media from 53% to 51% when compared to the 2014 report. Only trust in governments slightly increased from the low level of to 45% to 48% (see chart).

---

[3] „Der Kollaps der FIFA", Neue Zürcher Zeitung, 9 Oct 2015, frontpage.
[4] Res Strehle: „Auf FIFA-Präsident Joseph Blatter darf jetzt auch ein staubtrockner Funktionär folgen. Hauptsache: integer." Tages-Anzeiger, 9 Oct 2015, frontpage.

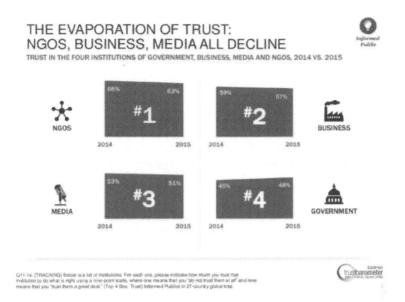

THE EVAPORATION OF TRUST:
NGOS, BUSINESS, MEDIA ALL DECLINE
TRUST IN THE FOUR INSTITUTIONS OF GOVERNMENT, BUSINESS, MEDIA AND NGOS, 2014 VS. 2015

The Edelman Trust Barometer 2014 asked 33'000 people from 27 countries about their trust in academics. "67% responded that they see academics as credible spokespersons, a particularly high mark in comparison to other groups. It is important for academics to be cognizant of this, and not to damage this reputation"[5]. The Trust Barometer also lists four clusters of 16 attributes that are key in building trust: integrity, engagement, products and services, purpose and operations.

---

[5] https://experientialcomms.wordpress.com/2014/01/24/trust-and-higher-education-lessons-for-academics-presidents-and-communicators/

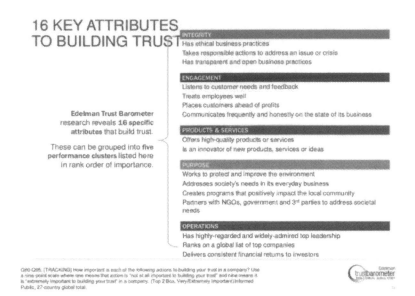

16 KEY ATTRIBUTES TO BUILDING TRUST

Edelman Trust Barometer research reveals 16 specific attributes that build trust.

These can be grouped into five performance clusters listed here in rank order of importance.

INTEGRITY
Has ethical business practices
Takes responsible actions to address an issue or crisis
Has transparent and open business practices

ENGAGEMENT
Listens to customer needs and feedback
Treats employees well
Places customers ahead of profits
Communicates frequently and honestly on the state of its business

PRODUCTS & SERVICES
Offers high-quality products or services
Is an innovator of new products, services or ideas

PURPOSE
Works to protect and improve the environment
Addresses society's needs in its everyday business
Creates programs that positively impact the local community
Partners with NGOs, government and 3rd parties to address societal needs

OPERATIONS
Has highly-regarded and widely-admired top leadership
Ranks on a global list of top companies
Delivers consistent financial returns to investors

Q96-Q95. [TRACKING] How important is each of the following actions to building your trust in a company? Use a nine-point scale where one means that action is "not at all important to building your trust" and nine means it is "extremely important to building your trust" in a company. (Top 2 Box, Very/Extremely Important) Informed Public, 27-country global total.

Trust in institutions and people is of specific importance in four sectors of each society because they are pillars for impartial opinion, truth and the promotion of the common good over individual interests: the judicial system, the media, educational institutions and religious institutions. Within these sectors, the leadership and governance structures hold a special responsibility.

2.3 Why a Global and Contextual Ethical Culture is Needed

Ethical, values-driven behaviour is needed in all societies. But in a globalized world, common values are needed since this world is highly interconnected and interdependent, linked by trade, information and communication technologies, fast social media, the free trade of goods and partially free movement of people. Global interaction needs a common set of values such as a sense of justice, fairness and peace and virtues such as respect and integrity. Without this common set of values with trust as the condition for exchange cooperation is not possible.

Open and distance learning educational institutions, which we represent here, are not exempt.

Open, globalized societies clash with manifold '–isms', such as nationalism, fundamentalism, ethnicism, racism, sexism, terrorism and egoism. Such ideologies are often a reaction to a loss of identity or to the fear of this loss. The openness that resulted from economic and technological globalization happened so fast that political, cultural and ethical globalization is lagging behind. New technologies such as mobile phones can profoundly transform the world within a few years, but to transform values and virtues needs a generation. Therefore, the technological and economic speed of globalization has to slow down a bit (decelerate) and the ethical, cultural and political globalization has to speed up substantially (accelerate).[6]

An open interdependent world needs common values in order to be sustainable. Unity with global values and diversity with contextual values belong together. Being global citizens *and* belonging to a specific nation, religious or ethnic group is not a contradiction, both are needed. Together they build the foundation for peace, sustainability and equality.

2.4 Why a Specific Role for Higher Education?

Higher education in general can and has to play a key role in this process of balancing global and contextual perspectives in building identities through research, teaching and training. Even if open and distance education seems to be delocalised and disconnected from a specific context, it can and has to promote contextual identities by reflecting and researching on it. In a more specific way, *ethics* in higher education is a central part of this objective.

---

[6] See Christoph Stückelberger, Global Trade Ethics. An Illustrated Overview, Geneva 2002, 158f.

Many professionals with a higher education are excellent specialists but moral crooks. After the financial crisis of 2008, business schools worldwide were called upon to revise their educational system to avoid producing managers who have been seen as contributors to the crisis. How can an ethical culture of integrity be systematically strengthened? How can the respective curricula be developed? How can values-driven behaviour be integrated into the process of staff recruitment? How can technological innovation be balanced with social and organisational innovation? How can distance education be combined with character development? How can values-driven students be supported in their first years of professional life when confronted with corrupt employers and societies?

University leaders, as global leaders, can and do play a key role in strengthening ethical values and virtues. University leaders are leaders of future leaders. The integrity and ethical values of leaders, institutions and of the curricula of higher education are crucial in building trust and credible professionals.

The currently high reputation of academic institutions as being non-partial, fair, objective and at the service of the whole community and of the common good of humanity is being threatened in ways that are deeply worrying. The cheating culture[7] is on the increase, academic fraud[8] and plagiarism is becoming more frequent than in the past, albeit partly thanks to the emergence and use of online publications and plagiarism software[9], corruption in educational institutions[10] has become

---

[7] David Callahan, The Cheating Culture: Why more Americans are doing wrong to get ahead, Orlando: Harcourt 2004.

[8] Eckstein, M. A. (2003) Combating Academic Fraud: Towards a Culture of Integrity, Paris: International Institute for Educational Planning.

[9] Marsh, B. (2007) Plagiarism: Alchemy and Remedy in Higher Education, Albany, NY: State University of New York Press; Creating the Ethical Academy: A Systems Approach to Understanding Misconduct and Empowering Change. Taylor and Francis. Kindle Edition, 2011, 10.

[10] Stephen P. Heinemann, The Concern with Corruption in Higher Education, in Creating the Ethical Academy: A Systems Approach to Understanding

so widespread that more and more employers no longer trust the validity of academic grades and certificates.

2.5 Reasons for and the Effects of Ethical Challenges in Higher Education

What are the reasons for and the effects of this development? Let me just mention four of them:

1) Pressure: For many parents and societies, higher education seems to be the only valuable goal. The pressure is so high that young persons and their parents use all means at their disposal to get a bachelor or master degree. The effect of this pressure and of one-sided public educational strategies is that we have millions of jobless academics and not enough young people with vocational training. But studies show that innovation of a country does not only depend on a strong academic sector, but on balanced educational instruments. Switzerland and Germany are examples: Switzerland is regularly rated among the most innovative countries in the world[11] but when compared with other countries it has a relatively low percentage of young people with a university degree and a high percentage of those who have vocational training.

2) Finance: in many countries, academic staff is not well paid compared to other sectors such as the private sector. With the minimum income, teachers are tempted to increase income by receiving bribes in the form of money and sexual services. The

Misconduct and Empowering Change, Taylor and Francis. Kindle Edition, 2011, 13-26; NATHAN F. HARRIS AND MICHAEL N. BASTEDO, Corruption at the Top. Ethical Dilemmas in College and University Governance, Creating the Ethical Academy: A Systems Approach to Understanding Misconduct and Empowering Change. Taylor and Francis. Kindle Edition, 2011, 115.
[11] World Economic Forum, Global Competitiveness Report 2014-2015, launched 30 Sept 2015, p. xx

effect is that students learn by example. It is a lesson that they are taught indirectly: in order to be successful in a profession, one needs to accept immoral behaviour. This then continues the vicious circle of corruption, low performance and lack of competitiveness that can also include losing lives: accountants, medical doctors, construction engineers, etc. put people at risk and even take lives if they have a diploma but not the knowledge to practice professionally. (Example: A professor of medicine in an African country told me he would never allow his son, who is a medical doctor, to treat him. I was surprised and asked why. His answer: "Because I know how he got his degree" [he meant bribes, without the need to explicitly say it]. A late confession.) In some countries and especially in public educational institutions, the salaries of teachers, including university professors, are not paid for months, which then leads to dramatic financial hardship and unethical consequences. A colleague of mine, a professor in DR Congo, decided to go hunger strike a few months ago because he was not paid for six months the salary that was promised and signed for by the government for his professorship at a university in Kinshasa (his name, like many others had been deleted from the salary list and replaced by the names of fake relatives of person responsible for managing the salaries in the public administration).

3) Privatisation: the boom of new, mainly private institutions of higher education in many countries is a positive sign that there is a need, a market and entrepreneurs and investors who are willing to make the most of the opportunity and to take the risk. But strong competition leads also to the temptation of fast success, cheap solutions, lack of qualified teaching staff with integrity and a lack of a sustainable ethical foundation of these institutions.

There is a need therefore not only for a strong academic, but also for an ethical rating of institutions of higher education.

4) <u>Technology</u>: Information and Communication Technologies (ITCs) represent a huge potential for higher education and are obviously the back bone of open and distance learning education. The advantages and future potential are still huge. But each technology is ambiguous when looked at from an ethical perspective. It can be used for good and for bad, to save lives and take lives, to democratise knowledge and to control or centralise knowledge. Excellent distance learning possibilities are improved with ICTs but at the same time cybercrime is increasing and cyber security decreasing. The ethical and legal development[12] is always behind technological development. That is why ethics in higher education needs to look at the ethics of technologies, especially ICTs.[13]

2.6 Which are the Values for a Global Ethical Culture?

A global ethical culture is based on common values. Before we divide human beings by colour, race, sex, religion, wealth and class, we have to remember that all human beings have similar basic human needs: physical needs such as food, water and housing, development needs such as the freedom to decide and implement, orientation needs such as education, social needs such as community and security, emotional needs such as respect, dignity and justice (fair treatment), spiritual needs such as a belief system that gives life meaning, energy for motivation, forgiveness for failures and dealing with major life

---

[12] See e.g. the many challenges listed at the international conference on Cyberlaw, Cybercrime and Cybersecurity in Nov. 2016 in New Delhi. http://cyberlawcybercrime.com/
[13] See: Globethics.net (Ed.), *Ethics in the Information Society*. The nine 'P's'. A discussion paper on the WSIS+10 process 2013-2015, Globethicsa.net Texts no 4, Geneva 2013. Free download here: http://www.globethics.net/texts-series

events such as birth and death. These needs lead to <u>core values</u> common to all human beings: <u>dignity, freedom, justice, equity, peace, security, community, inclusiveness, participation, forgiveness, reconciliation.</u> They together build the Tree of Values. Each main branch of the tree is a value. They belong together and are interconnected. In each culture, the interpretation and also the weight of each value is contextual, e.g. individual freedom is more or less relevant when compared with that of the collective community. Therefore, an intense dialogue and sharing of values is needed.[14]

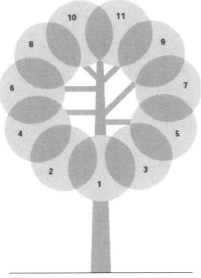

Tree of Values

---

[14] This is an ongoing process in Globethics.net. See many publications in the online library on ethics with 1,8 million full text documents downloadable for free: www.globethics.net/libraries. Specifically: *Principles of Sharing Values across Cultures and Religions*. Globethics.net Texts no. 1, Geneva 2013; Ariane Hentsch Cisneros/ Shanta Premavardhana (eds.), *Sharing Values. A Hermeneutics for Global Ethics*, Global Series no. 4, Geneva 2011*Globethics.net Principles on Equality and Inequality for a sustainable Economy*, Globethics.net Texts no 5, Geneva 2014. Download for free: www.globethics.net/publications.

Institutions of higher education are key drivers in promoting these values. Many mission statements of universities express the importance of values. Last week I visited the University of Nigeria in Enugu, Nigeria. Its motto is "Restore the Dignity of Man" with human dignity as a key postcolonial value. "The African University shaping futures in the service of humanity" is the vision of the University of South Africa Unisa. Graduates are there to serve society. This is the key value. In many mission statements, excellence is mentioned and envisaged. Excellence is important for higher education which claims to be of top quality. But excellence is not a goal in itself. Excellence in innovating new methods of criminal cyberattacks or more cruel chemical weapons is unethical, but excellence in developing new medicine against malaria or improved integrity in public administration is ethical. Therefore, excellence has to be specified by reference to values.

2.7 Which Virtues for a Global Ethical Culture?

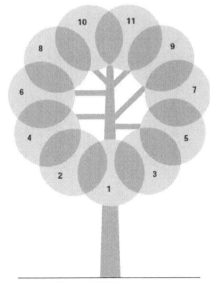

Tree of Virtues

For decades, as an ethicist, I have emphasized the importance of values and of embedding them in institutional structures such as codes of conduct and planning and monitoring mechanisms. But values as institutional and individual benchmarks need to be combined with virtues for individual behaviour. FIFA, Volkswagen or universities that have suffered reputation damage normally have good values statements. But they also need the individual integrity of their employees and especially of their top leaders. <u>Core virtues</u> for a global ethics are <u>honesty, compassion, care, transparency, accountability, reliability, respect, humility, courage, gratitude and generosity</u>. The list is not exclusive. And again, these virtues are common to all humans across cultures, but they have different contextual meanings and colour in the different value systems. On the international level, one virtue has become the most prominent: integrity. It is the sum of all the different virtues. A person with integrity is honest, credible, not opportunistic, but looking after and being faithful to the values of the institution and the community before looking for personal benefit.

2.8 Strengthening the Ethical Culture of Higher Education: Eight Recommendations

2.8.1 Individual and Interpersonal Level

Recommendation 1: Promote character education (for students and teachers) as a task of individual and interpersonal self-responsibility in order to become or remain globally responsible leaders.

A special challenge is how to combine distance education with character development. Face to face encounters are important for character education, but distance education offers many possibilities, especially through comments and by accompanying students.

2.8.2 Intra-Institutional Level

Recommendation 2: Develop within each educational institution ethics-related policies and respective institutional ethics units as key instruments.

How can an ethical culture of integrity be systematically strengthened? Within the institution, the role of charters, mission statements and specialised ethics and integrity officers are important. Ethics does not deal only with human resource management or research ethics, but needs a cross-sectoral approach throughout the institution. The following dimensions are part of it:

- Develop and integrate special ethics curricula in all faculties and reflect on aspects of values in all courses;
- Integrate in staff recruitment values-driven behaviour in addition to professional knowledge;
- Balance technological innovation with social and organisational innovation;
- Support values-driven students in their first years of professional life when confronted with corrupt employers and unethical decisions in society;
- Deal with corruption (financial, sexual, relational/ nepotism/favouritism) with a respective policy; [15]
- Develop (or review where existing) a policy on research ethics with a research ethics committee;
- Develop (or review where existing) a gender policy; and
- Develop (or review where existing) a policy on conflicts of interests [16].

---

[15] STEPHEN P. HEYNEMAN, The Concern with Corruption in Higher Education, in Creating the Ethical Academy: A Systems Approach to Understanding Misconduct and Empowering Change. Taylor and Francis. Kindle Edition, 2011, 13-26; NATHAN F. HARRIS AND MICHAEL N. BASTEDO: Corruption at the Top: Ethical Dilemmas in College and University Governance, idem, 2011, 115-132.

Many of the institutions present here certainly have already implemented a good number of these recommendations.

2.8.3 Inter-institutional Level

Recommendation 3: Include ethics in higher education in the accreditation and monitoring policies and training programmes of accreditation institutions and councils such the International Council for Open and Distance Education ICDE.

A encouraging example are business schools: The global financial crisis in 2007-2009, with its huge global economic damage, destruction of trust in financial institutions and criticism of business schools as producers of morally blind managers led to a period of self-reflection in business schools. The Globally Responsible Leadership Initiative GRLI, the World Business Council for Sustainable Development WBCSD and the Principles for Responsible Management Education PRME together developed the "50+20 Agenda", a model for renewed sustainable management education for the world. It was launched at the Rio+20 Summit in Rio 2012[17]. The values of "50+20" are "*to develop the well-being of all of us – and indeed of all living things – while respecting the limits of the planet*" and "Management education [is] designed … not being the best in the world, but for the world." [18] The 50+20 Agenda further states that "We envision three new roles of management education. First of all, we refocus education to ensure that we educate and develop globally responsible leaders. Secondly, we transform research into an applied field, with the clear purpose of enabling business organizations to serve the common good. Thirdly, we add a new role for management educators to engage in the transformation of

---

[16] Ethics matters in conflicts of interests. Discussion Paper of the Ethics Experts of the GSO SUN Project, main author Christoph Stückelberger, Geneva 2015.
[17] The 50+20 Agenda. Management Education for the World, without year (2012), www.50+20.org.
[18] Ibid, 1-3. Recommendations for practical implementation 31ff.

business and the economy by joining the ongoing public debate. As such, our vision is represented by the philosophy of a *collaboratory* – an open space for action learning and research."[19] Values in the 50+20-Agenda for business schools are: well-being of all, global responsibility, serve the common good and collaboration. EQUIS, in 2013, integrated ethical criteria in their accreditation standards for business schools[20] and the Association for the Advancement of Collegiate Schools of Business AACBS, one of the oldest American and now global accreditation institution of business schools, made a similar effort in 2013.[21]

---

[19] Ibid, 2.

[20] "In 2013 EQUIS revised its accreditation standards and established criteria for integrating ethics, responsibility and sustainability into business schools. The new standards suggest that ethical, responsible, and sustainable behaviour should be an integral part of business school's strategy and governance, as well as be reflected in their regular research, teaching, and service activities. These standards reflect the desire for business schools to contribute to the resolution of societal challenges and to act as 'good citizens' in the environments in which they operate." (GRLI - 50+20 Values in Action Group: Ethics, Responsibility, and Sustainability (ERS) in Business School Accreditation: Peer-Learning Perspectives, group of authors, Globally Responsible Leadership Initiative GRLI, Discussion Draft 7.0: September 10, 2014, 2.)

[21] AACSB: "The Association for the Advancement of Collegiate Schools of Business has been accrediting business schools for almost 100 years, first and mostly in the USA, today globally. In their most recent 2013 Business Standards they newly introduced ERS demands in their core values and guiding principles for accreditation. They demand "ethical behavior" ("The school must encourage and support ethical behavior by students, faculty, and professional staff.") and a "commitment to corporate and social responsibility" ("The school must demonstrate a commitment to address, engage, and respond to current and emerging corporate social responsibility issues (e.g. diversity, sustainable development, environmental sustainability, globalization of economic activity across cultures etc.) and challenges through its policies, procedures, curricula, research, and/or outreach activities."). Although the integration of ERS into the new accreditation standards is not as extensive in the case of AACSB, it is obvious that AACSB is moving in the same direction." GRLI 50+20, footnote above, 4. See also www.aacsb.edu/en/accreditation/standards/2013-business. aspx.

2.8.4 Political Level

Recommendation 4: Include ethical goals in the Framework for Action Education 2030 related to SDGs. Implement existing national and international legislation, anticorruption conventions, and policies on ethics in public administration to public and private institutions of higher education. Resist political pressure on admissions.

Most countries nowadays have extended legislation to strengthen transparency, accountability, to overcome corruption, protect whistleblowers, sanction sexual harassment, punish hacking and cybercrime, etc. But such legislation needs implementation in all sectors of society including in higher education. The cooperation between institutions of higher education and state authorities (in addition to the ministries of higher education also the ministries for governance, corporate responsibility, etc.) is promising.

A special challenge is political pressure on policies of higher institutions, e.g. to increase the number of students for political reasons even if it is at the cost of quality or even direct intervention of members of the government or parliament to admissions or scholarships. All of us could certainly report cases of pressure. In such cases the leaders of respective institutions of higher education need a very strong character of integrity and courage to resist temptations and pressure. Excellent instruments such as ICDE and the President's Summit also serve to strengthen the individual leaders in their responsibility and integrity.

2.8.5 Rating Level

Recommendation 5: Enlarge current rating systems of academic excellence by adding ethical criteria. Develop (Globethics.net with partners) a global ethics rating of institutions of higher education.

We have to redefine excellence. In the financial sector, companies and banks even with a triple A (AAA) rating have contributed to the profound crisis and disaster that has been happening in the sector since

2007. It mirrors the fact that AAA is a one-sided financial rating without enough social, political and environmental criteria. The triple A has to be replaced by a triple E (EEE): ethical excellence, environmental excellence, economic excellence (telling the economic truth of costs, including external costs).

Redefine Competition. Educational institutions should compete not only for academic, but for ethical excellence. Some already do this by positioning themselves as institutions with rigorous values. Parents look for it for their children (as the success of the ongoing campaign for corruption-free schools in five West-African countries which I co-initiated 15 years ago, shows). Publications in peer-review journals cannot be the main criteria for excellence nor the number of Nobel Prize winners working in an institution. University associations such as ICDE are well placed to push for a change in the rating and ranking systems of universities[22] and of individual staff. The "Academic Ranking of World Universities" ARWU developed by the Shanghai Jiao Tong University[23] is often criticized as being too oriented towards the sciences, publications and the number of Nobel Prize winners.

A few first efforts have been made to rank the ethics teaching and performance of universities or colleges, e.g. students' responses on ethics education in Business schools in US ranked Notre Dame as number one (2012)[24]. The UK students campaigning network "People & Planet" ranks UK universities on environmental and ethical criteria.[25] In 2015, the University of Cambridge (ranked worldwide no. 5 in ARWU)

---

[22] For a broad overview of ranking systems in higher education see Wikipedia article *College and University Rankings*, https://en.wikipedia.org/wiki/College_and_university_rankings.

[23] http://www.shanghairanking.com.

[24] http://www.bloomberg.com/bw/articles/2012-12-17/mba-rankings-top-schools-for-ethics.

[25] https://peopleandplanet.org/university-league: "People & Planet's University League is the only comprehensive and independent league table of UK universities ranked by environmental and ethical performance. It is compiled annually by the UK's largest student campaigning network, People & Planet."

is ranked 113 of 128, therefore ethically very low, and the University of Oxford (ranked worldwide no. 9 in ARWU) ranked 115 of 128!

Ethical ranking means a) to integrate the ethics performance of an institution in the ranking[26] and b) the ethical values of the ranking itself[27], the recommendations of ACE and AGB to conduct ethical audits and to establish conflict of interest policies[28]. Universities could also be ranked according to their level of ethical investments[29]. They could be ranked by ethics in their disciplines, e.g. colleges for their legal ethics[30], medical ethics[31], business ethics[32], etc. The University Codes of Ethics[33] and their implement ation would be of course be part of the rating.

---

[26] Patrick Loobuyck, What Kind of University Rankings Do We Want?, Ethical Perspectives 16, No 2 (2009), 207-224.

[27] The Berlin Principles on Ranking of Higher Education Institutions, published by the International Ranking experts Group in 2006, set criteria for participation of users, diversity of values and contexts: "1) Recognize the diversity of institutions and take the different missions and goals of the institutions into account (3); 2) specify the different linguistic, cultural, economic and historical contexts of the educational systems being ranked (5); 3) provide consumers with a clear understanding of all the factors used to develop a ranking, and offer them a choice of how rankings are displayed. The users of the ranking should have some opportunity to make their own decision about how the indicators should be weighted." (quoted in

[28] American Council on Education. (2008) Working Paper on Conflict of Interest (for review and comment), Washington, DC, 1. Quoted in. Creating the Ethical Academy: A Systems Approach to Understanding Misconduct and Empowering Change (p. 131). Taylor and Francis. Kindle Edition.

[29] Proposed by students in Canada in 2013, http://ubyssey.ca/news/macleans-975.

[30] http://law-schools.startclass.com/d/c/Legal-Ethics

[31] http://study.com/articles/Top_Schools_for_Medical_Ethics_and_Bioethics.html

[32] http://www.belmont.edu/business/ethics/

[33] See the broadest collection of codes of ethics at the online library of Globethics.net: Out of 895 articles, 41 are on ethics codes in higher education http://www.globethics.net/web/codes-of-ethics/overview?layoutPlid=4297674 (accessed 1 Aug 2015). An international comparison of University Codes of ethics: Heather Hilliard et al, International Educational Ethics: Asia, South Pacific, Europe, Canada and Latin America, Journal of Academic and business ethics, No. 3, 2011, 1-10.

The EEE Awards could be given ♛ for corporate excellence in balancing ethics, economy, ecology ♛ for transformative EEE leadership ♛ for EEE NGOs ♛ for EEE religious organizations, for EEE educational institutions.

2.8.6 Communication Level

Recommendation 6: Strengthen the communication strategy of the institutions for higher education so that integrity, credibility, responsibility and honesty are included.

Ethical communication does not mean talking about values and ethics, but to live values and virtues in a credible way, especially in crisis management. The Erdman team with its trust barometer showed what people expect from an ethical communication: "Communicate clearly and transparently (82%); Tell the truth regardless of how unpopular or complex the situation is (81%); Engage with employees regularly (80%); Be front and center during challenging times (79%); Support local charities and good causes (69%); Have an active media presence (53%)."[34]

2.8.7 Spiritual Level

Recommendation 7: Enable spiritual praxis of different faith communities on the campus of institutions of higher education as a foundation for ethical integrity.

Ethics is not only an issue of teaching and training, but spiritual praxes of meditation, yoga, prayer, choirs and study groups of Holy Scriptures are needed to build a culture of integrity and ethics. For example: the Indian Institute of Management Bangalore IIMB, one of the top Indian business schools, provide compulsory yoga exercises on its campus ground. Mahidol University in Thailand offers Buddhist meditation at the beginning of lectures, Christian and Muslim prayer

---

[34]   http://experientialcommunications.com/blog/2014/01/24/trust-and-higher-education-lessons-for-academics-presidents-and-communicators/

rooms and chapels on the same campus exist in many universities as they do in airports and railway stations. University campuses are important religious and interreligious learning communities and places to learn tolerance. Institutes of higher education have to define of course the rules for such activities in order to make them instruments for peace, caring and understanding and not weapons of fundamentalisms and hate speeches.

2.8.8 Action Level

Recommendation 8: strengthen values-driven behaviour not only by words, but also through individual and collaborative action such as community service.

To dismiss a teacher who accepted bribes to falsify the exam result of a student is stronger than 100 words and is an ethical testimonial of the leadership of an institution. The admission policies, fees structures or curricula testify to how much an institution supports equality, (through the opportunities given to get access to education), caring (for economically weaker students), etc. Compulsory community service and awards for research with societal impact are expressions of the value of responsibility in society.

An encouraging initiative for community engagement and peace happens in the USA: I had the opportunity to participate at a global conference at the White House in Washington, DC in the USA in autumn 2015. Five years ago President Obama started the interfaith community initiative for American colleges. Over 400 colleges already participate with the joint community engagement of students from different religious backgrounds, Muslim, Christians, Hindus, Buddhists, Jews, Sikhs, etc. The joint service for disadvantaged people strengthens mutual understanding and community. A month ago, the White House invited representatives from 50 educational institutions and networks including Globethics.net to cooperate on all continents in interfaith dialogue for community service. During the course of the conference and in particular during the exchanges with other participants I was struck by the wisdom, value and continuing potential of such an initiative.

2.9 Conclusion

All of the eight recommendations aim at strengthening what can be called the "Ethical Academy"[35]. It is not only a vision; it is a feasible and realistic plan which can be implemented also in open and distance learning institutions. It has to be an effort supported by the top leadership of an institution. It has to be promoted and monitored in an innovative way by the specialised units such as the Academic Integrity Officers and Academic Ethics Officers.

UNISA, the host of this conference, with the commitment of its Principle and Vice-Chancellor Professor Mandla S. Makhanya and under the dynamic leadership of Professor Divya Singh, Vice Principal Advisory and Assurance Services & Acting Registrar Governance (at the time of writing), in short "Miss Ethics" and also Director of Globethics.net Southern Africa, is a splendid example of the direction to go.

---

[35] Creating the Ethical Academy. A Systems Approach to Understanding Misconduct and Empowering Change in Higher Education Edited by Tricia Bertram Gallant, New York and London, 2011, Taylor and Francis, Kindle Edition. Dr. Tricia Bertram Gallant is the academic integrity coordinator for the University of California, San Diego.

HARMONY AS THE HORIZON
OF HIGHER EDUCATION

Paulachan Kochappilly

3.1 Introduction

In a world of cutthroat competition, education has almost become a business aimed at 'making money'; and the more, the better. In order to survive in this highly competitive sector, institutions and individuals play the game of money-spinning. Campus placement opportunity is the criterion of a best school, and character formation is almost a bygone ideal of education. The trend in education seems to be in producing or supplying the demands of the market. While some developed countries have made the concerted decision to increase student numbers, they employ a variety of practices including considerable investments of resources in foreign universities in developing countries. Education has become a booming industry, often at the cost of the values of education. Such an unbridled multiplying of educational institutions needs to be checked, lest the future of humanity be in jeopardy. The need is to pump the values of life into the veins of education in order to avert the impending danger of the extinction of diversity, democracy, and the dignity of community. Higher education should give adequate importance to holistic and integral formation of persons along with rigorous research and sincere commitment to address the manifold issues of our times.

3.2 Discussion

What follows is my reflection, based on the inspiration from my cultural and religious heritage, proposing a Seven Point Programme in view of this evolving integral, interdisciplinary, and interdependent programme of education.

> (i) WHOLE WORLD IS ONE FAMILY (*vasudhaiva kutumbakam*): Human consciousness is ever evolving and undergoing transformation in tune with the enlightenment and wisdom in the course of one's experiment with truth. Higher education and consequently responsible leadership depend heavily on the simple, refined, and the complexity of consciousness. Awakening of consciousness is the field of higher education. Education, ultimately, aims to bring out the best in a person to live in harmony with every reality out there. One is educated to fine tune the information and experiential knowledge into a beautiful melody of eternal music. Education is primarily and fundamentally to assist the seekers of wisdom to play the symphony of life – to celebrate life – using the given seven notes, on the stage of the universe. The saying, *vasudhaiva kutumbakam*, means that the whole world is one family, (*Maha Upanishad* 6, 72) is an epitome of human flourishing, the goal of all education. It is an invitation to live the ideal of universal sisterhood and brotherhood, attending to the needs and demands of every kith and kin, including the flora and fauna, the fish in the water, the birds in the air, the animals on earth, in this well-knit universe. The panoramic vision and friendly relationship celebrated in the *Canticle of Creation* of Francis of Assisi is a representation of this great ideal.

Education should give wings to the seekers to fly high in order to see everything with right reason and to act rightly as members of the same family. Another powerful imagery illustrating the oneness and relatedness of the whole universe is the metaphor of "different members in one body" (1 Cor 12:12) the microcosm, the miniature of macrocosm. The horizon of education has to grow into and go out to this all-embracing, all-flourishing, all-emancipating and yet bonding world vision. This world-family is the temple of learning, loving, and living our life with wider horizons and greater passion.

(ii) UNITY IN DIVERSITY (*Vividhata mein ekata*): The story of Kanhaiya Kumar, the Student Leader of Jawahar Lal Nehru University, New Delhi, one of the reputed universities in India, has been making huge waves in all spheres of life, triggering public debate on the question of dissent and democracy since 9 February 2016. Heated debate on nationalism and anti-nationalism is still gathering steam, even as I sit to write this note. Kumar was allegedly accused of shouting anti-nationalist slogans during a memorial celebration on the campus and was put behind bars for a fortnight. Later it was found that the video clipping produced in the court by the petitioner was a doctored one, and he is now out of prison on bail. By and large, Kanhaiya Kumar has been acquitted by both the public and the media. The whole debate opened up once again a fundamental, vital, and national issue of diversity and unity, the soul of Indian nationalism. The real is diversity. The ideal is unity. It is toward the ideal we need to walk and work together. It is in recognizing, respecting, and responding to the diversity that one can postulate unity. It is true of a nation. It is also true of a university. A university is known for its multiplicity and plurality. Any university exists because of its ability to be inclusive and integral in accommodating all noble thoughts and possible dreams. Unity in diversity is also the soul of the university, for it is a miniature form of the universe. While working for unity and universality in higher education, it is to be borne in mind that uniformity is not the ideal; instead, multi-polarity and transversality need to be adopted as the policies for responsible leadership in higher education. Identity, unity, and solidarity are to be the guiding principles in all walks of life, especially in higher education, because it is through education that generations are moulded and equipped.

(iii) TRUTH, GOODNESS, AND BEAUTY (*satyam shivam sundaram*): A mantle of truth, goodness, and beauty is the fitting garb of a responsible leader. These are not only the external outfit but are the values which a leader should adhere to and to which s/he must be moulded. A leader is one who seeks truth, speaks truth, and stands for truth. So also a leader must seek goodness, speak goodness, and stand for goodness. In thought, word, and deed a responsible leader has to work for the good. Similarly a leader is one who acknowledges, appreciates, and accepts beauty, wherever it is found. Truth, goodness, and beauty should guide his every step. The whole purpose of education is to help the pupil see the truth, goodness, and beauty in life and activity. These are the triadic values which should fill the ambience of higher education. These are to be arrived at through dialogue; they consist in an exodus – a movement in and a moment of going out – aiming high, going deep, and broadening one's gaze. Responsible leadership animates and accompanies people in awakening and expanding their consciousness. Truth sets people free; goodness moves them to dream; and beauty embraces differences and celebrates. Higher education is to support and promote these. Education is a lifelong journey or pilgrimage: in encountering truth, being enlightened by goodness, and always adoring the beauty.

In this journey of truth, goodness, and beauty, education is vital and fundamental to respect, protect, and promote life in its wholeness, fullness, and holiness. It seems, at times, research and study are compartmentalized and isolated, devoid of life and commitment to the myriad life issues, such as migration, abject poverty, rampant corruption, gender discrimination, human trafficking, wars, killings of the innocent and voiceless, crumbling families, disregard for the aged, communalism, religious fanaticism, terrorism, growing intolerance to the other, the environmental crisis, etc. In such a culture of death, higher education has the duty to attend to these realities and to explore the ways and means to inculcate a culture of life and a civilization of love. An apt slogan in this respect may be: All for life and life for all. This means that all our thoughts, words, and actions should be geared toward the good of all, including the least, the lost, and the last. In other words, truth, goodness, and beauty are not the monopoly of the elite alone, but they are the aspirations treasured and cherished by all regardless of gender, creed, colour, ethnicity, citizenship, etc. All is for all; everything is meant for everybody.

Higher education has a responsibility to the common good, to establish the dignity of all, and to ensure the fundamental human rights of all. Often in a market driven economy, generally, attention is paid to short-term benefits and to the interests of shareholders. There is an urgency to see the interconnectivity of all things; inherent interrelation of somebody with everybody. It is this education which is of paramount importance for our times, and responsible leadership has no choice but to pilot the project of a harmony of life, which assures health, happiness, and holiness.

The campuses and leaders of higher education should rediscover and revive this holistic and harmonious approach to education and leadership. Modern universities can trace their origin to such an organic, dynamic, spontaneous response to the emerging issues of life at their time of formation. Today the approach has become almost compartmentalized, fractured, and fragmented, which escapes the discussion on the fundamental good – life – and the common good – wellbeing – and is in need of our attention. This means that ethical and moral discourse has to be once again alive and active in the arena of higher education. Every action has an equal and opposite reaction. Whatever, wherever, whenever, whoever does has a repercussion on something, somewhere, sometime, and someone and is the truth one has to reckon with and respectfully respond to in our academic and public life.

> (iv) SPEAK TRUTH AND WALK RIGHTEOUSLY
> (*satyam vada dharmam chara*): At the close of the formal education in gurukula and at a function similar to convocation, the message of the teacher is *satyam vada dharmam chara* (*Taittireeya Upanishad*: 1,11). There is the opening line of the exhortation the master gives to his disciples in the ancient *gurukula* system of education (residential school). Higher education and responsible leadership have to invest much time and energy in inculcating the virtue of truth-telling and righteous behaviour. Education is formation; it is character formation. The adage "wealth is lost, nothing is lost;

health is lost, something is lost; character is lost, everything is lost", holds good even today. While imparting a lot of information for a professional placement, the teachers and institutions often neglect or ignore character formation of the students. In this regard, the principle of transformative education is: "preach the gospel, when necessary use words." Examples are better than precepts. Responsible leadership means good examples and attractive witness to the truth and righteousness. It is time that higher education has to invent the ways and means to attract the students to an ethical and moral life. Much time is invested in fulfilling the legal requirements, but not so much attention is given to moral formation. Mahatma Gandhi spoke of seven deadly sins, which are of great significance for our discussion. The seven deadly sins are: wealth without work; pleasure without conscience; knowledge without character; business without ethics; science without humanity; religion without sacrifice and politics without principles. These virtues are significant in the field of education more than ever before. All these and more should be part of the educational enterprise, for education is intended to bring the best out of persons; it is to churn out the nectar from the ocean of knowledge.

(v) TRUTH IS ONE, LEARNED SPEAK DIFFERENTLY (*ekam sat vipra bahudha vadanti*): Truth is that which exists. Truth sets us free. Truth will prevail. Truth is God. Yet who has the absolute grasp of truth? Who is right? Who is false? It is very difficult to ascertain the claim for truth. In fact, nobody has the absolute grasp of truth. Nevertheless, each one is true and shares in the truth. It is not to lead to relativistic understanding of reality, but to acknowledge the truth of the situation. The vedic saying, *ekam sat vipra bahudha vadanti* (*Rig Veda*, 1,164) is to the point. The truth is one and people behold it differently, for reality is greater than what one encounters. This approach does not absolutize any human statement out of proportion nor does it outright reject any point of view. According to this stance, freedom is guaranteed to all and naturally tolerance and reverence towards others' opinions are nurtured and fostered. The more people are educated, the more humble they become. Humility is the ornament of scholars. There is no room for arrogance and violence in them. Instead, there is a healthy exchange of ideas and perspectives. No coercion, but cooperation. Wondering together and walking together for wisdom is the ground for education. Dialogue of life takes place. Celebration of differences becomes the rhythm of life and progress. Higher education should enable and equip pupils and leaders not only to tolerate differences, but to appreciate and celebrate them.

(vi) "WHATEVER YOU WISH THAT OTHERS WOULD DO TO YOU, DO ALSO TO THEM" (Mt 7:12). The starting point of responsible leadership is to follow the golden rule. As educated people, this is a common minimum programme. Though there may be different goals in education, its primary end is to bring refinement and purification in thought, word, and deed. It is enhancing the excellence of the subject through ethical reflection that is of paramount importance in education. Allowing the noble thoughts to form a person is a sine qua non for an educational programme and its process.

Compassion and mercy towards all beings, especially fellow beings, should be the mantra of harmonious living. It is a matter of going out and reaching out to the needy, especially, the poor, the oppressed, the marginalized, the outcast. It is indeed doing justice, of going beyond the legal notion of it and walking the extra mile. Higher education should lay the foundation in the pupils not only to love their neighbour, but to love and pray for their enemies as well. Responsible leadership is to mould oneself in acts of compassion and companionship as a result of one's focused contemplation and communion with the whole world. The whole education policy and programme should reinvent a mood of joy in aspiring and acquiring of higher education. That is, to say, all educational endeavours should be guided by the principle of happiness. Every undertaking in education should have a touch of joy welling up in the heart of its takers and givers. The saying of Jesus might guide the steps of educators, "I have said these things, so that my joy may be in you and your joy may be complete" (Jn 15:11). It is this joy which should pervade and permeate all activities in the field of education.

(vii)   GLORY TO GOD IN THE HIGHEST, PEACE ON EARTH, AND HOPE TO HUMAN BEINGS: In this brief reflection, I have tried to convey that higher education and responsible leadership should have one focus and threefold relational directions. It is time for higher education to return to its roots and enjoy the fruits. It may not be wrong to state that the culture of education evolved in and around the ancient religious and spiritual ambience of the temples and monasteries and their worship. At the initial stage of the evolution of education there was no watertight compartmentalization of one discipline from the other; instead, they were considered to be parts of the integral whole. Therefore, there was unity and diversity. Thank God, an obligatory inter-dependence and inter-subjectivity of the reality is being reinvented and revived through the introduction of an interdisciplinary curriculum for university studies. Experiential learning and teaching is gaining momentum, especially education through service learning, which should be promoted by all means possible. These witness to the significance of the text and context in real education; there is a rediscovery of the source – experience – in the learning-teaching process. We are living in a world that cannot ignore or neglect the foundation of education - the realization of the wonder of life. Wonder takes us to the realm of work and work to the realm of awe and worship, which breaks the ground for wisdom. Hence, Dharmaram Vidya Kshetram has this motto in Sanskrit, *ishabhakti param jnanam* (devotion to the Lord is the supreme wisdom).

3.3 Conclusion

In my opinion, higher education has to discover and dedicate itself to a triadic relationship, namely with God, earth, and human beings. In other words, education is to develop a threefold relationship: oneness with the Other, rootedness with nature, and relatedness with neighbour. We are what our relations are. We cannot survive without land and other people, though some may be silent about God. In a world torn apart by war and terror, we long to see peace on earth. Our war on terror may not bring about peace. Instead, we need to wage war on error. No doubt, violence begets violence. *Ahimsa* or non-violence disarms the most powerful. Dialogue with culture, nature, and stature is urgently needed in our day. Peace is built on the basis of truth, justice, freedom, and charity. Hence these values are to be given prime place in higher education. In an age of increasing suicide and disintegration of human families, to breathe in hope is most urgent. While in promoting research in alleviating poverty and other ills of our society, higher education should pitch itself in injecting hope to humanity to overcome the imminent dangers and difficulties one has to face. A journey of faith can usher in necessary hope and courage to face the challenges squarely and bring about much needed peace on earth and hope to human beings. In short, higher education has to reclaim its holistic and integral programme, emphasizing God, creation, and our fellow beings, without which education is neither complete nor compelling.

To conclude, responsible leadership in higher education has a challenging call to coexist, cooperate, and celebrate with God, and with all people in the whole world-the key to harmony of life.

THE RELATIONSHIP BETWEEN THE SUSTAINABLE DEVELOPMENT GOALS AND THE ROLE OF HIGHER EDUCATION INSTITUTIONS: A SOUTH AFRICAN PERSPECTIVE

Avani Singh

4.1 Introduction

In his final judgment delivered as Deputy Chief Justice of the South African Constitutional Court, Judge Dikgang Moseneke began with the following words:[1]

"[1] Teaching and learning are as old as human beings have lived. Education is primordial and integral to the human condition. The new arrivals into humankind are taught and learn how to live useful and fulfilled lives. So education's formative goodness to the body, intellect and soul has been beyond question from antiquity. And its collective usefulness to communities has been recognised from prehistoric times to now. The indigenous and ancient African wisdom teaches that *"thuto ke lesedi la sechaba"*; *"imfundo yisibani"* (education is the

---

[1] *Federation of Governing Bodies for South African Schools (FEDSAS) v Member of the Executive Council for Education, Gauteng and Another* (CCT 209/15) [2016] ZACC 14 (20 May 2016).

light of the nation) and recognises that education is a collective enterprise by observing that it takes a village to bring up a child.

[2] Of this Aristotle, Immanuel Kant, Karl Marx, Mahatma Gandhi, Helen Keller, Nelson Mandela, Kofi Annan, Malala Yousafzai, the Holy Bible, Buddha, and the Holy Quran have said:

> "Education is an ornament in prosperity and a refuge in adversity." – Aristotle

> "How then is perfection to be sought? Wherein lies our hope? In education, and in nothing else." – Immanuel Kant

> "The education of all children, from the moment that they can get along without a mother's care, shall be in state institutions." – Karl Marx

> "If we want to reach real peace in this world, we should start educating children." – Mahatma Gandhi

> "Education should train the child to use his brains, to make for himself a place in the world and maintain his rights even when it seems that society would shove him into the scrap-heap." – Helen Keller

> "Education is the great engine of personal development. It is through education that the daughter of a peasant can become a doctor, that the son of a mineworker can become the head of the mine, that a child of a farmworker can become the president of a great nation. It is what we make out of what we have, not what we are given, that separates one person from another." – Nelson Mandela

> "Education is a human right with immense power to transform. On its foundation rest the cornerstones of freedom, democracy and sustainable human development." – Kofi Annan

> "There are many problems, but I think there is a solution to all these problems; it's just one, and it's education." – Malala Yousafzai

> "My people are destroyed for lack of knowledge." – The Holy Bible: Hosea 4:6

> "To have much learning, to be skilful in handicraft, well-trained in discipline, and to be of good speech – this is the greatest blessing." – Buddha

> "Are those equal, those who know and those who do not know? It is those who are endowed with understanding that receive admonition." – The Holy Quran: Surah Al Zumar 39:9

[3] Despite these obvious ancient virtues, access to teaching and learning has not been freely and widely accessible to all people at all times. All forms of human oppression and exclusion are premised, in varying degrees, on a denial of access to education and training. The uneven power relations that marked slavery, colonialism, the industrial age and the information economy are girded, in great part, by inadequate access to quality teaching and learning.[2]"

This universal recognition of the importance of quality education is further entrenched under Goal 4 of the Sustainable Development Goals (**SDGs**). As noted in a report published by the United Nations

---

[2] Ibid. http://www.saflii.org/za/cases/ZACC/2016/14.html

Educational, Scientific and Cultural Organisation (**UNESCO**), sustainable development post-2015 begins with education.[3]

An important development in the formulation of the SDGs is the express inclusion of higher education as part of the targets. Of the ten targets listed under Goal 4, the following are of particular relevance:

- By 2030, ensure equal access for all women and men to affordable and quality technical, vocational and tertiary education, including university;
- By 2030, substantially increase the number of youth and adults who have relevant skills, including technical and vocational skills, for employment, decent jobs and entrepreneurship;
- By 2030, eliminate gender disparities in education and ensure equal access to all levels of education and vocational training for the vulnerable, including persons with disabilities, indigenous peoples and children in vulnerable situations;
- By 2020, substantially expand globally the number of scholarships available to developing countries, in particular least developed countries, small island developing States and African countries, for enrolment in higher education, including vocational training and information and communications technology, technical, engineering and scientific programmes, in developed countries and other developing countries.

These targets speak directly to the complex and inter-related issues of accessibility and affordability, from both a quality and gendered perspective. It is clear that there is a responsibility to work towards the provision of higher education, but the question to be answered is: who bears this responsibility?

---

[3] UNESCO, "Sustainable development begins with education: How education can contribute to the proposed post-2015 goals" (2014) (http://unesdoc.unesco.org/images/0023/002305/230508e.pdf), at p 2.

The 2015/2016 academic year has been a fascinating period of reflection for the higher education sector in South Africa (as well as the country, generally). Notably, two popular student-driven movements – the Rhodes Must Fall campaign and the Fees Must Fall campaign – gave rise to difficult, and sometimes uncomfortable, questions about whether the state and higher education institutions were doing enough to achieve transformation in the post-apartheid era.[4] This has by no means been unique to South Africa, as student movements around the world have made it clear that business as usual will no longer be tolerated.

Certainly, the debate remains rife and ongoing, and demands critical engagement on how the targets set out in Goal 4 of the SDGs can be realised. As will be set out in more detail below, states remain the primary duty-bearers for the fulfilment of the right to higher education. However, it will further be argued that higher education institutions also have a crucial role to play – both in facilitating the realisation of the right to higher education, as well as in perpetuating sustainable development more broadly. This paper does not profess to have the answers to these complex and multi-faceted questions, and there can be no doubt that solutions must be found on a case-by-case basis. Rather, this paper seeks to contextualise the discussion within the domestic and international law framework in order to better understand the nature of the obligations in respect of higher education.

4.2 The Legal Framework for the Right to Higher Education

As a point of departure, the Constitution of the Republic of South Africa, 1996 (the Constitution) is the supreme law in South Africa.[5] It

---

[4] See, for instance, Mail & Guardian, "#FeesMustFall is just the start of change" (21 June 2016) (http://mg.co.za/article/2016-01-20-fees-are-just-the-start-of-change).

[5] Section 2 of the Constitution.

contains a justiciable Bill of Rights, and the state is required to respect, protect, promote and fulfil the rights in the Bill of Rights.[6] The Bill of Rights binds the legislature, executive, judiciary and all organs of state;[7] and may also bind a natural or juristic person if, and to the extent that, it is applicable, taking into account the nature of the right and the nature of any duty imposed by that right.[8]

The right to education is contained in section 29 of the Constitution. In terms of section 29(1)(b), everyone has the right to further education, *"which the state, through reasonable measures, must make progressively available and accessible"*. Unlike the right to basic education contained in section 29(1)(a), which is not so qualified, the realisation of the right to further education is expressly circumscribed by the principle of progressive realisation. However, unlike the other socio-economic rights contained in the Constitution that are also subject to progressive realisation, the wording of section 29(1)(b) does not expressly make the right subject to *"available resources"*.

The right to higher education is also well-established under international law.[9] Starting with the Universal Declaration of Human Rights (1948), article 26(1) thereof states that *"[e]veryone has the right to education. Education shall be free, at least in the elementary and fundamental stages. Elementary education shall be compulsory. Technical and professional education shall be made generally available and higher education shall be equally accessible to all on the basis of merit."*

---

[6] Section 7(2) of the Constitution.
[7] Section 8(1) of the Constitution.
[8] Section 8(2) of the Constitution.
[9] Section 39(1)(b) of the Constitution requires that, when interpreting the Bill of Rights, a court *"must consider international law"*; and section 233 of the Constitution requires that, when interpreting any legislation, a court *"must prefer any reasonable interpretation of the legislation that is consistent with international law over any alternative interpretation that is inconsistent with international law"*.

Under the African regional system, the African Charter on Human and Peoples' Rights (1981) (ACHPR)[10] provides in broad terms that *"[e]very individual shall have the right to education"*. The African Charter on the Rights and Welfare of the Child (1990) (ACRWC),[11] which South Africa has also ratified, makes express reference to the right to higher education:

> *"(1) Every child shall have the right to an education.*
> *[...]*
> *(3) States Parties ... shall take all appropriate measures with a view to achieving the full realisation of this right and shall in particular:*
> *(c) make higher education accessible to all on the basis of capacity and ability by every appropriate means."*

The ACRWC is framed in similar terms to article 13(2)(c) of the International Covenant on Economic, Social and Cultural Rights (1966) (ICESCR),[12] which states that *"[h]igher education shall be made equally accessible to all, on the basis of capacity, by every appropriate means, and in particular by the progressive introduction of free education"*.

It is clear, therefore, that a right to higher education exists – albeit on a qualified basis, subject to certain caveats. The framing of the right affords a measure of discretion to those responsible for the provision of the right to determine how to fulfil their obligations. This discretion is not, however, unfettered, and there is at least an implicit requirement that this must be done in a reasonable manner.

---

[10] South Africa ratified the ACHPR in 1996.

[11] South Africa ratified the ACRWC in 2000.

[12] South Africa ratified the ICESCR in 2015, subject to a declaration entered relating to the provision of basic education in terms of article 13(2)(a) and 14 of the ICESCR.

The United Nations Committee on Economic, Social and Cultural Rights (CESCR) has attempted to give content to the right to education in General Comment 13. In this regard, it provides that the right to education, in all its forms and at all levels, including higher education, must have the following interrelated and essential features:[13]

- Availability – which requires functioning educational institutions and programmes have to be available in sufficient quantity within the jurisdiction of the state;
- Accessibility – which requires educational institutions and programmes have to be accessible to everyone, without discrimination, within the jurisdiction of the state. This has three overlapping dimensions: non-discrimination, which requires that education must be accessible to all, especially the most vulnerable groups; physical accessibility, which requires that education must be within safe physical reach; and economic accessibility, which requires that education must be affordable to all;
- Acceptability – which requires that the form and substance of education, including curricula and teaching methods, have to be acceptable (e.g. relevant, culturally appropriate and of good quality) to students; and
- Adaptability – which requires that education must be flexible so that it can adapt to the needs of changing societies and communities, and respond to the needs of students within their diverse social and cultural settings.

General Comment 13 states further that "[w]hen considering the appropriate application of these 'interrelated and essential features' the

---

[13] Committee on Economic, Social and Cultural Rights, "General Comment 13: The right to education" (Twenty-first session, 1999), U.N. Doc. E/C.12/1999/10 (1999), at paras 6 and 17.

best interest of the student shall be the primary consideration".[14] However, little guidance is given on how to determine the "best interest of the student" standard. Arguably, students themselves should have a key role to play in determining how this standard is crafted and met, although the practicability of achieving a standard that all students agree on would be nearly impossible. At the very least, this ought necessarily to be a relevant consideration that permeates every level of the decision-making process.

It is apparent from the provisions set out above that there are clear and express obligations for the state. However, the next leg of the enquiry is what obligations exist for higher education institutions in achieving this.

4.3 The Role of Higher Education Institutions

As an organ of state, South African universities are expressly bound by the Bill of Rights. While the ambit of this has not yet been tested in South African law, it is submitted that there is an arguable case that this comprises not only the negative duties, but also the positive duties to achieve the realisation of the right. Indeed, through factors such as government subsidies, accreditations and oversight exercised by the executive, higher education institutions are provided with a social licence to operate, facilitated by the state in order for the state to realise the right to higher education.

Certain aspects of the right, such as acceptability and adaptability, more easily lend themselves to being achievable by the higher education institutions with limited state involvement; whereas other aspects, such as availability and accessibility, are arguably more dependent on cooperation with the state. In all circumstances, however, it is through the establishment and functioning of these institutions that the state

---

[14] Above n 4 at para 7.

complies with its constitutional and international law obligations to *"respect, protect, promote and fulfil"* the right to higher education.

The tangible role of higher education institutions can be seen, for instance, through the efficient use of resources, the availability of open source academic materials, the promotion of a safe and quality student experience, the attraction and retention of high calibre staff and students, and the fostering of good governance and management.[15]

However, the responsibility of higher education institutions goes beyond the facilitation of the state's realisation of the right. In this regard, it has been stated that:[16]

"Higher education institutions bear a profound, moral responsibility to increase the awareness, knowledge, skills, and values needed to create a just and sustainable future. Higher education plays a critical but often overlooked role in making this vision a reality. It prepares most of the professionals who develop, lead, manage, teach, work in, and influence society's institutions."

Over the years, there have been a number of sustainability declarations in higher education that have defined specific roles for universities to further sustainable development.[17] These defined roles have been summarised as follows:[18]

---

[15] OECD Forum for the Future, "Higher education for sustainable development: Final report of the International Action Research Project" (2007) (http://www.oecd.org/education/innovation-education/ centreforeffectivelearningenvironmentscele/45575516.pdf), at pp 15-20.

[16] Above n 11 at p 13, citing Cortese AD "The critical role of higher education in creating a sustainable future" *Planning for Higher Education* (2003).

[17] See, for instance, the Tbilisi Declaration (1977); the Talloires Declaration (1990); the Kyoto Declaration (1993); the Lüneberg Declaration (2001).

[18] GUNi, IAU and AAU, "The promotion of sustainable development by higher education institutions in sub-Saharan Africa: A survey report" (2011) at pp 8-9.

- Moral obligation: universities are morally bound to create change through preparing graduates to deal with environmental problems;
- Public outreach: universities should apply their knowledge in solving the problems of society in the communities in which they reside;
- Sustainable physical operations: greening the campus is considered a key component in becoming more sustainable;
- Ecological literacy: there is need for universities to aid the development of an environmentally literate people to help in understanding the functions of world, human impacts on the biosphere and the translation of understanding to action;
- Develop interdisciplinary curricula: subjects studies should show a link to the environment to help students become more environmentally literate;
- Encourage sustainable research: encourage research that contributes to local, regional and global sustainability;
- Partnership with government, non-governmental organisations and industry: this is an encouragement for coordination of efforts at all levels, since the university cannot necessarily create social change on its own;
- Inter-university cooperation: this will facilitate sharing of information and cooperation in pursuit of practical solutions to the sustainability problem.

Despite the expressed commitments, change on the part of the higher education sector has been slow. Some of the challenges that have been identified in relation to the implementation of sustainable development in higher education institutions include a lack of strategic leadership, drive and commitment in the institutions and government; low demand and perceived irrelevance from students and staff; limited staff awareness and expertise; academic and professional silos which inhibit cooperative efforts across disciplines and institutions; and poor communication within the higher education institution regarding the meaning and concept of sustainable development and how it applies.[19]

While some of these challenges are typical of the traditional challenges to organisational change, this view is short-sighted. Interestingly, there is significant overlap between the challenges and some of the opportunities that have been identified, including:[20]

- Inter-disciplinary nature of research in sustainable development;
- Zeitgeist, primarily attributed to climate change, but also the progressive awareness of other sustainability issues;
- Collaborations and partnerships to work together;
- Networks to learn from others;
- A proactive unit or individual within the higher education institution driving sustainable development with a clear plan.

There is clearly a role for higher education institutions to play, and indeed a responsibility on them to do so. Particularly in developing states, such as South Africa, where the provision of higher education by the state is unlikely to meet the demand given the available state resources, it is incumbent on higher education institutions to take concrete and targeted steps to address the shortfall. While higher education institutions may not be the primary bearers of obligations, the importance of the role that they can – and must – play cannot be gainsaid.

---

[19] Dawe G, Jucker R & Martin S, "Sustainable development in higher education: Current practice and future developments (2005) (https://www.heacademy. ac.uk/sites/default/files/sustdevinhefinalreport.pdf), at p 5; above n 11 at p 42.
[20] Above n 11 at p 42.

4.4 A Transformative Agenda

It has been recognised that *"[o]ne of the most important insights regarding development in the last 25 years is that knowledge and learning are at the centre of the process of economic growth"*.[21] The importance of education simply cannot be gainsaid, and underlies the realisation of various other rights – not least of all, the right to dignity. For many South Africans, and for many people the world over, it is the ultimate equaliser in a society that remains deeply unequal.

Education is not only an end in its own right, but also a catalyst for achieving a broader development agenda.[22] As explained by the CESCR in General Comment 13:

> "Education is both a human right in itself and an indispensable means of realizing other human rights. As an empowerment right, education is the primary vehicle by which economically and socially marginalized adults and children can lift themselves out of poverty and obtain the means to participate fully in their communities. Education has a vital role in empowering women, safeguarding children from exploitative and hazardous labour and sexual exploitation, promoting human rights and democracy, protecting the environment, and controlling population growth. Increasingly, education is recognized as one of the best financial investments States can make. But the importance of education is not just practical: a well-educated, enlightened and active mind, able to wander freely and widely, is one of the joys and rewards of human existence."

---

[21] United Nations Conference on Trade and Development, "The least developed countries report" (2007) (https://www.google.co.za/webhp?sourceid=chrome-instant&ion=1&espv=2&ie=UTF-8#q=unctad%20least%20developed%20countries%202007), at p 185.

[22] Above n 2.

Sustainability has been described as the reconciliation of three imperatives: (i) the ecological imperative, to stay within the biophysical carrying capacity of our planet; (ii) the economic imperative, to provide an adequate material standard of living for all; and (iii) the social imperative, to provide systems of governance that propagate the values by which we want to live.[23]   It is obvious that higher education institutions have a role to play in all three imperatives. Importantly, the challenge is about achieving real and meaningful change in both law and fact. Increasing the number of institutions or attendees does not in itself guarantee economic and social change if the quality of the education is lacking.[24] Higher education institutions have the potential to stand at the forefront of meaningful transformation and social upliftment for the global population, and the chart the course for the post-2015 period. However, in order to be transformative, the higher education sector needs to transform itself.

The SDGs give higher education institutions the springboard to do so, but it is for the institutions to develop strategic plans for sustainable development, taking into account their own unique features. Rather than being seen as a challenge, higher education institutions should embrace this for the incredible opportunity that it presents.

---

[23] UNESCO Bangkok, "Reinventing higher education: Towards participatory and sustainable development" (2008), at p 36.
[24] Above n 18 at p 51.

5

UNIVERSITIES, CULTURAL DIVERSITY AND GLOBAL ETHICS: OPPORTUNITIES FOR MORAL LEADERSHIP

Martin Prozesky

5.1 Introduction

A project that seeks to develop values-driven leadership presents today's universities with an important new opportunity. It was anticipated nearly a century ago when the eminent Harvard professor of philosophy, Alfred North Whitehead (1861-1947) wrote prophetically that the "task of a university is the creation of the future, so far as rational thought, and civilized modes of appreciation, can affect the issue." (Whitehead 1938, 1966: 171) Now, several generations later, the global future faces world-wide problems of a magnitude that were unknown in his day, including environmental degradation, global warming, gender discrimination, a deeply disrupted Middle East (as westerners call it), inter- and inner-religious fanaticism that includes the horror of video-taped beheadings, not to speak of the huge number of the poor, homeless and unemployed around the world.

In addition to these problems there is widespread evidence of another serious problem that is of great relevance to universities (and other institutions) as they work for a worthwhile global future, especially those in multi-cultural societies, as most now are. The problem is a growing concern that humanity's morality (a word used interchangeably with ethics) is losing ground in the struggles against violence, greed, discrimination and other evils.

The problem can be stated as follows. On a planet facing the serious world-wide crises mentioned above, the moral domain comprises a large number of separate, culturally embedded ethical traditions with important similarities but also important differences, many but by no means all being part of the world's multitude of religions. Using Lloyd Geering's helpful and instructive typology (Geering 2014: 17-18) we have the many surviving forms of ethnic morality – the kind that was once the world's only kind - such as traditional Zulu or Maori morality; we have what Geering calls the trans-ethnic moralities associated with the so-called great world religions that originated in India, China and the Middle East from about 2500 years ago, and we have the moves towards more inclusive, modern kinds of morality like the human rights movement that began about 300 years ago.

We can thus think of the world as a place of distinct and disunited moral provinces but no consciously shared, fully inclusive global ethic, inviting the belief that humanity's moral development has not kept up with the rise of a technological, global civilization beset by worsening world-wide problems. In this situation the opportunity exists to bring together two powerful forces to counter those problems: the global ethics movement and the contemporary, multi-cultural university, exactly as envisaged by Whitehead's view of the university, in quest of a multi-culturally created global ethic.

5.2 The Global Ethics Movement

The term "global ethics movement" can be taken to refer to a number of attempts at arriving at a set of ethical values that could be accepted across the globe. The account of them that follows is based on published research by Prozesky, suitably shortened, edited and updated. (Prozesky 2007: 141-44).

An early venture in this direction was given by the Catholic theologian, Hans Küng. Together with others he helped produce a statement of the values shared by the most widely followed faiths. (Küng and Moltmann, 1990) Based on this work Küng and his associates produced a document called "Declaration of a Global Ethic" with what they called "Four irrevocable directives", present to some extent in the various faith traditions. Firstly, there must be a culture of non-violence and respect for life. Secondly, people must commit themselves to solidarity and a just economic order. The third principle is that people must commit themselves to tolerance and a life of truthfulness. Commitment to equal rights and partnership between men and women is the fourth principle offered by the Declaration. (Küng and Kuschel 1993: 24-34).

It ends with some dramatic words:

"Together we can move mountains! Without a willingness to take risks and a readiness to sacrifice there can be no fundamental change in our situation! Therefore we commit ourselves to a common global ethic, to better mutual understanding, as well as to socially-beneficial, peace-fostering, and Earth-friendly ways of life! We invite all men and women, whether religious or not, to do the same."

(Küng and Kuschel 1993:36)

A problem with this approach is its omission of traditional African and other ethnic cultures, some feminist voices and secular approaches to morality (Prozesky 2007: 143). A rather more inclusive approach to global ethics was developed by the late Rushworth M. Kidder at the Institute for Global Ethics in the USA, using conversations with ethical leaders from different cultures plus surveys of the values rated most highly by people in a number of countries around the world. Kidder identified eight shared moral values: love, truthfulness, fairness, freedom, unity or inclusiveness, tolerance, respect for life and responsibility (Kidder 1994: 18).

These two ways of developing a global ethic, valuable as they are, cannot achieve maximum inclusivity because they use values common to the selection of faiths and cultures on which they draw. These involve only a part of humanity even if it is a large part. What about the rest of humanity? This limitation led Prozesky to explore a fresh path towards a global ethic, based on something shared equally by all people: human nature as revealed in cross-cultural experience, illuminated by human brain science and supported empirically by cultural evidence of moral convergence of the kind cited by Küng and Kidder (Prozesky 2007, 47-49, 2014: 283-301).

By nature people in all cultures want to thrive; they want to experience sustainable happiness and avoid as much suffering as possible. Experience shows that these desires cannot be achieved alone but depend on the support of others. Conversely, they can be harmed by the enmity of others, as we also all know from personal experience. Sustainable thriving therefore is a matter of understanding and managing our relationships with others in ways that increase the level of support we give and receive from one another, and reduce or even eliminate enmity. We can live selfishly and earn the enmity and at times bitter hostility of others, or we can live supportively and earn their friendship. The human brain provides us with the equipment to acquire from others, through our moral development, an understanding of this most fundamental of choices, make it and to learn from the results of whatever choice we make, which takes us from biology of the human brain into culture and the creation of the future (Prozesky 2007: 65-97).

From this bio-cultural approach to global ethics a set of core values can be deduced which is very similar to the findings of Kidder and Küng. Using the simple device of a distinction (but not separation) between the roles of the understanding and action, respectively, in doing what is right and good, the resultant set of core values can be grouped in two related sets: those that express the various main facets of beneficence (which means doing what is beneficial to others) and those that express the various facets of integrity, understood as a commitment to consistent truthfulness. Here are these values, slightly modified.

Beneficence values	Integrity values
Generosity	Truthfulness
Respect	Reliability
Justice and fairness	Trustworthiness
Inclusiveness	Self-knowledge
Responsible, caring effort	Open-mindedness
Freedom without harm	Wisdom
Beauty	Judicious criticality

(Prozesky 2007:131)

There is thus ample justification from human nature, from reflective experience across cultures, from philosophy, culture and religion for the following conclusion about global ethics: "Our separate histories, homelands and cultures have given the world a divided soul but not, at heart, a divided conscience" (Prozesky 2007:144). The core emergent principle of active concern for the common good provides an invaluable basis for negotiating a fresh, respectful and fully inclusive way to forge a truly inclusive global ethic and to handle the things about which our cultures differ. It is here that an important opportunity exists for the contemporary, multi-cultural university.

5.3 Universities, Cultural Diversity and Inclusivity

The contention of this part of the chapter is that the multi-cultural university of the 21st century, as a centre of thought leadership that creates and imparts conceptual and practical knowledge, is by its very nature ethical. There are three reasons for this contention. The first one derives its moral status from the integrity cluster of values in the table above. It asserts that the business of creating and sharing knowledge is itself a core form of ethical practice (as distinct from teaching about ethics, which may have no real impact on actual practice). Knowledge must be true to count as knowledge, and in every value-system accessed in the global ethics movement, truth is judged to be a central moral value. So to be in the knowledge business is to be in the ethics business whether our universities acknowledge this explicitly or not. Thought that is characterized by factual error, mere opinion, illogicality and partisanship and that is untested by the critical assessment of qualified peers is not thought leadership but an unpardonable waste of resources.

The second reason derives its moral status from both the beneficence and integrity clusters of moral values in the table above. It is that academics are key ethics players in their roles as researchers, teachers and in their community service. The examples they set both personally and in how they do their work are noted by their students and colleagues, and send out clear ethical (and sometimes unethical) messages. So we can ask how well our academics and administrators are equipped for their role in providing moral influence in the academy and beyond.

Like everybody else, university staff members all have the right to be religious or not, but the notion that they have the right to be professionally amoral if they choose, or that the right to freedom means that what they do off campus, like cheating on their income tax or on their partners, is nobody's business but their own, must be firmly rejected as a violation of the ethical principles of integrity and responsibility. How can it make sense to claim the right to be wrong?

The third reason for asserting that universities worthy of the name are by their nature ethical relates to the beneficence cluster of values in the table above. Universities are inherently social. They are places which cannot function without cooperation and inter-personal reliability. Staff members who prefer to let their self-interest outweigh their duty to act supportively towards their colleagues when that is needed harm this essential requirement. Universities are not places for the selfish any more than for the dishonest. The duty to increase knowledge is of course non-negotiable, but nobody ever does this entirely alone, without recourse to laboratories, libraries, learned journals, administrative departments and those who staff them. It will be clear that in drawing on these resources and those who work there, staff members who do so respectfully and considerately will help maintain the spirit of helpfulness that is essential for success, just as rude or inconsiderate behaviour damages that spirit.

Having set out these three reasons for defining the university as by its nature ethical, it is now possible to identify the most important challenges facing universities in connection with the further development of a global ethic. They are the inter-disciplinary and multi-cultural development of a maximally inclusive, multicultural value system as a contribution to the global ethics movement; the development of a values-driven pedagogy which will incorporate the values of the developing global ethic; and thirdly to develop leaders in any field imbued with those values, so fitting them for a moral impact in a globalizing, richly multi-cultural world.

The operations and structures of an ethically excellent, multi-cultural university will embody and practice agreed, basic ethical values such as those listed in the table above and avoid the opposites of those ethical qualities, above all dishonesty, injustice, mediocrity, selfishness, disrespect and laziness.

5.4 Practical Considerations for Universities

Ethics must never be just an impressive set of concepts and principles; it is pre-eminently something done, so this final section of the chapter provides guidelines and measures for implementing the kind of multi-cultural, global ethics project described above.   For convenience they are given in point form, starting with the underlying principles of an effective ethics programme in any multi-cultural organization but especially in universities.

- The essential foundation for institutional ethical strength is excellent thought leadership about ethics itself.
- Ethics must be understood in the light of all available knowledge about it. It is not the exclusive province of one or two historically dominant disciplines, nor is the gift of the west or of religion to the whole world.
- Ethical strength depends much more on commitment than compliance.
- Commitment requires that all those affected must be able to participate freely in enhancing the cthical quality of the university in question.
- There is no organizational quick fix for ethics: achieving and sustaining deep ethical quality is an ongoing, monitored process.
- Organizational ethical strength has three key aspects: workplace ethical strength, individual moral character, and exemplary ethical leadership.
- To achieve success in a multi-cultural society, the processes and values of ethical enhancement must be multi-culturally based.

- Top-down moralizing is fatal to an ethics project; instead it is essential to appeal to and involve the ethical strengths and experiences of the members of the university on a voluntary, respectful basis.
- All parts of the organization must be involved, including the leadership.

With these principles to guide the implementation of the ethics project envisaged in this chapter, here are practical steps that can be taken.

1) Constitute and authorize a task group with ethical and related expertise
2) to drive and manage the process under a respected leader.
3) Invite and enable all members to participate in discussing and defining the core ethical values and ethical nature of their institution, e.g. by means of sending inputs to the task group in response to drafts created by the task group. The drafts are then revised and a second version is sent to members.
4) Develop a careful, academically and ethically sound method of fostering moral motivation – i.e. the will to do the right thing at all times and communicate this to all members of the institution. A way to do this is summarized in the next paragraph.

From human brain science we learn that there are powerful structures in the brain-stem, the limbic system and hippocampus which drive (but do not coerce) us to actions that keep us alive and help us thrive, such as our pleasure, memory and feeling centres (Ashbrook and Albright 1997: 78-84). Uncontrolled by conscience, they easily lead to selfishness and even violence by those equipped to use it. A realistic institution must recognize this reality and curb its harmful potential by understanding the following. Policing, metaphorically understood as that which protects us from wrong-doing and from wrong-doers, must always be there in any institution. It requires two arms: external, in the form of effective, fair disciplinary structures, personnel and where necessary punishments, and internal, in the form of the moral sense or conscience of members.

The ideal situation is where individual conscience is strong, backed by a strong ethical workplace culture and by ethical leaders, and where these are supported by the minimum of effective external policing. The worst situation is where both internal and external policing are weak, for that opens the door to the evils of academic corruption.

To achieve the ideal situation it is not enough for the multi-cultural university to open its doors to people from any culture. It must enlist their commitment to participating in the project of creating a richly ethical, multi-cultural future for the academy and the world by understanding their backgrounds and needs, seeking to meet those needs and ensuring that the university they attend is not just inclusive in name but in reality.

For this to happen a special responsibility rests on the shoulders of the senior university leadership. Only they can set the right tone for a truly inclusive campus that embraces ethical values all can share. Achieving that requires of them the visible, consistent practice of three cardinal values: equality, respect and fairness. Equality means that everyone in the university is treated and valued equally as unique human beings with hopes, fears, frustrations, needs and feelings. Respect means accepting and valuing the reality that they come from diverse backgrounds, follow different faiths or none, and have different political loyalties. Fairness means relating even-handedly towards all, and that makes it essential that the leadership shows no trace of bias on grounds of belief, culture and political party. On this kind of basis our universities can do invaluable work to create a global future worth having.

5.5 Chapter References

Ashbrook, J.B. and Albright, C.R. (1997): *The humanizing brain: where religion and neuroscience meet.* Cleveland: The Pilgrim Press.

Geering, L. (2014): *Reimagining God: the faith journey of a modern heretic.* Salem, Oregon: Polebridge Press.

Kidder, R. (1994): *Shared values for a troubled world: conversations with men and women of conscience.* San Francisco: Jossey-Bass Publishers.

Küng, H. and Kuschel, K. (eds). (1993): *A global ethic: the declaration of the Parliament of the World's Religions.* London: SCM Press.

Prozesky, M. (2007): *Conscience: ethical intelligence for global well-being.* Pietermaritzburg: University of KwaZulu-Natal Press.

Prozesky, M. (2014): "*Homo ethicus:* understanding the human nature that underlies human rights and human rights education." In *Journal for the study of religion*, volume 27, number 1, 2014, pp. 283-301

Whitehead, A. (1938, 1966): *Modes of Thought.* New York: The Free Press.

6

INFUSING ETHICS INTO EVERYDAY PRACTICE IN HIGHER EDUCATION

EM Lemmer

6.1 Introduction

Ethics in academia can be broadly understood as decision-making, associated with the university's tripartite mission of teaching, research and community service, which is based on moral principles or values, and which determines how members of the university community behave and treat others: with a view to the common good (Wagner, 2011). During the last three decades explicit debate about the role of ethics and values in higher education has gained prominence (Keenan, 2015) as evidenced in the proliferation of written codes of ethics and value statements, the establishment of ethics committees to grant clearance for research activities and the appointment of legal experts to deal with misconduct litigation, which ranges from professional misconduct, cheating, plagiarism to the misuse of university resources and misappropriation of funds (Heyneman, 2011). Notwithstanding gross violations of ethical behavior, what comprises everyday ethical academic conduct is not clear-cut and academics may differ in the identification and classification of appropriate values in higher education (Dill, 1982). The difficulty in setting out a uniform code of ethical conduct for academics lies in dilemmas of definition: what constitutes the academic profession and who are its members (Dill, 1982). In the professions of law and medicine written codes of conduct guarantee the integrity of members who are engaged in private practice and date back centuries. In contrast, scholarship is a communitarian activity, practised in discipline-based departments, colleges or faculties broadening out to the university as the larger community (American Association of University Professors [AAUP], 2009). To address this gap, national organization such as the AAUP (2009:111-112) developed five general standards for professional conduct of the academic profession in the United States. The standards are as follows: the commitment to the advancement of knowledge above all subsidiary interests; the promotion of learning in university students by appropriate pedagogy and role modelling; loyalty to the community of scholars including willingness to participate in university governance; a commitment to the roles of teacher and scholar as practised foremost within the institution; and the responsibility to balance rights and responsibilities as private citizens with rights and responsibilities as scholars committed to freedom of inquiry and speech and academic freedom in the public sphere. In addition, individual institutions and communities of scholars can develop their own codes or statements of professional ethics. In spite of this, professional self-regulation of ethical conduct in this context remains complex although not absent (Felicio, 1999).

6.2 Ethics in the Current Context of the University

Ethical conduct on an individual and an institutional level is problematized by the current context of higher education in an age of super-complexity (Barnett, 2000). The university has shifted from the so-called 'ivory tower' model of the collegial university to become the economic engine of societies whose future wealth and material well-being is based on knowledge which has intrinsic value only as a marketable commodity rather than as a cultural and scientific resource (Santiago, Tremblay, Basri & Arnal, 2008). In this environment, traditional collegial patterns of decision-making and loyalty to core academic values have been blurred by corporate models of leadership, governance and management (Sporn, 2006). Further, post-World War II massification continues unabated (Altbach & Forest, 2006), which places financial and infrastructural strain on institutions. Further, technological development has introduced changes in pedagogy, course delivery and communication in virtual academic communities (Scott, 2009). This has made the university an arena of competing discourses implicit in the language and everyday practice (Foucault, 1985). Discourses are value-embued and may be frequently ignored but function nevertheless (Hook, 2001). Dominant discourses, which arise from and drive the business university model generally adopted worldwide, are characterised by performativity, instrumentalism, corporatism and consumerism. Coexisting with these discourses are the more appealing discourses of care, service, servant leadership, integrity and trust, which are more likely to be overtly identified in mission statements and other codes of behavior prevalent in university branding and marketing (Visagie, 2005). However, it is arguable that the 'softer', more appealing discourses are merely paid lip-service as they jostle for recognition among the realities of a high-stakes accountability environment, which is managed by hard systems of hard 'control' and surveillance with their own rewards and penalties. Venter (2006a) contends that this increasing subordination of higher education to the forces of technicism and economism implies a reductionist view of the university's character and mission with far-reaching implications for university educators and students. The intellectual enterprise of the university is dehumanised in the interests of the new ideals of techno-economic progress (Venter, 2006b).

In South Africa post-1994 higher education transformation currently reflects these global trends as well as local imperatives (Mapesela & Hay, 2005). The Higher Education Act, No.101 of 1997 (Republic of South Africa [RSA], 1997) created a unitary, state-steered and quality-assured system of higher education, further shaped by institutional closures and mergers (Ministry of Education [MoE], 2001). A National Qualifications Framework (RSA, 2008) linked to an outcomes-based philosophy steered curricula into an outcomes-based format. New funding mechanisms re-orientated university offerings to address national, regional and local education and training priorities (MoE, 2003). Universities have also seen radical change in student and staff composition caused by the massive increase in black students, many of whom are underprepared for the demands of higher education (Du Toit, 2010) and the redress of racial imbalances throughout the ranks of university employees through equity policies (Hall, 2010). Organizational processes, partly in the wake of global trends and partly as a tool to control and regulate institutional change, are managed according to a managerial-corporate style by an increasing corps of university bureaucrats (Mapesela & Hay, 2005).

In sum, these developments, local and international, constitute a new crisis for the very idea of the university (Barnett, 2000) and have far-reaching challenges for ethical behaviour in academe. Decision-making based on moral principles is raised to new levels of complexity and the intensity of temptations to compromise, if not ignore, moral principles under high-stakes pressures particularly the financial, is increased (Wagner, 2011). By way of illustration, institutions may lower admission standards to enroll large numbers of students with a view to obtaining tuition fees which will increase university revenue. As Barnett (2004:v) observes, "The contemporary climate of 'performativity', with its insistence on demonstrable outcomes – preferably with a monetary gain – is threatening to reshape academic life in terms of an ideology of calculation."

6.3 Ethics and the University: the Educator's Multiple Roles

The professoriate operates in this vortex and any debate on ethics should grapple with this reality. Traditionally, the task of the academic is broadly arranged according to the tripartite mission of teaching, research and community service but teaching/transmission of knowledge is its overall distinguishing feature (i.e., as contrasted to a researcher employed in research institute or a community worker or instructor employed by a service organisation) (Boyer, 1990). Others suggest more complex and diversified role sets for the academic (Arreola, Theall & Aleamoni, 2003). However, even if only taken at the level of the more traditional three roles, the implications for ethical issues emerge. As teacher, the university educator communicates values to students, although some would argue that these are subverted or at least masked by the substantive issues of the discipline or field (McFarlane, 2004). In the teaching role university educators should be diligent in the lecture room and current in their subject matter (Scriven, 1982). Professional development should be directed towards producing quality teaching not only career promotion. As assessors of student work, university educators should be fair, unbiased and thorough. Similarly in the role as peer evaluator, the university educator must be unbiased and judge on merit only. These are but a few ways that ethics penetrates everyday academic life. In the role of researcher, aside from the clear requirements to meet the well-accepted ethical standards in field or laboratory work, other issues exist which are more subtle and these are related to the privileged position held by research production in most universities due to the potential of the research endeavour for wealth creation (Brewe & Lucas, 2009). Translated into the everyday life of the academic, research and publication assume far greater importance than teaching, contributions to service or internal university governance. According to Bexley, James and Arkoudis (2011:14) academics in Australia expressed a sentiment commonly encountered in most universities elsewhere, "Even though there is a spoken acknowledgement that all three (teaching, research and service) are important, every academic knows there is a hierarchy with research sitting on top." Thus, the tension between teaching and research manifests itself in decision-making revolving around a how the academic spends his/her best time and resources – in quality teaching or in quality research with its lure of material incentives at the expense of the teaching task. Although such dilemmas will seldom, if ever, bring an individual academic into contravention of an official code of ethics, they are nonetheless real in terms of moral decision-making. Thirdly, the service role also may also present the university educator with choices between non-profit community projects and lucrative consultancies or large scale funded projects privileged also by university administrators in pursuit of a source of third stream income.

6.4 Concluding Comments

Institutionalisation of ethical checks and balances, while necessary, run the risk of mere 'paper ethics'. To create a pervasive ethical culture in the current context of the university fraught with ambivalent, jostling discourses and among the competing role sets of the professoriate, principles and values hinge on the internalisation and the transmission of an ethical habitus, that is, an embodied ethics (Bourdieu, 1970) or an 'ethics from below' (Dill, 1982). This is of particular importance as universities receive continually new cohorts of academics who should be socialised in ethically sound and rigorous communities of practice. In this regard university educators would benefit from a code set, such as the ethics of knowledge developed by Clark Kerr (1994:13), former president of the University of California. Kerr advocates ethical principles for academe based on care – for intellectual property, for intellectual freedom and discourse, for academic merit and performance, for human and animal subjects in research, for position and resources and for students and colleagues. To reach this kind of consensus about core values that penetrate academic daily life far beyond the stated requirements of a clearance committee, the conditions of an ethical contract or the rigours of a plagiarism-checking device, collective self-scrutiny is necessary. This would also resolve the dilemma of the perceived tensions between so-called "business" ethics and disciplinary based ethics.

6.5 Chapter References

Altbach, P.G. & Forest, J.F.F. (2006): Introduction. In: Forest, J.F.F. & Altbach, P.G. (eds.) *International handbook of higher education. Part one.* Dordrecht: Springer.

American Association of University Professors [AAUP] (2009): Statement on Professional Ethics. Available at: https://www.aaup.org/ report/statement-professional-ethics, retrieved on 20 May 2016.

Arreola, R.A., Theall, M. & Aleamoni, L. M. (2003): Beyond Scholarship: Recognizing the Multiple Roles of the Professoriate. Paper presented at the 83rd Annual Meeting of the American Educational Research Association. Chicago: April 22. www.cedanet.com/meta/ Beyond%20Scholarship.pdf, accessed 20 May 2016.

Barnett, R. (2000): *Realizing the university in an age of super-complexity.* London: Society for Research into Higher Education & Open University Press.

Barnett, R. (2004): Foreword. In: McFarlane, B. *Teaching with integrity: The ethics of higher education practice.* London: Routledge Falmer.

Bourdieu, P. (1991): Universal corporatism: The role of intellectuals in the modern world. *Poetics Today*, 12(4), 656-666.

Boyer, E.L. (1997): *Scholarship reconsidered: priorities of the professoriate.* San Francisco: Jossey Bass.

Bexley, E., James, R. & Arkoudis, S. (2011): *The Australian academic profession in transition.* Melbourne: Centre for the Study of Higher Education, University of Melbourne.

Dill, D.D. (1982): The structure of the academic profession: towards a definition of ethical issues. *Journal of Higher Education,* 53(3), 256-267.

Du Toit, A. (2010): Social justice and post-apartheid education in South Africa. In: Featherman, D.L., Hall, M. & Krislov, M. (eds.) *The next 25 years: Affirmative action in higher education in the United States and South Africa.* Ann Arbor: The University of Michigan Press.

Felicio, J. (1999): Ethics in higher education: Red flags and grey areas. *Feminism & Psychology*, 9(1), 53-73.

Foucault, M. (1985): *The use of pleasure.* London: Penguin.

Hall, M. (2010): Nothing is different, but everything has changed. In Featherman, D.L., Hall, M. & Krislov, M. (eds.) *The next 25 years: Affirmative action in higher education in the United States and South Africa.* Ann Arbor: The University of Michigan Press.

Heyneman, S.P. (2011): The corruption of ethics in higher education, *International Higher Education,* Winter, 8-9.

Hook, D. (2001): Discourse, knowledge, materiality, history: Foucault and discourse analysis. *Theory and Psychology*, 11(4), 521-547.

Keenan, J.F. (2015): *University ethics: How colleges can build and benefit from a culture of ethics.* Lanham: Rowman & Littlefield.

Kerr, C. (1994): Knowledge ethics and the new academic culture, *Change* (Jan/February), 9-15.

Mapesela, M. & Hay, H.R. (2005): Through the magnifying glass: A descriptive theoretical analysis of the possible impact of the South African higher education policies on academic staff and their job satisfaction. *Higher Education*, 50, 111-128.

McFarlane, B. (2004): *Teaching with integrity: The ethics of higher education practice.* London: Routledge Falmer.

Ministry of Education (MoE) (2001): *National Plan for Higher Education. Government Gazette,* Vol. 4. No. 22138. Pretoria: Government Printers.

Ministry of Education (MoE) (2003): *Funding of Public Higher Education. Government Gazette,* Vol. 2, No. 2002. Pretoria: Government Printers.

Republic of South Africa [RSA] (1997): Higher Education Act, 1997 (Act No.101 of 1997). *Government Gazette*, Vol. 390. No. 18515. Pretoria: Government Printers.

Republic of South Africa [RSA] (2008): The National Qualifications Framework Act, 2008 (Act No. 67 of 2008). *Government Gazette*, Vol. 524, No. 31909. Pretoria: Government Printers.

Santiago, P., Tremblay, K., Basri, E. & Arnal, E. (2008): *Tertiary education for the knowledge society.* Paris: OCED.

Scott, P. (2009): Markets and new modes of knowledge production, In: Enders, J. & De Weert, E. (eds.) *The changing face of academic life: Analytical and comparative perspectives.* London: Palgrave Macmillan.

Scriven, M. (1982): Professorial ethics, *Journal of Higher Education,* 53(2), 308-317.

Sporn, B. (2006): Governance and administration, In: Forest, J.F.F. & Altbach, P.G. (eds.) *International handbook of higher education. Part one.* Dordrecht: Springer.

Venter, J.J. (2006a.): A creative humane university: coping with the business model. *Koers,* 71(2), 357-395.

Venter, J.J. (2006b): A humane "university": Resisting scientism, technicism and economism. *Koers,* 71(1), 275-318.

Visagie, J. (2005): Deconstructing the discourse of community service and academic entrepreneurship: The ideological colonisation of the university. *Acta Academica,* 37(1), 222-237.

Wagner, J.W. (2011): What we mean by ethics. Paper presented on 2 February, 2011 at the Second Annual Academic & Industry Intersection Conference, Emory University, Atlanta, Georgia Conference Center.

SECTION 2

Responsible Leadership

7

RESPONDING TO THE CHALLENGES OF GENDERED CAREER ASPIRATIONS: RESPONSIBLE ACADEMIC LEADERSHIP IN SUPPORT OF THE GOLDEN TRIAD OF ACCESS, EQUITY AND JUSTICE

Divya Singh

7.1 Introduction

The triad of access, equity and justice in higher education has been discussed, analysed and debated at numerous forums, today finding expression in both global and national policy documents, regulating frameworks, and action plans. The UNESCO *World Declaration on Higher Education for the Twenty First Century: Vision and Action* (1998: 1) and the Sustainable Development Goals Post 2015 are but two examples. The Preamble to the *World Declaration on Higher Education for the Twenty First Century: Vision and Action* states unequivocally:

> "On the eve of a new century, there is ... an increased awareness of its [higher education] vital importance for sociocultural and economic development, and for building the future, for which the younger generations will need to be equipped with new skills, knowledge and ideals."

There is no gainsaying the correctness and enormity of this directive in a world characterized by continual change and a higher education sector undergoing disruption. In this milieu, university leaders are called upon to ensure that the teaching and learning agenda remains true to these aspirations and that the students they produce are true global citizens competent to understand and engage both discipline-specific issues as well as ethical, cultural, political, and social problems.

However, before they become graduates, for many potential students lies the challenge of access and admission to university. In both of the aforementioned signal global instruments, nothing is said about promoting a better gender balance in higher education. This may be because, in the developing world from the second to the third millennium, gender balance in higher education has in fact greatly improved. With the emphasis on open and equitable access for previously disadvantaged groups facilitating their entry into higher education, the number of women entering the higher education system and university specifically has increased manifold. However, notwithstanding the open access paradigm, a particular area of emphasis, globally indicated, is that women often constrain themselves, giving preference to particular career choices "perceived to be traditionally suitable for females" (Obura and Ajowi 2012: 149). Similarly, Momsen (2010: 65) describes the "subject ghettos" as nursing, education, and social work for women and remonstrates that courses leading to the best paid jobs such as medicine, law and engineering continue to be dominated by men.

The purpose of this paper is to open a discussion on whether the gendered mindset to career choices by women remains real, and if indeed true, then what informs such thought and decision-making processes in the twenty-first century, and is there anything that universities can (and should) be doing to influence and facilitate a different way of thinking and practice among women entering the university sector?

7.2 The Research Survey

In 2013-2014 the University of South Africa (Unisa) undertook a (limited) Student Education and Career Aspirations Survey at the request of the author. The final report was prepared by Dr Molapo based at the Unisa Directorate: Institutional Research. (Molapo & Mapolisa 2014) 1793 students participated in the survey and the participation analysis is reflected below:

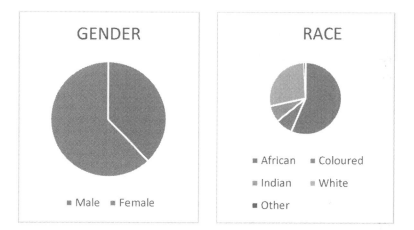

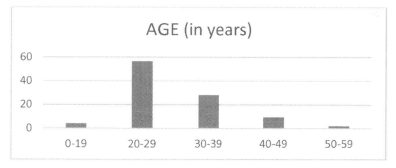

Graph 1: 56.5% of the participants were African, 7.6% were Coloured, 7.4% were Indian, 27.8% were White, and 0.7% fell into the category Other. The researchers confirm that the participation distribution by race was reflective of the institutional demographic. Graph 2: The gender participation indicates 37.9% were male and 62.1% female; and Graph 3: provides an indication of participants by age.

The study used a social constructionist approach building on the work of Momsen (2008) and Mutekwe and Modiba (2012) which posits that (i) gender is a social phenomenon and (ii) gender influences social and cultural practices and expectations (Molapo & Mapolisa 2014: 9).

Data collection was through an online survey questionnaire as well as face-to-face interviews. The survey instrument included both structured and open-ended questions which directed the respondents' focus whilst not completely limiting the expressions of their views, which were recorded in the responses to the open-ended question.

7.2.1   Results

Students were questioned on their career aspirations and career choices, as well as the underpinning factors that swayed and/or informed their final decisions. The results indicate that *inter alia* (i) particularly with regard to subject choices in secondary school, the majority of the respondents indicated that they had chosen their own subjects in secondary school (46.4%), followed by 20.6% who indicated being influenced by their mother or a female guardian. Other role-models included siblings (6.9%), friends (11%), school teachers and counselors (29.5%), others (5.9%) (Molapo & Mapolisa 2014: 21). With specific reference to study at university, a majority of the respondents (33.3%) indicated that they had made their own decision to register at university, followed by those influenced by their mother or female guardian (17.6%) with the influence of the father or a male guardian registered at 14.5%. 49.5% of the respondents noted that they had individually chosen their subjects and career path at university, whilst 10.1%

received guidance from their mother or a female guardian and 8.4% were influenced by their father or a male guardian. Siblings, friends, school teachers and counselors, and others made up the difference (Molapo & Mapolisa 2014: 21).

The respondents were specifically challenged on the opportunities available to male and female students and the results were an unequivocal 72.3%: 14.6% disagreement with the statement that male and female learners were not afforded the same opportunities in high school, whilst 13.1% of the respondents were unsure. There was also disagreement (45.5%: 27.2%) that male learners necessarily performed better than female learners in mathematics and physical science in high school. 62.0% of the respondents were certain that men and women could enter a career in any field of their choice (Molapo & Mapolisa 2014: 34).

Notwithstanding the above opinions, when making a gender comparison about the suitability of specific fields of study, a majority of respondents were of the opinion that some areas of study were predominantly male-oriented and less suitable to women. The results are tabulated below:

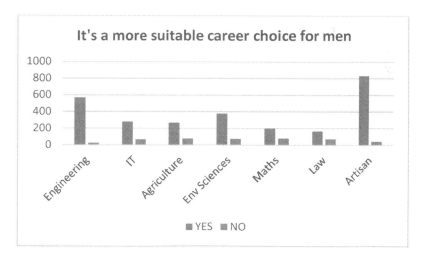

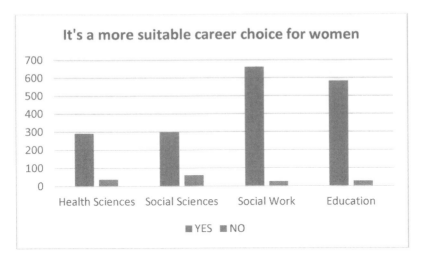

From the sample surveyed, females clearly outnumbered males in education (77.8%:22.2%), human sciences (73.8%:26.2%), economic and management sciences (62.8%:37.2%), and agricultural and environmental sciences (57.4%:42.6%). There was a much smaller difference in law with women exceeding men by 51.9%:48.1%. However, there was a notable difference in science, engineering and technology where the males outnumbered the females by 70.1%:29.9% (Molapo & Mapolisa 2014: 33).

Finally, on the overall gender and perceptions of career choice, the findings are set out below:

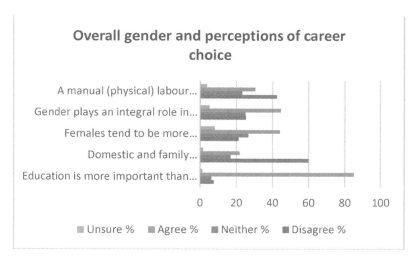

(Molapo and Mapolisa 2014: 36)

An interesting consideration is the point that the higher number of respondents who agreed with the statement that "gender plays an integral role in the career choices made by males and females' may be indicative of the respondents" own decision-making: however, this matter was not further tested in the survey.

7.3 Discussion

The literature confirms that there is indeed a difference in the manner in which men and women make career choices. There is no evidence of a single factor that influences career choice: rather what one sees is a multiplicity of values of both psychological and sociological character that underpin the identified variances. Behrend et al (2007:1) suggest that one way in which students - both male and female - make career decisions is by gauging their perceived overall 'fit' with the chosen career specialty.

In understanding this notion of "fit" Obura and Ojawi (2012: 150) found that one of the significant factors impacting on "fit" especially when subject choices are made, is school performance. In their study amongst students in Kenya, the poor performance of females in the training setting when compared with their male counterparts led women to make particular career choices because of the perception that "some careers are better suited for males".

The Unisa study also reveals the importance of family/guardian representatives in influencing career choice, repeating the recommendations of the social constructivist theory, specifically the influence of learning through observation and imitation (Ernest 1994: 63). Using the principles of social constructionism helps understand how and why many women choose specific careers, explains why children identify with parental norms and expressions of experience from within the communities in which they grow up, and often take onboard and internalize expressed gender stereotypes and opinions as their own. Interestingly, the study showed far more clearly that amongst the respondents canvassed, a significant majority had made their own career choices, persuaded by neither parent: however, social and community influence was a significant factor. This is not incongruent with social constructivism for as Ernest (1994: 63) notes, "Knowledge and perception of reality are socially constructed and we are socialized in our upbringing to share aspects of that perceived view."

The Unisa study found that mothers have a slightly higher influence on career choices and aspirations of their children - both male and female – as compared with the father or male guardian. The impact of the mother or maternal guardian on career aspirations reiterates the findings of Bojuwoye and Mbanjwa (2006) and the much earlier studies by Mickelson and Velasco (1998) who also identified a similar result. However, Mickelson and Velasco go further to point out that not only were mothers more influential in guiding occupational selections but that daughters' career choices were often closely aligned with that of the maternal parent. Hurtado and Gauvain (1997: 514) looked at influencing factors on "college attendance" (as opposed to career choice) and suggest that from their study, it was evident that amongst the Mexican American youth the role of the mother is far more emphatic, whilst amongst the Euro-American adolescents it was the fathers' education that played the stronger part. They did not provide any reason for the difference.

In studying women's reasons for going to College, Astin (1990: 484) found that it was "both *intellectual* and *occupational*." Whilst factors such as "employability" and "making more money" were important considerations for the women surveyed by Astin, of equal interest to them was the need to "learn more" and "gain a general education and appreciation of ideas". On the other hand, the men surveyed ranked "wanting to make more money" as a consistently higher trigger than "the need to learn more". Sax (1994) and Perry (1996) also found a similar mindset recording that whilst women were more concerned with the social good of their career choice, men's aspirations appeared to be inherently driven by financial empowerment.

However, whilst women appear to indicate a stronger inclination to supporting the common good when making career choices, as early as 1990, Astin (1990: 485) found that in the U.S.A. almost one-third of high school females were already beginning to make choices for careers in business, law, medicine and engineering, with only one in 10 women expecting to pursue a teaching career and fewer looking to careers in the arts. (1990: 489). Obura and Ajowi (2012: 157) confirm the funneling of the career aspiration disparity between men and women finding, for instance, that amongst the youth participating in their study, the main career choices for male respondents was law, medicine and engineering whilst amongst female respondents it was also medicine and law, with nursing as the third option. With specific reference to medical study, Behrend *et al* (2007) found that *within* the discipline there are aspirational differences with women being much more inclined to specialties focused on primary care over other areas of medicine. They attributed the choice differentiation to "a function of gender differences in the values that affect students' career choices" and continue, "One such value involves the desire to give comprehensive care for ones patients" which includes "providing treatment that that encompasses psychological and social aspects of patient well-being in addition to biological aspects" (2007: 1). The conclusion they draw is that primary care, chosen over all other specializations, is essentially because it is "relationship-focused" as opposed to "treatment-focused". This outcome is synchronous with the findings of the study by Clancy and Dollinger (1993) whose results revealed that when asked to choose photographs that described their lives, women chose photos of others whilst male participants selected more photographs of themselves, reinforcing the view that woman have a greater tendency to define themselves based on social relationships and connectedness compared with men. (Clancy & Dollinger 1993: 488) Similarly Obura and Ajowi also found that amongst Kenyan youth, female respondents were more inclined towards careers that were "biological-science" based whilst the male respondents were inclined towards the physical-science based occupations. (2012:157) The Unisa survey corroborates the findings in the literature that the social and care-giving disciplines tend to be dominated by females.

Very often the differentiation that culminates in career selections is initiated in the school environment where under-representation of females in particular subjects has concomitant consequences for occupational under-representation. The sciences are a very good example of this manifestation and it explains the current limited number of women in the areas of science, technology, engineering and mathematics (STEM) in university and the workplace. Obura and Ajawi point out that math-related and scientific and technical subjects have traditionally been seen as male activities and, coupled with the stereotype of women being seen as less competent than their male counterparts in these areas, it may have led to "girls being less confident than boys in their general intellectual abilities and to have lower expectations for success at difficult academic and vocational activities." (2012: 160) Against this stereotypical backdrop, girls may be even less inclined to choose such subjects, particularly if they do not find them especially interesting and important (Obura and Ajawi 2012:160).

However, over the years there has been an increasing interested amongst girls in school in the subjects of science, technology, engineering, and mathematics, which is confirmed by the growing numbers of women (i) registering for STEM disciplines in, and (ii) graduating from universities in these disciplines. Hill *et al* agree but raise the nagging concern that notwithstanding the growing numbers, there still remains a pattern amongst female school-leavers of diminishing interest from high school to graduation. They note specifically that in high school, as many women as men show an interest in pursuing science and engineering programmes at university, yet fewer women *actually* do so (2010:xiv) and, similar to other studies, they identified that the disparity becomes greater when the biological sciences are not included (2010:7). Their findings are that, by graduation, the numbers of men completing the qualification outstrips women in almost every science, engineering, physics and computer science programme. The representation of women in science and engineering drops even further in the transition to the workplace and they confirm that men continue to outnumber them especially at the upper levels of the profession. (Hill *et al* 2010: xiv; 9-11; 18-19)

Margolis and Fisher (2006) looked particularly at computer science as a career choice, and found that the image of the "the computer geek" - whose only interest is the computer - is particularly damaging to women "who, instead of the singular obsessive interest in computing that is common to men, require a balance of multiple interests" (2006:6).

This image and the concomitant social reaction shapes the assumptions of who will succeed and who belongs to the discipline. The suggested challenge is, however, not insurmountable but Hill *et al* make it clear that in addressing the issues, universities must avoid the traditional approach of trying to fit women in to computer science: rather what is required is to revise perceptions of computer science at an overall level. In response Margolis *et al* (2006:6) suggest one simple inducement to attract women into the discipline - Computer Science Departments should consider creating "a more conducive and balanced environment where social spaces and interactions are promoted" thereby mitigating the perception of computer science students as isolated, asocial personality types, and social misfits.

The research also demonstrates that limited familiarity coupled with negative experiences and an incomplete understanding of the broad employment market and professional *milieu* as well as the available opportunities and prospects for success may also contribute to career choice decisions, especially amongst women in minority and previously disadvantaged groups. Astin's study on career choices amongst women from "minority" groups' is however, more hopeful as she notes that over time there has been a far more focused shift in career choices towards professions that "demand increased preparation and training, and occupations that require greater commitment" amongst women from minority groups. (1990: 489) This accelerated shift that was identified by Astin may be explained by (i) increased exposure of minority and previously disadvantaged groups to the different and better opportunities and careers, and (ii) a recognition of past and current socio-economic challenges and the consequent hope of a better life and future.

Against this background, however, the point made by Shumba and Naong (2012: 169) must not be lost – they caution that whilst context is important, personal aptitudes are also a critical factor in the decision-making process. Therefore, as schools and universities focus on women in science, it must be understood that not every girl is geared for science, just as not every boy will not choose to enter a career in science or technology. That being understood, at a principle level, if the identified challenge that constrains women's career aspirations is to be addressed by the university sector specifically, it is crucial that academic leaders understand the influencing factors that contribute to how career choices are made by men and women, how racial and ethnic dynamics contribute to the final selection of occupation by many women, and that they are able to respond to these individual constraints.

7.4 Recommendations

Effective solutions to this conundrum will require responsible and responsive leadership. Stuckelberger and Mugambi (2007:1) define such leadership in the following terms: "A leader is responsible when he or she is responsive to the needs, concerns and interest of those whom one aspires to lead." Responsible leadership recognizes the various issues and the diversity of demands, the opportunities and the challenges, it requires the necessary sensitivity that therefore ensures that decisions, plans and strategies are mutually reinforcing and serve the interests of all stakeholders.

Women's participation in higher education has seen an extraordinary growth with policy imperatives in many countries specifically focusing on this issue. From school, girls are being encouraged to study science and mathematics and enter careers that were previously part of the male-oriented stereotype. Employment opportunities for women have undergone unprecedented change as a result legislation and policy directives. Thus, there is no gainsaying that in recent years one is seeing a widening of career aspirations as well as work-related expectations from women and a clear trajectory of convergence in the occupational choices of men and women. Women are now more prepared to enter fields previously occupied by men and take the opportunities on offer. The Unisa study found that among other choices, the majority of the respondents – both male and female – indicated that they chose their current career paths because they are interesting and fulfilling (83.4%), have prospects to improve their economic welfare (70.7%), and are relevant to the job market (63.1%) (Molapo & Mapolisa 2014: 37-38).

Further, notwithstanding the growing trends in women's empowerment, the stereotypical choice aspirations still pertain – as is indicated by the Unisa survey and other studies – and it would be premature to believe that true equality has been attained. There is still much work that needs attention during basic education and secondary school, as well as from university leadership to provide the enabling environment that addresses the constraining forces that perpetuates specific stereotypes for women, and ensures a totally desegregated labour market. If higher education is aimed at a collective and individual good and is recognized as a core lever for social development and global citizenship, the doors of higher education must be opened wider and all those who wish to study and are capable of studying should be able to. If the commitment to the Sustainability Development Goals is to be realized, equity and access will require greater impetus focusing on race, economic standing, and gender. The studies analysed recognize that women are inclined to choose career opportunities that are more 'social' and relationship-orientated (as opposed to investigative and technical): however, what can higher education offer to better attract women into these less-chosen areas and disciplines identified as being strongly male-dominated? In the STEM disciplines, for example, if there is indeed a veritable commitment to growing the number of women in the profession the test for leaders in education is to identify innovative solutions to encourage women to enter these career disciplines and to persist and graduate. The "nudge theory" provides an interesting option in positive reinforcement – where universities will take the bold step of reviewing the teaching and learning space in identified disciplines, deliberately inculcating and nurturing a growth mindset which reinforces the belief that men and women are equally capable of succeeding in the chosen occupation. In the mathematics discipline, for example, Hill *et al* motivate the importance of reassuring young students both at school and at university that mathematical ability is really a "learned skill" rather than a "gift" (2010: 34; 20). Similarly, Dweck's (2006) research points to men having greater inherent spatial skills than women, influencing their success in the STEM disciplines. Poor or under-developed spatial skills often deter girls from pursuing mathematics or science courses or programmes: however, Hill *et al* point out again that spatial ability can be learned and 'dedicated courses in the curriculum aimed at improving spatial-visualisation skills of affected students, [have] rendered very positive outcomes (2010: 20). Positive reinforcement in the classroom is crucial as it inclines towards a twofold progressive impact. Hill et al confirm that firstly, with positive reinforcement and support women stayed in the programme and completed their studies; and secondly, that they were less susceptible to the negative stereotypes that presented at university and even when they became part of the work environment (2010: 34; see also Frome, Alfeld-Liro & Eccles undated). Anecdotal evidence submits that competent women in a male job are often found 'less likeable' and experience an unwelcoming and 'chilly' working environment (Seymor 1995). However, if men and women are made aware of this prevalent prejudice, they can prepare for it and/or consciously work at expunging such a mindset. Supporting women in male-oriented disciplines and raising awareness amongst the men of the environmental prejudices, also requires universities to consider a more holistic and integrated approach to the learning paradigm, focusing on discipline-specific teaching whilst also preparing students for the workplace with the concomitant cultural and contextual biases and stereotypes. This will of course require deep research and a thorough understanding of the profession: rather only the limited focus on the discipline of the programme.

There is no denying that if science is the discipline of choice, students entering university need a sound foundation and this begins in the school. In South Africa, for example, if the challenges experienced in the schooling system which have resulted in the under-preparedness of school leavers particularly in the areas of mathematics and science are not addressed, "this will continue to have an impact on learners" choice of study, with fewer being academically prepared to tackle science and engineering degrees (Coetzee et al 2012: 23). As Ernest (1994: 63) notes: "both social processes and *individual sense making* have central and essential parts to play in the learning of mathematics"; [my emphasis].

This does not mean that students cannot succeed in the university, with the appropriate didactic and pedagogical reforms in place this is achievable: however, the challenge at university level is in attracting school leavers to the STEM disciplines when the high school learning experience has already been one that was negative.

On a more positive and hopeful note, Astin (1990: 489) found that over her 13 year longitudinal study (1975-1988), the degree aspirations of minority women had increased far more significantly than those of white women with a far higher proportion aspiring to careers in medicine, law and engineering as opposed to teaching and the arts. This bodes well for the global future. However, that said and given the global policy imperative, government intervention with appropriate encouragements and incentives will probably be one of the strongest catalysts for change. Financial aid, bursaries and scholarship for women seeking to study for degree programmes in areas highlighted as male dominated will be a material inducement for women, particularly in countries like South Africa where affordability of higher education is a critical constraint for the majority of the population. Leadership internships and learnerships for women leaving university – focused on addressing her specific contextual and social realities – will positively reinforce an informed decision to take on business and leadership roles and to remain in position even after marriage and a family.

A very important signal for change is role-modelling – children making secondary school subject choices and career choices at university need to see positive reinforcement that quashes the perceptions of specific careers being for men or women and household chores being the prerogative of women. A small improvement that will yield big results is for universities to ensure that in the specifically identified disciplines, they attract more successful women as faculty, who will in turn be role-models and mentors to young students.

Notwithstanding Momsen's affirmation (2010: 4) that the beginning of the third millennium has seen a "greater voice of women in both their public and private lives", a concern that cannot be underestimated is the belief amongst many men and women that the mother has the primary role of caregiver in the home. The task of balancing demanding career aspirations as well as a full burden of responsibilities in the home often results in role overload for many women. (Astin 1990:491) Universities can play a crucial role in enhancing social equality - creating spaces for discourse, engagement, disagreement, and debate, enabling men and women to hear each other, and to understand that running a home is a joint responsibility. There is no gainsaying that gender equality requires change from both men and women. Universities and the university leadership regime should be at the forefront of leading such social change imperatives, promoting activities and engagements that acknowledge the need to adjust both at the deeper personal and communal levels, as well as through ensuring curriculum transformation and gender mainstreaming in the university programmes and projects.

7.5 Conclusion

If one accepts the proposition that (a) we are in a modern economy – the so-called "knowledge era" – where education is the key driver, and (b) women are central to global development, then it follows that *all* plans and strategies geared to future growth, well-being and sustainability need to include a focus on gendered abilities, rights and needs. Momsen (2010: 251] warns though that "[i]nvesting in women is not a global panacea." However, it will set a springboard for future generations to be treated equally, fairly and justly. However, the caution by Tomlinson (2007: 287) must be underscored namely that women are not a monolithic group and the way in which students approach their career choices is incredibly subjective and "value- and identity-driven, relating to the graduates' own disposition and biographies." Thus career aspirations are ultimately a confluence of communal experience, economic reality, and very importantly individual identity. There is no one-size fits all solution but an open door and a level playing field will be a critical enabler for equity and access of women in higher education.

7.6 Chapter References

Astin, H.S. (1990): Educating Women: A Promise and a Vision for the Future. 98. *American Journal of Education*, 479-493.

Bojuwoye, O. & Mbanjwa, S. (2006): Factors impacting on career choices of technikon students from previously disadvantaged high schools. 1. *Journal of Psychology in Africa*, 3-16.

Clancy, S.M. & Dollinger, S.J. (1993): Photographic depictions of the self: Gender and age differences in social connectedness. *Sex Roles*. 29. 477-495.

Coetzee, M., Botha, J., Eccles, N., Holtzhausen, N., & Nienaber, H. (Eds). (2012): *Developing Student Graduateness and Employability.* Knowledge Resources Publishing Pty (Ltd). Randburg, South Africa.

Ernest, P. (1994): *Constructing Mathematical Knowledge: Epistemology and Mathematics Education.* Taylor and Francis. Bristol.

Fromes, P.M., Alfeld-Liro, C., & Eccles, J. Undated. *Why don't young women want to pursue male-type occupational aspirations? A test of compelling hypotheses.* www.rcgd.isr.umich.edu/garp/articles/eccles961.pdf, accessed 21/05/2016.

Hill, C., Corbett, C., & St Rose, A. (Eds). (2010): *Why so few women in science, technology, engineering and technology?* AAUW. Washington.

Hurtado, M.T. & Gauvain, M. (1997): Acculturation and Planning for College among Youth of Mexican Descent. 19. *Hispanic Journal of Behavioral Science*, 506-516.

Kao, G. & Tienda, M. (1998): Educational Aspirations of Minority Youth. 106. *American Journal of Education*, 349-384.

Moapo, M. & Mapolisa, S. (2014): *Student Education and Career Aspirations Survey and Report.* Directorate of Institutional Research. Unisa. South Africa.

Margolis, J. & Fisher, A. (2002): *Unlocking the Club House: Women in Computing.* Massachusetts Institute of Technology. Cambridge.

Mutekwe, E. & Modiba, M. (2012): Girls' career choices as a product of a gendered school curriculum: the Zimbabwean example. 32. *South African Journal of Education*, 279-292.

Momsen, J. (2010): *Gender and Development.* Routledge. London.

Obura, C.A. & Ajowi, J.O. (2012): Gender and Students' Perceptions of Career Aspirations in Secondary Schools. 1. *Academic Journal of Interdisciplinary Studies*, 149-163.

Perry, N.M. (2006): Factors influencing career choices of adolescents and young adults in rural Pennsylvania. 44. *Journal of Extension*, 1-6.

Sax, L.J. (1994): Retaining tomorrow's scientists: Exploring factors that keep male and female college students interested in science careers. 1. *Journal of Women and Minorities in Science and Engineering ERIC*, 45-61.

Seymour, E. (1995): The loss of women from science, mathematics, and engineering undergraduate majors: An explanatory account. 79. *Science Education*, 437-473.

Shumba, A & Naong, M. (2012): Factors Influencing Students' Career Choice and Aspirations in South Africa. 33. *Journal of Social Science*, 169-178.

Stuckelberger, C. & Mugambi, J.N.K. (eds). (2007): *Responsible Leadership Global and Contextual Ethical Perspectives*. Globethics.net Global Series No. 1, Geneva.

8

CHANGE LEADERSHIP, ETHICS AND THE FUTURE OF HIGHER EDUCATION

Maxim Jean-Louis

8.1 Introduction

Leaders in higher education face a great many responsibilities and an equal if not greater number of challenges. Amongst the numerous responsibilities of a higher education leader today is the expectation that they lead change, and do so strategically, sustainably and ethically. In our work as Contact North | Contact Nord with publicly funded colleges and universities in Ontario and in our interactions around the world, we can see these challenges "up close and personal" for Vice Chancellors, rectors and other leaders tasked with leading and directing academic and administrative success in the global higher education system.

Five strategic challenges in particular are at the heart of the changing realities for institutional leaders:

1) *Costs and Competitiveness* - several universities and colleges are facing financial challenges due to declining revenues from Government, changed market conditions and shifts in student demand. Others are looking at mergers and there are likely,

between now and 2030, to be significant structural changes in our systems of higher education.

2) *Structural Complexity* - With the pursuit of massification of higher education since the mid 1960's, there has been a growing expectation that more and more individuals will attend college and university and that the percentage of individuals in the workforce with a post-secondary qualification will continuously rise. Indeed, some countries have committed to this as a strategic intention. In 2015 there were significantly more universities and colleges around the world than there were in 1985 and 1995. Canada, for example, now has 98 public universities and over 130 public colleges. This has led to a very complex system which has on its own created some noteworthy barriers to learner articulation and mobility.

3) *Changing Student Expectations* - As students pay more of the costs of their own education, they demand more in terms of quality, relevance and engagement. More specifically, students are seeking high quality courses and programs which are work-relevant (but not solely focused on employment competencies) and engaging. Students today are much more critical of the quality of their education than many of their predecessors. As governments reduce their per-capita expenditure on higher education (following the trend they have pursued over the last twenty years), these expectations will increase.

4) *Technological Development* - Since 2000 there have been many changes in the technological landscape. Hand held devices now surpass desk-top computers in terms of ownership and use. Growing access to broadband (but still not universal) has changed access to knowledge, information, services and support. The emergence of online learning has transformed access to

learning for a great many students and has changed the dynamics of higher education.

5) *Global Competitiveness* - it will get more difficult over time to recruit, retain students as the market for these students becomes increasingly competitive and value sensitive. What is more, Governments will assess institutional performance by their ability to sustain themselves while offering less financial support per capita: expectations will grow while resources available to meet these expectations shift from government to more varied sources of revenue.

There are other factors too – demography, a rapidly changing knowledge base, new 'political correctness' sensitivities – but these five dominate the conversations of leaders. How they respond to the inter-related impacts of these challenges determines the extent of their ability to lead and the sustainable impact their leadership may have on their institution. Change leadership – the management of significant change and the ability to focus and align their colleagues on needed change – has become the key work of leaders. Not all are well equipped for the journey – the number who do not complete their contractual first term or seek a second term is on the rise and it is becoming more difficult to recruit to such leadership positions.

8.2 The Ethics of Change Leadership

Most faculty members, administrators and support staff do not especially like change. They are suspicious both of the outcomes and the process and will usually question the motives for change, especially if the rationale for change is presented in terms of external factors (financial, competitive factors, etc.) or in response to emerging technology. They are fearful for their future, both in terms of employment and security, but also for the design of their day to day work. Change is generally resisted, always questioned and sometimes seriously challenged. While similar sentiments may be found in business and other organizations, universities and colleges appear unable to engage and accelerate change, given that there are few incentives for them to do so.

Ethical behavior in the management of change is key to the success of any change initiative. This takes five key forms:

1) *Trust in the Message and the Information on which it is Based:* Stakeholders need to know that the information on which the change work is based is "the best it can be" and that there is integrity about the data, the analysis of these data and the options for change being presented. When there is a sense of bias, mistrust in the evidence base for change, then there will be mistrust in the process of change.

2) *Genuine Engagement Rather than Tokenism:* stakeholders feel that their voices are heard and that their suggestions are carefully considered and, where appropriate, included in the plan for change. They know that their voice carries weight.

3) *Development of a Values Driven Change Process* – the change journey is planned and designed so as to leverage and support the values of the organization. These values are articulated and the plan for change is tested against them.

4) *A Sense of Shared Outcome – The Change will Benefit More than a Few:* The change plan has consequences but these consequences seek to improve outcomes and performance for all not just a few. While some may be more impacted by change than others, the intended outcomes are aligned with the mission and values of the organization.

5) *Clarity About the Journey – No Surprises:* Once the change plan is made and communication lines established, organizational members do not receive constant surprises or

sudden requests for action. They know what they have to do and why.

These ethical principles are the bedrock of an approach to change which others have called "planned change" (Burnes and By, 2011). In this approach there are focused outcomes agreed by stakeholders and the journey to these outcomes is negotiated with stakeholders, who feel a true sense of engagement. This contrasts with a different approach to change, known as "emergent change" (Burnes and By, 2011) where new decisions are made which surprise stakeholders and the information base on which the change is being made keeps changing. Indeed, the emergent model is one in which change is a serial set of surprise activities as opposed to a set of inter-related and planned moves leading to agreed outcomes. Some changes in higher education institutions can be seen as planned and others as emergent.

One key difference between these two kinds of change – planned and emergent – is the ethical bases of the change. In planned change ethics are front and centre and are guiding the process of change. In emergent change expediency and urgency drive the process, with ethical behavior sometimes sacrificed for a "quick win". This leads to very different sense of stakeholder engagement and a very different focus for leadership. In emergent change, leadership is often focused on mediating between conflicting groups whereas in planned change the focus is more on engagement with all stakeholders on an agreed journey and destination. One is built on trust and the other is built on mistrust.

Given the commitment to collegiality and peer decision making within the higher education sector, planned and ethical change seem to fit culturally, especially if coupled with a strong use of empathy and evidence based decision making. Emergent change is often seen in a higher education context as expediency and is generally done with poor or no consultation and a lack of genuine engagement.

8.3 Managing Change

Change leadership is a fraught process, especially in higher educational institutions where professional autonomy is strong and tenure, supported by collective agreements written and agreed to at a different time, a reality for leaders to deal with. In many situations, managing by consensus is not possible, and so tensions and anxiety are very real. Also very real when faced with significant challenge, threat or uncertainty, is genuine and deep anxiety.

Effective change leaders have three main roles. These are, according to Moujaes et al (2012):

- *Thinking Ahead* – thinking back from the future, having undertaken cross-boundary learning and explored global and local developments. Using this work to develop a shared sense and shape of the future.

- *Leading Across their School and System* – demonstrate focused, ethical and effective leadership within their institution and system through their openness, personal mastery and passion.

- *Delivering Within* – ensuring that the institution continuously improves its performance, not just for some but for all. Driving performance with passion and being systematic, focused and mindful in leading change and measuring results.

These three managerial behaviours need to come from a stronger catalogue of leadership dispositions, such as these:

- *Practice personal mastery:* They have high integrity and view self-awareness as a prerequisite for leadership. They work hard to develop their capacity to innovate, and to inspire others to join them in making the world a better place and their school a great place for all.

- *Apply a glocal mindset:* They have a keen sense of history and seek a holistic understanding of changes taking place on a global scale. They use this global perspective as they address local challenges and seize opportunities (global and local – hence "glocal") to connect their work and that of others in the school to developments taking place elsewhere.

- *Accelerate cross-boundary learning:* They constantly seek to satisfy an intense curiosity about every facet of human life, past and present, scientific and artistic, technical and social. They guide others in distilling meaning from a morass of information, and efficiently apply their learning in creative ways to nurture innovation and drive improved performance.

- *Think back from the future:* They are readily able to imagine and articulate alternate futures and work back from there – connecting with lessons from the past to better understand the present and choose among possible paths to the future they see.

- *Lead systemic change:* They are systems thinkers who seek out patterns, interconnections and interdependencies. They are skilled in seeking common ground and nurturing productive collaboration across diverse parts of a system – be it an organization, a sector, a community, a network – to solve complex problems and drive large-scale change in their own school.

- *Drive performance with a passion:* They care that their leadership makes a substantive and sustainable difference, and are relentless in their commitment to performance. They articulate clear (and high) expectations of themselves and others, create focused strategies for innovating to achieve these ends, and are disciplined about assessing progress.

These six characteristics, developed by Murgatroyd and Simpson (2010), are not listed in order of importance nor are they intended to be complete – it is the list we have arrived at on this stage of our understanding and learning. It is becoming more difficult to recruit and retain such leaders (Selingo, 2016).

Underlying all of this work is the challenge of being an effective, focused communicator – engaged in communication that conveys determination, optimism, conviction, integrity and realism. Such communication cannot be "command and control", but has to lead to engagement, involvement and action.

8.4 Conclusion

As we look at the beginning of a transformative period in higher education – what some are seeing as a renaissance for learning and our colleges and universities – we need to ensure that institutional leadership focuses on change skills and competencies and ethical, planned change. If change is to occur without disruption and lead to improved learning outcomes for learners, greater equity and the most effective use of available resources, planned change is essential. While business leaders can simply exercise authority and demand change – something we can see in some private educational institutions and publishing organizations – universities and colleges do need to bring their people with them to ensure the sustainability of change.

What makes this work more difficult is the increasing austerity and financial challenges which higher educational leaders now have to cope with. Reduced per capita funding coupled with demand for greater student numbers, better quality, more work-ready skills, more commercially focused innovation and research – leaders are challenged simply to maintain what they have, especially in terms of people, buildings and infrastructure. As more change happens, leadership will be under considerable pressure. It would be easy to respond in an emergent rather than planned way. Yet time and time again in the study of effective, sustainable organizational change we see the importance of engagement, building ownership of a plan and making decisions with an evidence and empathy base. In higher education we need a high quality of leadership with the necessary skills and capabilities for this work. They are not always easy to find.

8.5 Chapter References

Burnes, B. and By, R.T. (2011) Leadership and Change – The Case for Greater Ethical Clarity. *Journal of Business Ethics*, Vol 108(20), pages 239-252.

Murgatroyd, S. and Simpson, D. (2010) *Renaissance Leadership – Leading and Rethinking the Future.* New York: Lulu Press.

Moujaes,C.N., Hoteit, L., Hiltunen, J. and Sahlberg, P. (2012) *Transformation Leadership in Education – Three Key Imperatives for Lasting Change.* New York: Booz & Co.

Selingo, J.J. (2016) The Job Nobody Can Seem to Keep: College President. *Washington Post*, July 15th

9

LEADERSHIP AND ETHICS IN HIGHER EDUCATION: SOME PERSPECTIVES FROM EXPERIENCE

N. Barney Pityana

"A return to first principles in a republic is sometimes caused by the simple virtues of one man. His good example has such an influence that the good men strive to imitate him, and the wicked are ashamed to lead a life so contrary to his example."

– Niccolo Machiavelli (1532).

"Leadership is communicating to people their worth and potential so clearly that they come to see it in themselves."

– Stephen R Covey

9.1 Introduction

It is a well-attested fact that the challenge of the modern century is the crisis of leadership. It is leadership that steers the course in war and in peace, that ensures that objectives are met, and hopes and aspirations realized. Yes, it is leadership that brings nations to the heights of exhilaration, sense of pride and belonging, and yet, it is a failure of leadership that brings people to the depths of despair and loss. Although leadership has become an all-pervasive study of the human condition in our times, it is remarkable that leadership has tended to be studied largely in relation to business, and politics, but rarely for its own sake.

The purpose of this paper is to demonstrate ways by which ethics has become essential component of good governance in higher education management. The paper draws extensively from the author's own experience as a manager of a large higher education institution, and from his long association at leadership level at higher education leadership. The paper, nonetheless, seeks a theoretical undergirding of ethics in higher education management. By so doing the paper seeks to move the ideas about leadership away from the constructs established in business and management sciences, and draws in large measure from philosophy, behavioural sciences and ethics.

9.2 Discussion

9.2.1   Underpinning Markers of Leadership

Leadership surely entails the capacity to galvanise, or mobilise people by a strategic utilization of available resources to achieve set objectives. The resources, both financial and human, but also the ability to strategically read human psychology, and to understand timing and place are the tools in trade for a study of leadership. To that extent therefore, leadership facilitates and enables. But Leadership is about people – their anatomy, their psychology and their gifts, and their skills[1]. The amazing thing is that almost everyone exercises leadership in one aspect of life or another, even at one time or another – in the home, in community or neighbourhood, and in various aspects of human endeavour. Leadership is an abiding constant in human life. It is unimaginable that there could be any human activity that happens without leadership. We all somehow and sometimes exercise leadership.

It is to recognize the skills, intelligence and effort that are required of us in different environments of leadership that we get to understand how best we can help achieve what is the best. (Shisan: 1937)

I need to express myself with a bit more care and nuance. We speak so often about "achievement". We are inclined to be "driven" by "success", by a profit or benefit motive, sometimes referred to as leadership by objectives. Often we fail to measure that element of leadership that is about human fulfilment, the capacity to realize one's human worth, and for the potential to be unleashed are not easily quantifiable or identifiable. That "worth" may not immediately translate into the bottom line or cash value, but nonetheless it cannot be said that it is without achievement. In other words it is at the level of the confluence of three categories of being that we find Leadership "success": human worth, realization of potential and meeting declared targets or strategic objectives.

Many of the studies on leadership have been about strategies that work to bring about the intended ends. Such studies are often about the social psychology of working with people, designing vision and mission, inspiring people to achieve, working together as a team or as a collective, checking and directing progress, assessing results.

Leadership is also not just about personality, or the position (in African language, 'a stool' the "leader" occupies). Leadership is more than just the personality, or character of the person who bears a title. It is about the values or the content of leadership – in other words, what does the leader stand for? It is at that point that one has to look beyond the leader to those who follow: who are they? Why do they follow? It is important to understand the people who are led or who follow the leader. They have certain personalities that may affect or influence the tenor of leadership. They are the ones who shape the quality of leadership, otherwise there is no point in being a leader without followers. Leaders and followers together do so in order to achieve shared objectives.

Leaders must also understand the people they lead. Followers are not mere passive receptacles of the wisdom of leaders, they shape and inform leadership, and they can make or break leaders. One must share with them something of a vision, and understand what makes them "tick", and internalize the context. In sum, then, however much technology, globalization and the science of humanities have developed, it remains universally accepted that Leadership Matters.

Modern scholarship has now moved from the psychology of leadership, or the behaviourist conceptions of leadership, to leadership by values, or leadership as reflective of, guarantor and creator of the values systems of the community, sometimes also referred to as "leadership by design". It has become apparent that the cost of leadership must also be assessed. In other words it is just as important to know how goals are achieved as the fact that they are achieved at all. In other words the topic that refers to "Leadership" *and* "Ethics" misses the point. In many respects one can hardly talk about leadership without factoring in values or ethics. Ethics is the necessary means by which leadership achieves goals by paying attention to ways and means, and not just to the ends. It is to understand that leadership is best exercised in an environment of checks and balances, in a responsible and accountable manner, under limitations of law, good order and morality. In other words the driving ambition must never be allowed to become the final arbiter, regardless of what rights and responsibilities are trampled upon in the process.

Leadership must be exercised in a fair and just manner mindful of the human dignity, the environment and rights of others that may be affected. In other words leadership can hardly be achieved without regard to the principles of "goodness" or "the common good". It is my submission therefore that there can hardly be any leadership if it is devoid of values and ethics. Failure to have this would result in unimaginable risk and damage to reputation, limit the probable contribution to the wellbeing of society, and might also risk loss to the bottom line.[2, 3] By its nature leadership is about values. These may be values as received or shared, or values of a community, or values that seek to ensure that declared outcomes are met. In other words values should not be just about "just" ends but also about "just" means. It can be stated, therefore, that leadership is ethics in practice.

9.2.2 Leadership Values and Morality

All that may be too theoretical. It is my view that in South Africa we are guided by the Constitution and the values enshrined therein. Those values are set out in the Preamble to the Constitution that speaks of the goal of the Constitution being to "improve the quality of life of all citizens and free the potential of each person." In the first paragraphs of the Constitution we are told that South Africa is one sovereign, democratic state founded on the following values... human dignity, the achievement of equality and social justice. This suggests that whatever the actions of state or the agents of public power might be, it is about enhancing the quality of life and dignity of others. This also means that leadership and public resources are at the disposal of the state to advance and enhance the purposes clearly set out in the Constitution.

It is worth taking notice that the South African Constitution (1996) prefigures that the South African state is founded on "values". That therefore means that public power and governance are exercised on the basis of values – meaning, an ethical standard of conduct, of decision-making or a way of life founded on good and right thinking and actions. One observes as a matter of concern that some of the judgments of the justices of the Constitutional Court fail to draw on the intricate relationship between law and ethics that one believes is embedded in our

---

[2] UNESCO. 2015. *Rethinking Education: Towards a global common good.* Paris.
[3] World Bank. 2012. *Constructing Knowledge Societies: New Challenges for Tertiary Education.*

Constitution. The argument advanced in this paper is that ethics in leadership means that ethics serves not just as a means of accomplishing stated goals but that it also restrains the tendency to exercise the power of leadership for purposes other than those that can be considered "good" in objective terms. This governance by ethics is well stated in s.1(d) of the South African Constitution, 1996 when it says that government under the constitution seeks "to ensure accountability, responsiveness and openness."

One example is the recent case[4] on the application of the regulations on pregnancy by learners. The principles of legality and constitutionality were considered without regard to the ethical issues that are as much the mission of the school environment as are the rights and best interests of the learners. Of course the issue of law and morality is a vexed matter in jurisprudence. Nevertheless, especially in a country where values are entrenched in the Constitution, and where one ought to be mindful of the social environment of conduct in public life, schools are an important if not vital area for the practice of moral life.

South Africa's judiciary ought to be mindful of words once stated by Lon Fuller that "internal adherence to the internal morality of law would, in practice, significantly inhibit a government's ability to engage in grossly immoral behaviour..." (1993:283). What is under question in our country at the moment is whether people believe that the "internal morality of law" has currency any longer. I wish to suggest that that "internal morality" of law is expressed in our Constitution, but its lifeblood is in the practice of law and governance.

I disagree with many others who decry the fact that South Africa is not possessed of a unifying vision and a compelling idealism. I believe that Nelson Mandela was able to rally this nation away from its sordid past towards embracing reconciliation as the means by which we could

---

[4] Head of the Department, Free State Department of Education v Welkom High School & Another; Head of the Department, Free State Department of Education v Harmony High School & Another (CCT103/12), delivered July 2013.

continue to live for and realize the vision of the liberation struggle and the benefits of the historic negotiated settlement. I believe that Thabo Mbeki, likewise, captured the imagination of this nation with his eloquent statement "I am an African..." African Renaissance thus became a rallying cry for connecting South Africa with its inner being and search for an African identity founded on the values of *ubuntu*, and to be conscious of itself as an African country with a shared destiny with the rest of the Continent.

For both former heads of state there was this sense of decent government, kind and caring especially to the poor and needy - the soft side of politics that is designed to enhance human value and to lift people towards a higher value of themselves. In other words the focus had to be on honest living, peaceful co-existence, and a pursuit for peaceable relations with others. The picture that emerged was therefore not one of power as brute force, but of power as an inner resolve to be good and to do good, therefore power as a means of facilitating service in the interests of others rather than as a means of self-enrichment. To be a nation at peace with itself, and seeking to be an influence for peace and goodness in world affairs was an ideal former President Nelson Mandela often articulated during his term of office. This element of the pursuit of the good is often lost sight of. But it was in my view that understanding that as South Africans we were capable of being good for the sake of the other that elevated the moral quality of the newly emergent South Africa post-apartheid.

South Africa can do without the aggressive and angry conduct that has become our national pastime, violence-ridden, selfish and self-centred, living with distrust and mutual suspicion. We could live to pursue genuine equality as a common project, and address the pathologies of inequality. We could be a caring nation that is outraged both by the debilitating poverty that surrounds us as well as by the obscene wealth that gets flaunted by those of excessive means. We could address the plight of the unemployed by electing governments and for corporates to be prepared to take lesser profits. We could achieve more by treating our fellow South Africans as fully human, men and women of dignity who may be silent for now but who are never without voice. The politics of our country could reflect the "decency" that our Constitution and laws promise. That it does not happen can be attributable to bad leadership. Besides bad leadership there is a meta-narrative that undermines development and promotes dependency and clientelism. The messages of "The Big Man" or the Big Party" can only induce despondency about our political and social life. The problem we have these days in South Africa is that governance tends to proceed in a peripatetic fashion like a drunken sailor without direction, form or order, and certainly without evidence of a driving, overarching, organizing principle, or vision. The result is Leadership of diminished value.

Of course, leadership should never simply be about the lone ranger mentality. There is not likely any longer to be anything like a messianic leadership. That is because leadership reflects the values of the society it comes from but with this difference: Leadership calls us to our higher values and best possibilities, rather than to wallow with us at our most base instincts. It is not just about popularity or approval per se. It is rather about that capacity to be moral and to call the nation to be self-corrective about the values it wishes to espouse, and how such values are representative of its nature and character. Leadership is responsibility.

I trust that, though unstated, the argument above is clear enough that one should avoid the tendency to valorise "leadership" as if it is a characteristic that is fixed, and unchanging, necessary and of value of and by itself. In the higher education environment, especially, leadership can become the means for maintaining outmoded conventions, oppressive ideas, and power relations over others. In particular, at higher education leadership can be self-serving, if not it could be in the service of certain interests that are conservative and of dubious motives. All claims to and aspirations towards leadership must be subjected to ethical examination. What are the theoretical foundations for any examination of the notion of leadership?

9.2.3 Leadership in a Space of 'Lived Reality'

The German Philosopher Immanuel Kant talks about the "categorical imperative". It is a principle that says that "I am never to act otherwise than so that I could also will that my maxim should become a universal law." If it is good enough, it must be good to be shared. That is my idea of a common good. This Kantian adage is really about living in practice that which one believes, to share with others that which one holds dear, and to act at all times with moral consistency. In this regard one cannot but express alarm at times at the moral bankruptcy in public life both in matters of state and well as in the private sector. For some reason, words have lost their meaning.

One listens to politicians decry to high heaven the incidence of crime and threatening that action will be taken against any found guilty of corruption. In truth, we know, that in the same vein the same politicians are actively engaged in corrupt dealings, and that the resources of the state are being diverted to non-legitimate purposes. Huge infrastructure programmes have less to do with a desire to improve the wellbeing of people and create employment than with huge deals that are to be made, and the private sector aids and abets corruption by engaging in corrupt dealings to divert the resources of the state. No wonder therefore that the word "honour" no longer has any meaning, as ministers and senior public servants are engaged in a culture of corrupt activities. The real danger, though, is that this will all become so inane (meaning, without significance, empty or void) to ordinary citizens that they have come to expect no better from politicians and immoral behaviour becomes the common signifier of being a South African. When people become cynical and get to expect no better from leaders and from politicians, then we are on course to make of our national life the Wild West. A leader therefore has no choice but to be the exemplar and model of the nation's best idea of itself.

In a recent article in *Al Jazeera on line,* Hamid Dabashi, a scholar of Persian Studies at Columbia University had this to say:

> "Therefore the agent "must" act according to a "model" which he would like to see diffused among all mankind (*sic*), according to a type of civilisation for whose coming he is working-or for whose preservation he is "resisting" the forces that threaten its disintegration (2013:3)."

It is precisely that self-confidence, that self-consciousness, that self-assuredness, that audacity to think and plan ourselves into an unimagined future that the seeds whose birth lie embedded in the loins of present time, are brought to birth. If only leaders would think not just of the present time, but recognize that they are indeed planting the seeds that may cause the nascent future to become aborted, then they would recognize that their present conduct makes the future they wish to see dim. Jim Wallis in his book, *The Soul of Politics* (1994) says that without the value of moral conscience, our political life quickly degenerates into public corruption, cultural confusion and social injustice. It is not enough just to mouth a vision. The vision must however be compelling on one's conduct because the vision must direct the way we act. This is perhaps what may be referred to as "transformative ethics". In other words leadership that must be possessed of the imagination to think radical ideas that go to the heart of the matter, that are imbued with idealism that dares to imagine the unimaginable and to desire only that which is the best. Leadership ethics should be by its nature transformative because it is capable of challenging given norms and orthodoxies to a better ideal of itself.

Understandably there are some voices in South Africa who have been advocating African values in leadership. Reuel Khoza[5] is probably the main proponent of African values in leadership. Sometimes, this is articulated under the umbrella of *Ubuntu* meaning a philosophy of life, sometimes ethical values, that are drawn from traditional African culture. Besides Archbishop Tutu[6] who had been promoting this from his earlier years as a scholar of African Christian Theology, *Ubuntu* found its way into the Post-amble of the Interim Constitution of the Republic of South Africa (1993), and consequently became the *ratio decidendi* for our earlier judgments in the courts of our country.

The problem, though with the concept, *Ubuntu* is that it has become rather nebulous, a referent for all things that may sound vaguely good. It transpires that for many people who articulate it, *Ubuntu* refers to some distant ideal that makes us feel good but that there is no danger of it might becoming applicable today, otherwise its demands could be unbearable and onerous. This is the reason, Nigerian philosopher Emmanuel Chukwudi Eze[7] has declared that *Ubuntu* is both "not enough" and "too much". This is what he says:

> "Ubuntu is too much because... as an ideology it relies too much
> on the *extraordinary*: luck, miracles and an ambiguous concept
> of natural goodness. Ubuntu is not enough because it fails to
> supplement – or one might say, to moderate – its innate optimism

---

[5] *Vide Let Africa Lead: African Transformational Leadership for the 21st Century Business (2006);* and *Attuned Leadership: African Humanism as Compass* (2012); Penguin.

[6] See Battle M: The Ubuntu Theology of Desmond Tutu in Hulley L, Kretschmar L & Pato LL: Archbishop Tutu: prophetic Witness in South Africa; 1996, Human & Rousseau, 93ff. On a more detailed treatment of the philosophy of *Ubuntu* see Leonhard Praeg and Siphokazi magadla (Editors): UBUNTU: Curating the Archive, 2014; UKZN Press, Scottville, and Munyaradzi Felix Murove (Editor): African Ethics: An Anthology of Comparative and Applied Ethics, 2009; UKZN Press, Scottville.

[7] Reason, Memory and Politics, 2008, Unisa Press, at 111 and 114.

about natural goodness of humankind with what I will call *the
ordinary* (111)."

His conclusion is that as a moral philosophy *Ubuntu* is deficient
because it promises what it cannot deliver. The tension here is between
the world *as it could be* or as it *ought*, or the world as it has *become* –
between *is* and *ought*, between *being* and *becoming*. The moral
challenge, ethicists will tell you, is to move from *is* to *ought*, without
appearing to be preaching *pie in the sky*. If one were to assume a
deontological supposition, one still has to justify what rules or how one
arrives at the rules that shape one's moral outlook.

My own reservations stem from a different perspective. In fact it is
much more as a warning to me than a rejection of the concept. I fear that
in pointing to some imaginary past, that does not appear to be grounded
in present realities of life, *Ubuntu* may be guilty of undermining the
challenge of revolt and critical consciousness and lead to paralysis and
atrophy that Karen van Merle in her chapter, *Lives of Action, Thinking
and Revolt: A Feminist Call for Politics of Becoming in Post Apartheid
South Africa*, talks about[8].

> "a complacent society where political action, thought, eternal
> questioning and contestation are absent and replaced by an
> understanding of freedom as mere commercial/economic
> freedom and of thought as calculated and instrumental (2007:34 -
> 58)."

As the unwritten moral law and practice of the peoples and
communities of Africa, Ubuntu calls for a taken-for-granted rendition of
moral conduct. In reality there are two factors that do not always get
taken into account. One is that by whatever name it is stated Ubuntu is
an ethical compass that subsists in all communities and cultures. Africa

---

[8] In Roux W & van Marle K: Post-Apartheid Fragments: Law Politics and
Critique; 2007, Pretoria, Unisa Press; 34-58.

does not have the monopoly of Ubuntu practice. Ubuntu is not unique to Africa. It is a universal ethical practice. However, it does not cease to be universal by reason of its becoming rooted on African soil. Africa shares with the world community a common outlook on life that arises from a common humanity.

Secondly, Ubuntu must be observed in varying cultural, economic and technological circumstances. For example, it is arguable that modern society may no longer be unquestioning and compliant in terms of expectations, cultures are a lot more intermingled in our time, and there is a lot more reliance on modern technologies that affect human conduct. Ubuntu for those reasons may no longer be as abiding as was once assumed. Ethical practice thus can no longer be assumed or taken for granted but must be interrogated. Even the ideas of goodness, harmonious relations, love and peace are idealisms that are continuously tested in real-life living by people including Africans who may be under the influence of a variety of cultural and philosophical presuppositions.

Where should such leaders come from? How does society produce and reproduce its best? I start by mentioning that good leaders distinguish themselves by "intelligence", by that capacity to have insight, possessed of the power of deep discernment, and wisdom to aspire to higher ideals and resolve, and to be able to "read" the signs of the times. Prof. Hellicy Ngambi[9] of Mulungushi University in Zambia takes the statement below to make the point by reference to my paper published previously:

> "… there is most likely to be a tendency from leaders who are without intellect to also lack in moral fibre because they fail to understand the limitations of governance, but also that they may be incapable of drawing from their own capabilities to provide the nation with a new, compelling and confident vision of itself

---

[9] Cf. forthcoming publication to mark the 70th Birthday of President Thabo Mbeki.

and idealism, to be, at times above the fray, and help guide the nation in its most difficult moments (Pityana, 2012:7)."

It is not unusual that poor leaders are often without intelligence, poor readers of human character, who govern by fear and distrust and are ruthless to opposing views. Such leaders never act with an ethical impulse but are often driven by self-preservation.

But leaders are also "entrepreneurs" who make something out of nothing, bring out the best in others and create a "buy-in" by others into the common pot of ideas. But the "entrepreneurship" must be driven by ideals, if it is not to be merely commonsensical or commodification of material wants. It should be less about the self in interests and enrichment, or merely of those close and dear to one, but genuinely "the common good". That common good must also derive from the context and real-life situations of those who are to be beneficiaries. In a place where the greatest social challenge is poverty and unemployment and inequality, then surely the common drive has to be devoted to finding ways and means of addressing those challenges to the benefit of the people.

This paper is written against the background of unprecedented student protests in South Africa since the onset of the democratic state in 1994 and the end of apartheid. The protests have engulfed virtually all higher education institutions. The protests began in March 2015 at the University of Cape Town as a protest against racism on campus,. It was a call for the decolonization of the university in its symbols and images, teaching, curricula, and to establish a university environment that is not alienating to black students especially, but also to women, but also one that is welcoming and friendly if it is to encourage and promote effective study, teaching and learning. The protests that began, characteristically as #RhodesMustFall ended the year with a spirited campaign #FeesMustFall calling for free higher education. Cecil John Rhodes, the benefactor of the University of Cape Town was a notorious

19th Century colonial politician and businessman whose views on British colonial and imperial expansion were undisguised, and so were his racist views about the people of Africa in general. To varying degrees in the course of 2015 and into 2016 the protests ebbed and flowed, but at certain points they captured the imagination of the people of South Africa. On 23 October 2015, President Jacob Zuma partially conceded to the demand about fees by undertaking on behalf of the government and universities that there would be a 0% fee increase in 2016. He also established a commission of inquiry into the feasibility of providing free higher education for all in South Africa.

Universities responded to the protest movement that was at times violent and determined to disrupt to the maximum the ordinary operations of the universities by acts of arson, intimidation, occupations as well as blockages. It was noticeable that at its most violent, the protests were not led by the elected student leaders, but by an informal, ad hoc coalition of students, who were in no mood to negotiate, refused to recognize the university authorities and were determined to make demands and back up their demands by causing maximum chaos and actual damage.

The university Vice Chancellors responded variously by seeking court injunctions, enhanced the presence of campus security augmented, at great cost, with hired private security agencies. Universities tried in vain to keep the lines of communication with the students open, but they made concessions at times. For example, the Council of the University of Cape Town voted to remove the statue of Cecil John Rhodes from its prime location on campus. That was done on 9 April with the support of the Heritage Council. Universities also conceded a later demand from the students being the end to the outsourcing of the non-core services of the university e.g, security, catering, cleaning and gardens. They set in motion mechanisms to address the problem of outsourcing. It was also agreed that while fees would not be increased in 2016, universities would be more flexible about meeting the requirements for upfront payments for fees. But still disruptions continued, and protests escalated. What, in essence, was the issue? Is it transformation? Is it disillusionment, ignorance about the idea of a university? Or is it about anger, about the political and economic state of the nation?

It is evident that under the rubric of *transformation* much of the protests are emotionally charged. A great deal of the anger has to do with perceptions that the university is stubbornly untransformed. In reality the concept of transformation is ill defined. On the matter of racism as well as the alienating, oppressive environment students insist that is their daily experience on campus, universities have done much to begin to attend to this, but it also true that this is not a matter that is resolvable instantly. The same can be said about other critical issues like Africanisation, curriculum reform, employment equity and institutional culture are all long term goals. The demand for an end to out-sourcing is a governance matter that requires engagement not just with Council but also to ensure the financial sustainability of any reforms that are made. There did not seem to have been any mechanism for any meaningful engagement towards negotiations and resolution of matters in dispute.

Arguably the greatest casualty of the pandemonium at university campuses across the country has been the stature, authority and leadership of the office of the Vice Chancellor. It is painful to observe that the Vice Chancellor as the executive leader and manager of the institution is treated with so much disdain, disrespect and disregard in the institutions, by government, staff and students, and in some instances, by University Councils. This begins not just with the students but the way in which government undercuts the authority of the Vice Chancellor, but it has a lot to do with the diminishing authority that Vice Chancellor exercises in our higher education institutions. Students have clearly shown disrespect and no regard for the person of the Vice

Chancellor, in the manner of addressing the Vice Chancellor, and in their demeanour towards the Vice Chancellor, for example.

The Minister of Higher Education and Training, Dr Blade Nzimande, MP often makes *ex cathedra* pronouncements about matters that are in the domain of governance and management. At times, the current Minister expresses undisguised disrespect for Vice Chancellors, meets with Chairs of Councils, and student leaders without reference to the Vice Chancellor. It is no wonder then that student leaders prefer to deal directly with the Ministry about institutional matters. A typical example is the manner in which the President communicated a decision arrived at about the '2016 No Fee Increase' concession on 23 October 2015, personally through the media, and not through University Councils whose domain it is to set fees and as stewards of the finances of the university. The proposed amendments to the Higher Education Act whereby the Minister seeks to give himself power to make directives to university managements about transformation is another instance. Clearly this is a management and governance matter, and not directly a matter of policy.

Ultimately authority is given by the office one occupies, but respect is earned. The Vice Chancellor is the institutional leader and exercises authority subject to oversight by Council. That means that the Vice Chancellor must earn the respect of staff and students by the manner in which she or he exercises leadership on campus and in society. The Vice Chancellor is a visible presence, someone with gravitas, an intellectual and moral authority, and a person of vision and quiet influence in the affairs of the institution. The tone for the culture and moral stature of the institution is set by the Vice Chancellor. It is the Vice Chancellor who, leading by example, shapes the institutional discourse, translates that into strategic objectives of the institution, communicates these and seeks the widest possible consensus for the institution to journey forward together to achieve such objectives. To achieve any of that, the Vice

Chancellor must be an empathetic communicator, a listener and a decision-maker.

From observations, one senses that so many Vice Chancellors in the country throughout these events have come across as overwhelmed, very weakened, indecisive, compromised even into making ill-considered decisions, a diminished power to exercise authority, in general isolated. Who would not be in similar conditions! It is imperative that the Vice Chancellor prioritises meetings with various structures of the community, to be in constant communication in formal and informal ways, to show respect for students at all levels without being deferential, delivering on what is promised, and keep your word! To that extent, the Vice Chancellor's role is unashamedly political.[10] In the prevailing circumstances what could be the political influence of the Vice Chancellor? In what way is her or his leadership looked upon for guidance and wisdom? Higher education leadership and management have been sorely tested by these events. Have we learnt any lessons from this debacle then? Time will tell.

In circumstances like these, how does a leader in a higher education institution, one presumably founded on a common search for truth, and seeking alike to discover knowledge and in the process all can grow in stature and esteem, conduct the business. There is a sense in which building confidence and trust in the Office of the Vice Chancellor is a critical prerequisite. The process of trust building does not happen at the heat of the moment or in the midst of conflict, it has to be a badge of honour and practice in the ordinary daily practice of campus leadership. In that way one learns respect by one abiding by principle and the truth at all times, listening, however, deeply and intently to all opinions, consulting meaningfully and ensuring that decisions taken are ones reflective of and to the benefit of the wider community of students and scholars. Finally, it is important that the university communicates and publishes a moral outlook that everybody trusts, that is consistently applied, if not deviations can be explained and that becomes the reference point for the common life of the institution.

All this has to do with *Ubuntu*. It both sets out an abiding ethical principle, but that it also recognizes the limitations of that principle. For example, in pursuit of the common good and harmonious relations at all times when and how does the enforcement process available to the university get resorted to? By the way, the love-principle that is inherent in *Ubuntu* does not mean that punishment and retribution have no role in appropriate circumstances especially in order to bring matters into equilibrium.

In the South African setting, one has to be mindful of two things. One, that universities cannot be seen in isolation; and two, that the idea of a university is contested. The university is affected by societal tensions, disputes and political cultures. This is more so in the current environment where clearly the university is powerless to effect the changes that are demanded short of making room for wholesale revolution! The idea of a university is an ongoing debate for which different generations of students and academics will approach differently. What must remain constant though is the moral fibre of the institution, and its ethical legitimacy must be acknowledged. Of course, much of this has to do with a variety of matters: fairness in employment policies, fairness and equality in remuneration practices, integrity in academic systems and transparency in decision-making including financial dealings of the university. While all that may be critical, ultimately, though, the institutions should cultivate an environment of open discussion and debate about all issues. Recent studies at international level throw light on developments and renewed thinking on the ethics of public life. It is to that that we now turn.

9.2.4 Responding to the Challenges of Higher Education

The UNESCO Study *Rethinking Education: Towards a Global Common Good* (2015) re-introduces the idea of the "common good" in relation not only to basic education, but also to tertiary and technical education and training. It is suggested that all education, formal and non-formal, is essential for human living. This, of course, goes beyond education as a parental responsibility, or family endeavour, or the means for accessing material benefits, or is it the task of the community for its own renewal. It is also the case that education becomes a necessary good for humanity to thrive and to prosper, and indeed, for humanity to be able to achieve her potential and to make the best of the opportunities available to them. The study goes on to say that "the creation of knowledge, as well as its acquisition, validation and use, are common to all people as part of a *collective and societal endeavour*" (2015:11). It is refreshing in my view to move away from the previous individualistic notions of education, or the simple utilitarian notions, back to the idea that education has a purpose in and of itself.

It is now accepted, as the World Bank study *Constructing Knowledge Societies: New Challenges for Tertiary Education* (2012) says, that tertiary education must be viewed as of value beyond preparing young men and women for useful service to society in the world of work. "It also involves", says the World Bank, "developing a person's ability to reason systematically about critical questions and issues, to place facts in a broader context, to consider the moral implications of actions and choices, to communicate knowledge and questions effectively, and to nurture habits that promote life-long learning behaviours outside of the formal academic setting" (2012:31). If this is so, what then does that say or prescribe about higher education leadership? It means, in my view, that a higher education leader must embrace these perspectives in her/his vision not just for the university but for society, and understand the relationship between the academy and the society it seeks to serve. In other words, then, for me higher education leadership places at the centre of its consciousness the idea of the human – in the service of being and becoming human.

The world in which we live in and universities to no less an extent, in the pursuit of serving humankind, has to balance the dialectical pulls of both particularity and universality. It means that universities must recognize the uniqueness of students as well as staff, and at the same time draw them to a higher calling and a common future. In some respects approaches to this differ. At one level how does race and culture specificity find a place in an environment where common life should be the rule. How does the university provide a language and culture that affirms the humanity of all, without degenerating into a religious, linguistic or ethnic essentiality. I suggest that if one takes the view of *Ubuntu* that I have just expressed, then one recognizes that within each and everyone of us is a kernel of truth that we can never exist in isolation. We exist in community and are bonded by relationships that are a part of our human nature.

In a recent TB Davie Academic Freedom Speech at the University of Cape Town (2015), Kenan Malik drew attention to the dangers of identity politics that seemed to be presenting a new suspicion about the universality of values, and the essentialisation of the particular, e.g. identity, race, tribe, language, or nation or religion. He also seeks to defend the universal values that serve both to give a common or shared vision to the world, and to restrain those propensities that seek to elevate selfish or national, or group interests above all others. Universal norms and standards are necessary, he believes, as a restraint to a propensity for the use of naked power in world affairs. Malik observes, sardonically, that people have come to understand values less in terms of ideals than in terms of identity. One has to watch against the trap of identity, he believes. It may well be true that this suspicion about universal values and a too easy resort to identity is what lies at the root of the demands placed on higher education in South Africa today.

The view adopted in this paper is that the purpose of education, especially higher education, has to cultivate that critical mind that discerns the societal trends, and applies a critique that seeks to sustain the values of freedom, critical consciousness and human prosperity. It is suggested that such values are now entrenched in the recently adopted 2030 Global Sustainable Development Goals by the United Nations General assembly in 2015. It is also suggested that once one embraces these ideals one can then approach the questions of the opportunities and challenges for leadership in higher education institutions.

I have prefaced this address in the manner that I have done because I sincerely believe that the role of a leader in higher education institutions is not about dictatorship but rather it is recognition that higher education institutions are spaces for free thought and radical experimentation. They exist as places where ideas are challenged and received notions are tested, and new knowledge(s) emerge. This is what makes higher education leadership unique, exciting and challenging. It begins with the one who leads. She/he has the burden of setting the tone for the institution as a whole.

It is challenging for a different reason. It is that a leader and manager of a higher education institution is not and should not be elected by popular will. This brings the freedom of knowing that one is not beholden to any interest groups from within or without. But to govern without the democratic will of one's peers, also holds the prospect of having support withheld, sensing a lack of confidence in one's abilities or motives and, ultimately, having to contend with open rebellion. The head of the institution manages with the confidence of the highest governing body of the institution, the Council of Governing Board and with the support of the academic community, mainly through Senate. The institution must establish and the community must honour transparent systems of governance such as to ensure mutual accountability and to achieve agreed outcomes. It is a good idea for the institution to commit itself to the reporting templates set out for example in the King Codes or the Global Reporting Initiative (GRI), and to honour the reporting mechanisms set out by the Minister of Higher Education.

Finally, however much one might seek to inculcate a common vision, much of that might be challenged and debated in the academic environment (and so it should, but that could be frustrating and may appear to set one back!). I therefore believe that the role of a higher education leader and manager is a modest one. It is to facilitate and create an environment where a discourse of ideas for the creation and development of knowledge can take place, as well to seek buy-in and understanding of the ethics of the institutions and institutional culture all seek to establish. It also means that the leader is just as bound by rules and policies as anybody else. The President or Vice Chancellor commits to abide by the laws of the institution and to deal with colleagues at all levels with dignity and respect. On that score, Claudio Fernadez-Arnoz is correct to say, "an organisation's ability to choose the right leaders is one of the most important controllable factors in creating and destroying the company value" (HBR; October 30, 2012). In other words "controllable" must be understood also as a "risk factor" that must be anticipated and managed. Proof, he says in the title of his article, that leaders matter. Often the fit between the culture and aspirations and competencies of the institution and the candidate are important markers of possible success, or failure.

That is perhaps easier said than done. The assumption behind this is that it is possible that such a consensus could be found among such a diverse community and interest groups as can be found in a university. You might think not. At any one time the Vice Chancellor or President of an institution represents the mind of the institution at a certain point in time. This might change as the critical personnel change, as in changes in the composition of Council or governing body set in, or in policy change from government or Council that has to be implemented and does not necessarily come from management. Changes could seemingly erupt suddenly as a result of prevailing political winds, or gradually out of planned interventions. In other words, the consensus that is presumed to exist in liberal society between the higher education institutions and the state such that institutional autonomy is guaranteed, academics are assured of academic freedom, and the institution in return establishes a reputation in scientific activities, and the state guarantees funding from the public purse to assure the operations of the institution, may no longer hold.

In a neo-liberal world or in authoritarian systems where universities are expected to take orders from the political masters, the value of higher education institutions may constantly be questioned, as well as justifications for the money spent on higher education may no longer be guaranteed. In the extreme, politicians may seek to compromise the standing of the institution, and co-opt elements of the institutions to a narrow political purpose and/or the institution may be accused of political bias. All this brings a great deal of pressure and uncertainty that might affect the extent to which the institution may succeed in its mission. In other words, there can be no leader without followers. It is the responsibility of a leader to understand those to whom one has been placed in charge to lead, and to be open to listen, study and to read the signs of the times. Indeed where such cross-currents threaten to derail the university from the course already agreed, the Vice Chancellor has a duty to calm fears where one can, resist and seek broad support, if that becomes necessary, and ultimately to pay the supreme price for taking a principled position, resign.

In the culture of a higher education institution, the Vice Chancellor or President must also embrace the culture of learning of the institution.

He/She must cultivate thinking clearly and carefully and exercise leadership and make decisions with discretion, always bearing in mind the best interests of the institution as expressed in the resolutions of Council and Senate. It is to be expected that the Vice Chancellor or President must also understand the academic project either through his/her own knowledge activities, but in any event must have a passion for and understanding of the academic activities that the researchers and teachers are engaged in. The academic leader must also keep abreast of developments in higher education management.

Notwithstanding all that, the leader of an academic institution presides over an institution whose very nature is unpredictability. In South Africa currently higher education institutions face the challenge of a messy and unstructured campaign for transformation. The problem is that by their nature higher education institutions are both conservative and transformative. They are conservative in that they are built on traditions and conventions that may appear archaic but without which they may cease to deserve the name "university". They also base new or acquired knowledge on achievements of the past critically examined. There is also a sense in which higher education institutions do not flourish in environments of instability and uncertainty. Students on the other hand are in a real sense a transient community even though they have a valid right to create out of the institution in their generation something that reflects their own ideals and perspectives, mindful always in such cases that change is an ever present constant. The task of a leader is to keep that balance. Perhaps we should accept that the university is never going to be the most ideal place where revolutions are to be launched from.

Yet, students are not and cannot be the sole barometer of the culture that must shape the institution for ever, as that shape alters and changes with each generation of students that occupies campus. Higher education institutions must also needs be citadels of transformative values. Higher education institutions are meant to change lives for the better. Research and teaching by their nature should be about discovery and confronting received ideas. Knowledge thrives in an environment of experimentation and testing of ideas. Higher education sits very uncomfortably in environments of rigid ideology and dogma, or in irrationality and refusal to think, or by purveyors of violence in order to impose one's will. The extent and the limits of transformation are matters that must be debated and mediated within the institution, and where policy matters, a national consensus may be necessary.

Many an institution and academic manager is labouring under the weight of what has become known as "managerialism". Often expressed among academics in a disparaging manner, what it means is not simply that academic managers spend all their time loading academics with the burdens of administrative functions, demanding accountability for resources put at their disposal, and managing and assessing performance. In part there is justifiable hostility to what is considered an inappropriate importation of business management-speak into an ill-fitting organizational model. The situation, however, is that society has changed. Expectations are rising and accountability is the requirement at all levels of society. Academics cannot claim exemption from these standards. The truth is that from the point of view of institutional management, governments are also increasingly demanding more and more precise record keeping and financial reports. Donors and other funders also require detailed reporting. The institution is bound to be in a dilemma about this from all levels. It also increases tension between managers and academics. In a sense, the distinction between the administrator and the academic is being breached because more and more administrative duties are also being performed in the coalface, in the context of academic functions.

"Managerialism" is often understood as the manner in which professional managers and administrators in an institution of higher learning impose on the academics their own values, methods of operation, time-lines, and accountability, without taking account of, and understanding the value and priority of academic performance, or making room for it or giving support to enable academics to perform according to their core duties. Often unstated, there is resentment that the administrators assume a hierarchy of authority and impose expectations that cannot be met.

My only plea is for an understanding and acceptance that higher education institutions have become as big as the business conglomerates that are referred to. It is also correct to accept that a badly managed institution will put at risk not just the academic project, but also the livelihoods of many staff including academic staff. Higher education institutions therefore must meet the demands for accountability, a prudent management of resources and a crafty management of human capital, ensure financial efficiencies and nurture the academic reputation of the institution. As long as government remains the main funder of higher education institutions this requirement of accountability for the public purse must remain. Besides government, higher education institutions have other stakeholders or interest groups to bear in mind. These include the donors, benefactors and alumni of the institution. In my experience what helps to bridge this gap is by making sure that management is transparent in what it does, consults exhaustively, places before the community all the options and acts in a manner that is consistent with reported undertakings. In other words it is about building relationships of trust within the institution.

Management experts tell us the obvious, that successful managers must possess three overarching qualities: basic knowledge and information, skills and attributes, and meta-qualities. The so-called "meta-qualities" are perhaps vital. They include, among others, as the book by Mike Pedler, John Burgoyne and Tom Boydell, *A Manager's Guide to Self-Development* (1986) puts it, a manager as critical learner who processes ideas and applies them; a manager as a critical thinker, "this ability – which is sometimes known as a *helicopter mind* – enables managers to generate their own theories from practice, and to develop their own practical ideas from theory" (1986:29).

9.3 Conclusion

In conclusion I wish to point out that higher education management everywhere in the world is taking place in the midst of a dangerous and unpredictable world. Unpredictability has to do with the availability of resources necessary to make the university function effectively, but also about uncertainty due to the currents and cross-currents of culture and politics, ideas and philosophies, and of science and morality. In recorded history there can never have been a time when universities lived through calm and peace times. It is equally correct that universities can never be islands of calm in a sea of storms. Tsunamis uproot both nature, people and establishments. It is understandable, not least because universities work with a clientele of young minds much sought after in war, on the streets, in commerce at home and abroad. For that reason young people may be moved by a variety of influences, and so will the academic staff.

The context in which these ideas and challenges are placed is the South African higher education landscape of 2015/2016. The art of leadership has been tested, and as a result new learning and strategies for leadership are developing in South African higher education. The submission in this paper is that all leadership is at its best when it is tested. The clarity of ideas on which it is founded, the moral questions that drive leadership, and the intended outcomes and the effect on those who are participants, have been examined.

What this paper seeks to establish, though, is that universities survive because they are founded on the will of the people, and they reflect as fully as they can that sense of commitment to human flourishing.

Because at the centre of being university is this idea of the human, so also a university has to build relationships, express community, and to do so on ethical principles as the glue that holds community together.

Finally, and that is the subject of this paper ethical leadership is the driver who holds the road map, ensures that there are conditions safe and viable enough to navigate, as well as the resources to reach the destination.

10

LEADERSHIP AND EPISTEMOLOGICAL RESPONSIBILITY IN AFRICAN UNIVERSITIES IN THE 21ST CENTURY

Catherine A. Odora Hoppers

10.1 Introduction: Eurocentric Thought and "Otherness"

The era of the Empire, weak and strong at the same time, declared Africa to have nothing. Its knowledge systems were irrelevant. We were unsuited for the modern world. The Imperial, twisted parochial mythologies taught us in Africa that a handful of countries in Europe dominated all thoughts and actions, and naturally set the pattern for the world. They mangled Darwin's theories of evolution into a populist racist, political narrative of progress and race; and they used it to justify their untold violence on Africa and the Third World saying all the while that is was a manifestation of scientific destiny. So they intentionally headed everything from table manners and dress codes to economic methods, political philosophy and governmental administration, to notions of civilizational truth and destiny (Saul 2014, Odora Hoppers 2003).

Thanks to the pen of Herbert Spencer's "survival of the fittest" in 1864, suddenly public debate in Europe was full of scientific truisms were neither scientific nor true. By 1870, we had social Darwinism which helped to shape more empire mythologies from the Europe to the US and Canada.

The combined narratives ruled Africa up to now. Europeans insisted that their principles in particular were universal. The details of universality as mediocrity are always fascinating. They make sense because behind them lie the European national imperial schools of philosophy which are still "put" and anchored around the world in *THEIR (meaning "OUR) universities...* taught as universal. Their narrative of history, cuisine, of civilization, of fashion spread wide during the violence of colonization – all apparently universal. Educational curricula were filled with these absurdities. They then went to mount attacks on indigenous cultures and peoples and demean them by banning languages, cultures, rituals and all things spiritual. The illegal, unethical moral acts followed. Myriad laws regulations and administrative structures were created and amended in order to install a legal infrastructure and punishment, both social and economic (Saul 2014, Memmi 1965).

Reason began abruptly to separate itself and to outdistance the other more or less recognized human characteristics – spirit, appetite, faith and emotion, but also intuition, will and most important – experience. This gradual encroachment of the foreground continues today. It had reached a degree of imbalance so extreme that the mythical importance of reason obscures all else and has driven the other elements into the marginal frontiers of doubtful respectability (Saul 1993).

Through this imaginative strategy of difference, European universities created an artificial construct of humanities and spread it throughout humanity (Memmi 1965) leaving behind multiple legacies of trauma, fear and dread. No ecology, no culture, no people and no psyche remained untarnished. The technology of social control and oppression remained everywhere. The damage inflicted on the national and international policy frameworks have been well documented, but little has been understood (Henderson 2008; Odora Hoppers 1998).

To quote Jean Paul Sartre in his "Materialism and revolution" in Literary and Philosophical Essays (1968):

> "Everyone has felt the contempt explicit in the term "native" used to designate the inhabitants of a colonized country. The bankers, the manufacturer, even the professor in the home country, are not "natives of any country: they are not natives at all. The oppressed person, on the other hand, feels himself to be a native; each single event in his life repeats to him that he has not to right to exist"

> (Sartre 1968:215 London, Hutchinson)

10.2 Inwards to Outwards: What has this Meant for Strategies for Leadership in Africa?

While history tells us that the 20th century was the century of Africa's political independence, the 21st century is the century of Africa's *reclaiming of human agency, and of her status in world citizenship as a subject, not object.* The 21st century will be one in which the political freeing of the continent from various strands of colonial control as an act linked with the attainment of political sovereignty transforms and metamorphoses into *being free as a creative act of the spirit.*

But if by attaining political freedom and sovereignty the continent attained the right to act politically, awareness of freedom in the 21st century brings with it what Béji has called *"a greater consciousness of our duties"* (Béji 2001:286). The attainment of Africa's political freedom does relieve the world and especially the West, of a great moral burden of its historical injustices it meted out to 86 countries of what we now know of in deficit and hierarchized terms as the "Third World", and in generative language as the "global South".

By attaining "independence", the West can now say, "we gave them sovereignty" and thus share some moral dividends that would have eluded it had independence never been allowed to the colonies. But awareness of spirit and of being free as a creative act of the spirit takes us far beyond the cries of reparation and claims of injustice against a historical experience that was cruel and in some instances actually evil. It goes beyond the dictates of modernity and enlightenment in which all nations of the world are locked into the grids of the European experience; to quite a different place, *in which that freedom in the 21ˢᵗ century now meets the requirement of the common good and the demands of common well-being... of new futures of a different kind.*

In other words, a key question for Africa in this century is precisely *how active and fully knowing human agency is to be realized in an ethically cognizant dispensation?* On the one hand, we can clearly see that political freedom creates a strange handicap and incoherence, an intimate juxtaposition of past and present that Africa represents. On the other, what this does is that it puts Africa in a unique position in relation to both human history and human destiny from which position *she can articulate the contours of that new dispensation, and herald the new social compact on a global scale.*

Where Europe destroyed and dehumanized with elation, *Africa must weigh carefully its methods of transcending the realms of that bondage* i.e. she must go beyond naming what she is *fighting against*, to courageously naming what she is *fighting for*. Where Europe needed to destroy and subjugate so many, Africa must *define new formulas for its reconstruction* (in relation to the historical destruction of course*!); name the new icons symbolizing its points of departure*; and articulate the kind of energy she will bring to bear in the *building of its future in the new more humane dispensation.*

10.2.1 Example 1: From Humiliation to Dignity

As she confronts the dysfunctions of modern and European-programmed notions of progress and its off-springs development, progress, rationality, it becomes clear that it is Africa that is now in control of the definition of 'time', lived time that needs to be humanized. It is therefore Africa that, in transforming the contours of its struggles from archaic resistance to domination, holds the key to the world's future.

But to do this, a lot depends on how she questions her past (one which still painful) and the kind of future she would like to see unfold, not just for herself, but also for humanity at large. Much will depend on how she articulates herself out of the experience of humiliation suffered in the hands of colonialism, and *avoid adding to self-perpetuating cultural cycles of violation and vindication which would seem to say, "I have the right to be angry and make others suffer forever because someone hurt me in the past".*

How can Africa generate less humiliation entrepreneurs like Hitler and more Nelson Mandelas who interrupt the cycle of humiliation by triggering new cycles of dignity? How can we, together cultivate enduring instruments and practices that can disarm this singular weapon of mass destruction – *HUMILIATED HEARTS AND MINDS, and turn them into weapons of mass creativity and solidarity?*

In the context of post-colonialism, we have seen how in some instances, the new cultural pride becomes a new nook for intolerance providing seedbeds for new forms of discrimination. Traditions threaten to offer unitary radicalism in which it is not always evident that tolerance and political commitment to diversity will be guaranteed. Human dignity is easily circumscribed in terms of ethnic, national, or religious identity – in short, allegiance to a deterministic primacy (Béji 2004:29).

The illusion of self-expression seems to supplant the faculty of mutual understanding, while the disinherited of the earth employ the same devices to exist as the privileged do to dominate. Modern culture has become characterized by the fact that human rights of all kinds are turned into inhuman codes. Sovereignty is replaced by supremacy, and tolerance, which is the rejection of the intolerable, has become the right to practice the intolerable. Many a-times, humanitarian action which professes to be on the side of the weak, comes with superpower backing which quickly turns it into providential inhumanity. Anti-racism becomes as intolerant as racism, and the rights of the weakest are modelled on the abuses of the rights of the strongest, with the result that the rights of the victims are turning into a morality of cruelty (Béji 2004:31).

Culture no longer offers access to humanity or the foundation for the ethic of recognition. Ethnic consciousness has liquidated ethnic awareness creating a costly humanist deficit in which decolonization fails to live up to the promise inherent in its cultural potential – that of creating a more viable model of civilization.

In other words, because the confrontation between tradition and modernity remains locked in the suspicion and resentment that each has of the other, the confrontation and the poverty of heuristics inherent in it threatens to deprive both of inspiration in that it has stimulated them ideologically, but discredited them morally. They both converge in terms of the shadows -- not of light they cast, and the destruction, not the creation that they produce. That is the challenge we have to face now and into the future!

But it is here also that the perspectives, methodologies and breakthroughs in unpacking these gross shadows that are threatening to overwhelm humanity, must be deployed with urgency – to precisely reverse this decline and plant new thought experiments in a transversal and transdisciplinary dispensation such as what the Department of

Science and Technology Research Chair in Development Education hosted by Unisa is now doing.

Some of these include:

a. putting knowledge in the plural,

b. asserting the right to a multiplicity of times;

c. of citizenship as a hypothesis;

d. placing human development rather than employment at the centre of education,

e. linking epistemology and democracy;

f. bringing in robust theorizations around freedom, innovation, cosmology, constitution, citizenship, community and syllabi; and

g. Cognitive justice and the right of traditions of knowledge to co-exist and unfold without duress.

10.2.2 Example 2: The Story of Indigenous Knowledge Systems in South Africa

Background

Indigenous Knowledge Systems is referred to in different ways in different parts of the world, under different circumstances. Related conceptions include "Traditional Knowledge Systems" (TKS), "Endogenous Knowledge Systems" (EKS) and in some instances "Classical Knowledge Systems" (CKS). Each of these refers to the same content, but with particular slants.

South Africa has so far chosen "Indigenous Knowledge Systems" as a capping concept for that system of knowledge in philosophy, science, technology, astronomy, education, mathematics, engineering etc. that are grounded in the total "cultural" (very broadly defined) heritage of a nation or society, and maintained by communities over centuries. An interlocking web of ethical, social, religious and philosophical sub-systems that determine broad cognition patterns, provide the rational essence and emotional tone that underlies these systems.

In the context of countries like China, IKS provides the bedrock of its scientific and technological advancement, witnessed in the clothing and textile, food, medicine, architecture, construction from which base it can choose which aspect of foreign knowledge or technology it needs or wishes to incorporate into its development strategy.

However, in parts of the world such as Africa and in most of the so-called Third World where colonialism not only went deeper, but was accompanied by European nationalism, all the knowledge systems that people had used for generations were unilaterally declared unfit, irrelevant, primitive, or even evil. The religious ideology posited the belief in the Christian god as the only god and forced people to laugh at their own gods, and even to denigrate it. Not infrequently, science was used ideologically within the framework of colonialism to demonstrate not only the superiority of the Caucasian race, impose the developmental trajectory of the west onto those colonized societies, but also to imbue the knowledge generation process with a mechanistic, dualistic, materialistic, instrumentalist and linear way of seeing and doing (Ani 1994).

Most of these violated key precepts that under-girded the systems in Africa, Asia, and non-western societies, and led to the alienation and objectification of nature, a fundamental de-spiritualization of human development, and the privileging of an extractive and exploitative relationship with nature and non-European peoples in general. It not only created fundamental cognitive deficiencies in billions of people, generated insecurity and self-doubt within dominated groups, but also denied them the right to ontological experience and a sense of being (Ani, 1994). More seriously, it pre-empted or even stunted the natural development path that these systems of knowledge would have undergone had they been allowed their natural evolutionary and development path in what may, in IKS terms, correctly be referred to as "the lost years". On the other hand, the world also lost its opportunity to learn from other societies the basis upon which an ecologically coded, and human-centered development had been cultivated for centuries (Odora Hoppers 2002).

A focus on IKS therefore implies the archeology and re-appropriation of those knowledges that were not allowed to "be", in order to enhance our understanding of it, develop, protect, and promote it. Most challenging in a context such as South Africa's and the African continent as a whole, is the challenge of developing appropriate protocols, codes of conduct, and terms under which any integration and dialogue should occur.

For scientists and academics, it also implies taking community holders of knowledge as fellow experts and reorganizing research and development strategies and ethics accordingly, including a serious consideration of issues of the protection of Intellectual Property Rights, economic benefit sharing, poverty alleviation, and employment creation. For all the disciplines, it mandates a rethinking of the tenets and limitations of existing disciplinary arrangements, while for sector ministries, it implies broadening the operational parameters of existing policies including the implementation strategies that accompany them.

While at a systems level, IKS demands the establishment of an ethically sound and ecologically constituted way of thinking, the affirmation of the multiplicity of worlds and forms of life, the creation of a shared paradigm shift, self-reflexive praxis, becoming critical explorers of human and societal possibilities, the establishment of new evaluation and appraisal criteria, and the transformation to new futures (Odora Hoppers 2001).

10.3 Implications for Policy and Institutions for the IKS Initiative in South Africa

Soon after a call was made from the Parliamentary Portfolio Committee on Arts, Culture, Language, Science and Technology for the

Heads of the Science Councils to explore the role of the social and natural sciences in supporting the development of indigenous knowledge systems (1998), it was clear that this was not quite as simple a task as it initially appeared. Then located at the Human Sciences Research Council, I was tasked to develop a framework for developing, coordinating, managing and prioritizing Science Council's activities in IKS.

The driving question behind the responsibility was: How can indigenous knowledge systems impact on the transformation of knowledge generating institutions such as science councils and higher education institutions?

It quickly became clear to me that engaging in IKS would, of necessity firstly, have to entail commitment to the collective creation and recreation of several aspects of history, of practice, and of cognitive frameworks guiding thinking at present.

Secondly, it would require the development of freedom to envision a generative African future capable of developing practical strategies for human development based on knowledge resources reposing in its diverse peoples, and from that base drawing upon the power of modern science and technology towards the value addition objective.

Thirdly, it would be self-evident that there cannot be a people centred development without accepting that those we have so easily labelled as poor are not "tabula rasa", might actually be "knowledge rich…only economically poor (Gupta 1999)".

Fourthly, it would mean that we have to consider that while the integration of content would require cultivating basic knowledge of both IKS and western knowledge, the development of bi-cultural experts, and re-aligning such knowledge for direct policy formation and formulation have to become urgent priorities. An important step in this should be an investment in developing a language, a philosophy, a framework and perhaps a well-grounded rationale for addressing this issue – i.e. the central core around which multiple initiatives can hang.

Finally, it would require the systematic codification of a language and paradigm of articulation that is buttressed in human rights as enshrined in the international Bill of Rights and International Customary Law.

The implications of this initiative also had to be contemplated among which would include:

- the questioning of the present definition of what constitutes "Knowledge" with the intention of developing more inclusive policies and strategies for generating, legitimising and accrediting knowledge;
- who is the "subject" and what constitutes the "object" of scientific research with a view to humanizing research and halting the extractive and exploitative tendencies in present research regimes;
- de-museumizing, and de-formaldehyding African culture as a strategy of linking culture to science, and exposing the science behind every culture,
- scrutinizing the juridical domain within which science works in order to make sense of the intolerance, indifference, and culture of social triage that make scientists at times so oblivious to the consequences of their work on people.
- Even more than this, is to help draw attention to the manner in which the exclusion of other traditions of knowledge by reductionist science is itself part of the problem: at the *ontological level* (in that properties of other knowledges are *simply not taken note of*); at the *epistemological level* (in that other ways of perceiving are simply *not recognized* even where they should); and at the *sociological level* (in that the non-specialist, the non-expert is deprived of the right both to access to

knowledge and to judging claims made on its behalf) ... and to assist in the necessary rectification of this situation.

It short, this became a process that would help develop a mission statement on the emancipation, development, integration and protection of IKS; where emancipation is a necessary precondition for its integration with other knowledge systems; and protection is a strategy of vigilance against exploitation by dominant world orders.

Protection had then to be defined both as negative, and as positive protection where the first is protection from the "wolves" out there, and the latter is the incubatory protection that would enable the weak and the vulnerable knowledges to regain their strength and capability to incubate, develop tools for critical self-evaluation in the light of changing global situations, as well as the terms under which it can dialogue or refuse to engage with others.

10.4 What this Effort Enables in Scholarly Terms

- 4.1 It enables us to *move the frontiers of discourse* and understanding in the sciences as a whole, and *open new moral and cognitive spaces* within which constructive dialogue and engagement for sustainable development can begin.
- It also enables us to "clear space" in order to *enable new issues* in science development to be generated and fostered and thus determine new directions for the philosophy and sociology, as well as political economy of the sciences.
- IKS enables us to begin to understand the political economy of "Othering, thus permitting us to begin to develop a clearer sense of the ethical and juridical domain within which science works.
- It enables the articulation of IKS as a system of knowledge whose *intrinsic efficiency* and *efficacy* as tools for personal,

societal and global development needs to be identified and accredited as necessary.

- It further enables us to realize that it is this ***recovery*** of indigenous knowledges, and the systems intricately woven around them that will enable the move towards a *critical but resolute re-appropriation of the practical and cognitive heritage* of millions of people around the continent and elsewhere in the world.

Not all discomforts can however, be easily erased. For instance: *How do we handle the ambiguous situation of Pavlov and his dog, when the dog previously electrocuted without qualms in the name of "science" and "progress" has come out of the cage, and is demanding a discussion on the nature of science?* But that is a question for each of us to contemplate.

10.5 Facing the Public Policy and the Academic System

10.5.1 New Paradigms of Thought

In facing the public policy system, IKS brings to bear on discourse, the interface between cognitive justice, democracy, epistemology and sustainable human development. It questions the knowledge base informing policy, the knowledge legitimation and accreditation culture and procedures; the shortfalls in disciplinary arrangements in universities in their responsiveness to diversity (including cosmological); the issue of introducing legislation on intellectual property in a context of cultural diversity on the one hand, and the forces of globalization on the other; and the issue of human rights and identity (i.e the right to "be").

10.5.2 Developing Holistic Knowledge Frameworks

It means going beyond the appraisals of the work of individual scientists, beyond the output of particular research teams, and the competitive acumen of individual research institutions and towards creating an integrated and holistic knowledge framework for societal progress and development that seeks to *make whole that which was partial, incomplete, in large measure stunted, and thereby also stunting* (Hountondji 1997).

10.5.3 Generating New Paradigms of Development

It helps generate a vision of development other than the one that is pre-occupied with what the *people do not have*. This thinking has been trapped in a *negative dependency orientation* that it generates rather than motivating society to become constructively engaged in moving forward. If development is endogenous however, then the people are the subject. They are not trapped in the cold condescending gaze of the rich upon the poor, because *endogenous development begins at the point when people start to pride themselves as worthy human beings inferior to none*; and where such pride is lost, *development begins at the point at which this pride is restored, and history recovered.* (Odora Hoppers 2002)

10.5.4 Questioning Theoretical Habits of Thought

Clearly, a tremendous challenge is posited to academic disciplines across the board to revisit their core perceptions of African society, to question their theoretical habits and images of thought, and especially the normative and conceptual backgrounds that shape the rules and define parameters for what is considered "real" knowledge in academic work.

10.5.5 Rethinking Some Tenets of Academic Disciplines

For starters, for the *human and social sciences*, there is the issue of how to begin to take down Africa from the double cross upon which it has been haplessly hung (i.e. the Hobbesian picture of pre-European Africa milling with brutal savages AND the Rousseaurean picture of perpetual infantile people). For *anthropology*, some soul searching as to how the "savage" is to become an active knowing participant (Mudimbe 1988). For *history*, a scrutiny of the semantic shift that turned the illiterate from one ignorant of the alphabet, to a complete ignorant (Hountodji 1997). In *education*, questions of values, value education, history, the nature and manifestation of science, mathematics education, and the overall cultural orientation in curricula etc. would need transformative work.

10.5.6 Taking in the International Bill of Rights

In doing this, we are reminded of International Customary Law and the International Bill of Rights (Human Rights Convention) which spells out to us the fact that the appropriation of knowledge of indigenous communities and people by industrialized firms and scientists both locally and internationally without fair compensation or reward or explicit recognition *contravenes* fundamental moral, ethical, and legal norms that protect people from any form of ecological, political, and social abuse. We, as local institutions, often through inertia, have been proxies in this abuse, and middlemen in this untrammelled exploitation.

We must take a stand accordingly.

10.5.7 Taking in the Tenets of the Budapest Science Agenda

In this document is found strong injunctions and guidelines that are invaluable as we rummage our environs for creative ways around the impasse we find ourselves in. it states that what the world most needs is:

- a more inclusive, a more responsive, and a more dialogical science

- that there is a need for a vigorous and informed, constructive intercultural and democratic debate on the production and use of scientific knowledge
- that ways must be found to link modern science to the broader heritage of humankind
- that any kind of central monitoring, whether political, ethical, or economic, needs to take into account the increasingly diverse actors entering into the social tissue of science (Unesco 2000).

10.6 Confronting the Epistemological Irresponsibility

So what are those emerging propositions and conceptual reversals that are emerging in the groundswell of an alternative project of globalization in confronting the epistemological triage?

Here I will outline several new points of departure in rethinking the future of knowledge, innovation, social justice and human agency within a new conception of knowledge economy and information society; in other words, epistemological responsibility.

10.6.1 Knowledge and Innovation

Innovations go beyond the formal systems of innovation done in universities and industrial research and development laboratories. For proper development to occur, innovations *from below* have to be taken into account and appropriate support at national level accorded (Mashelkar R.A. 2002).

By innovation from below is meant taking into account the *full participation of all producers of knowledge including in informal settings of rural areas.* Indeed many societies in the developing world have nurtured and refined systems of knowledge of their own, relating to such diverse domains as geology, ecology, botany, agriculture, physiology and health. Within this, the emergence of terms such as "parallel", "indigenous" and "civilizational" knowledge systems are also expressions of other approaches to the acquisition and production of knowledge.

Indigenous knowledge and innovation systems must therefore be sustained through *active support to the communities who are keepers of this knowledge,* custodians of their ways of life, their languages; their social organization and the environments in which they live.

10.6.2 Bio-diversity Erosion, Sustainable Ethics, and Livelihood

While innovations promise to be a key factor in promoting equitable and sustainable development, it is recognized that there is a gross asymmetry in the rights and responsibility of those who produce Indigenous Knowledge in local communities and those who go about valorising it in the formal sector. This brings to light the issue of the *ethics of extraction and responsibility* (Gupta 1999). This must be reversed.

In this context, it is important to understand the fact that biodiversity erosion starts a chain reaction. The disappearance of one species is related to the extinction of innumerable other species with which it is interrelated through food webs. The crisis of biodiversity is therefore not just a crisis of the disappearance of the species which serve as industrial raw materials with potentialities for spinning millions of dollars for corporate enterprises. It is, more basically, *a crisis that threatens the life-support systems and livelihoods of millions of people in developing countries.* Yet, efforts to build upon knowledge systems of people who have maintained their natural resources so far are quite inadequate (Shiva 1997).

The issue of value addition to innovations going on in local communities is key to authentic development. In the area of bio-diversity, value addition will help local communities co-exist with bio-diversity resources by reducing primary extraction and generating long term benefits. There is also a need to connect creative people engaged in generating local solutions, which are authentic and accountable, thus facilitating people- to-people learning. The discussion on bio-diversity can only become authentic if we probe deep enough into knowledge traditions of each part of the world to discover the roots of the *sustainable ethics.*

But this discovery requires preparing our minds for visions which may collide with the dominant materialistic world view. Local communities are "knowledge-rich, but economically poor" (Gupta 1999). The search is therefore for a middle way in the development of the linkage between IKS and the formal processes, including the development of clear strategies that aim at the development of IKS specifically.

10.6.3 Renegotiation of Human Agency

Social justice is seen as that ideal condition in which all members of a society have the same basic rights, security, opportunities, obligations and social benefits. It is based on the idea of a society which gives individuals and groups fair treatment and a just share of the benefits of society. But when it comes to deciding what is "fair treatment" and what is a "just share", *alas! it has been found that social justice has still been largely defined by whatever the strong decided.* Social justice is therefore both *a philosophical problem* and *an important issue in politics.*

The recognition of what diversity poses compels us to propose that the true challenge before us is understanding the political significance of diversity (Hiley 2006) – or, as Seyla Benhabib has well put, it is the challenge to democracy of difference (Benhabib 1996). It is here that insights from post-colonial theorists that cultural difference is an important heuristic that has the capability to gradually corrode the grand narratives of evolution, utilitarianism and evangelism as technologies of colonial and imperialist governance, becomes inescapable.

According to Homi Bhaba, history is now taking place on the outer limits of the subject/object, giving rise to new moments of defiance that rips through the sly civility of those grand narratives, exposing their violence.

Subaltern agency emerges as a process of reversing, displacing and seizing the apparatus of value coding which had been monopolized by the colonial default drive. According to Bhaba, it is the contestation of the "given" symbols of authority that shifts the terrain of antagonism. THIS he states is the *moment of renegotiation of agency*. It is the voice of an *interrogative, calculative agency, the moment when we lose resemblance with the colonizer*, the moment of rememoration, that turns the narrative of enunciation into a haunting memorial of *what has been excluded, excised, evicted.* (Bhaba 1995).

10.7 Conclusion

The twenty-first *century* has been called the century of knowledge and of mind. Innovation is no longer contained within the laboratories of formal scientific systems, to innovations from below including knowledge systems of diverse people. A core need that is emerging is that for us to understand the conditions for the modernization of these knowledge systems in a just and fair manner (Mashelkar 2002).

As has been stated in the UNESCO World Report on Knowledge Societies, to remain human and liveable, knowledge societies will have to be societies of shared knowledge (Binde 2005). Today, we can say that the knowledge paradigms of the future are beginning by reaching out to those excluded, epistemologically disenfranchised, to move together towards a new synthesis.

In this synthesis, 'empowerment', it is recognized that shifting of power without a clear shift of paradigms of understanding that makes new propositions about the use of that power in a new dispensation leads to vicarious abuse of power by whoever is holding it – old or new (Venter 1997). In this new stream, modernization proceeds, but without necessarily following Western values (Huntington 1998) or sequences, but rather with a re-strengthening of core values from different traditions of knowledge and living.

It is about equal access as citizens of a nation and of the world into the mainstream society, with an emphasis on equality – i.e. the right to participate on an equal footing in a negotiating partnership. Western modernization, progress and thought is seen as a temporary epoch in human history with both advantages and disadvantages which must, and is seeking to re-engage with the more holistic integrated conceptualizations of sustainable life held by cultures that have, fortunately, not been down the path of "westernization".

In other words, it is a rapprochement of modern and older cultures, including modern culture's older roots where each complementing the other opens up the possibility of a viable future for humankind (Huntington 1998, Fatnowna & Pickett 2002).

I end this paper by quoting Howard Zinn in his book: *A People's History of the United States,* who states that there are several paths available to the historian. One can lie outright about the past. Or one can omit facts that might lead to unacceptable conclusions. Or, one can take what has become a fairly "safe" way: i.e. mention the truth quickly, then proceed to bury it a mass of other information.

This third option, Zinn states, is the way to say to the reader with a certain infectious calm: yes, mass murder took place, but it is not that important - it should weigh very little in our final judgements; it should affect very little what we do in the world.

He argues that while it is a useless scholarly exercise to indulge in accusations, judgements and condemnations, *the easy acceptance of atrocities as a deplorable but necessary price to pay for progress* (imperialism, colonialism, Hiroshima, and Vietnam – to save Western civilization; Kronstadt and Hungary to save socialism; nuclear proliferation to save us all) *is still with us*. One reason why these atrocities are still with us is that we have learned how to bury them in a mass of other facts.

Because this kind of calculated indifference, coming from the apparent objectivity of the scholar, or development expert, is easily accepted and ingested, it is therefore more deadly. The quiet acceptance of conquest and murder in the name of progress is only one approach to history, in which history is told from the point of view of the conquerors, and this single fact has underpinned the essence of the struggle of what can be called the African, or at times the "Third World" perspective since the beginning of the anti-colonial struggles to the present.

The rummage of the victims, tainted with the culture that oppresses them, as they seek to find some way out of the impasse of dehumanization that surrounds them, may at times lead to divergent fact surrounding the aspect of history; OR, be witnessed in the victims turning on other victims. This cannot be condoned. Neither can we stand by as spectators.

As Zinn poignantly recapitulates, *the cry of the poor is not always just, but if you do not listen to it, you will never know what justice is.* And in such a world rummaging for sources of life and hope, a world of apparently never-ending conflicts, a world of victims and executioners, *it is the job of right thinking people,* as Albert Camus suggested, *not to be on the side of the executioners* (Zinn).

10.8 Chapter References

Ani M. (1994): Yurugu: An Africa-Centred Critiques of European Cultural Thought and Behavior. Trenton, NJ. Africa World press.

Attran S. (1987): Origin of the Species and Genus Concepts: An Anthropological Perspective. In *Journal of History and Biology*, 20, 195-279.

Béji H. (2001): Tomorrow. Women. In Bindé ed. 2001. Keys to the Twenty-first Century. Paris. Unesco, 286-288.

Benhabib S. (1996): Democracy and Difference. Contesting the Boundaries of the Political. Princeton. Princeton University Press.

Bhaba H. (1995): In the Spirit of Calm Violence. In Prakash 1995. After Colonialism: Imperial Histories and Post-Colonial Displacements. New Jersey. Princeton University Press, 326-346.

Bindé J. (2005): Towards Knowledge Societies – UNESCO World Report. UNESCO Publishing.

Brush S.B. (1996): Whose knowledge, Whose Genes, Whose Rights? In Brush S.B & Stabinsky D. eds 1996. *Valuing Local Knowledge. Indigenous People and Intellectual property Rights.* Washington DC. Island Press, 1-24.

Esteva G. (1992): Development. In Sachs W.ed. 1992. *The Development Dictionary. A Guide to Knowledge as Power.* London Zed Books Ltd. 6-25.

Fatnowna, S & Pickett, H (2002). The Place of Indigenous Knowledge Systems in the Post-Postmodern Integrative Paradigm Shift. In: Odora Hoppers, C. (2002): *Indigenous Knowledge and the Integration of Knowledge Systems: Towards a Philosophy of Articulation.* New African Books (Pvt) Ltd, Claremont, South Africa.

Gupta A. (1999): *Conserving Biodiversity and rewarding Associated Knowledge and Innovation Systems: Honey Bee Perspective.* Paper presented at the World trade Forum. Bern. August 27-29th 1999.

Henderson, J.S.Y (2008). Indigenous Diplomacy and the Rights of Peoples. Saskatoon. Purich Publishing.

Hountondji P. (1997): Introduction. In Hountondji P. 1997 ed. Endogenous Knowledge. Research Trails. CODESRIA.

Huntington S.P. (1996): The Clash of Civilizations and the Remaking of World Order. New York, Simon & Schuster.

Luyckx M. (1999): The Transmodern Hypothesis: towards a dialogue of cultures. In *Futures*. Volume 31 Numbers 9/10. November/December 1999, 971-983.

Mashelkar R.A. (2002):The Role of Intellectual Property in Building Capacity for Innovation for Development: A Developing World Perspective. In: Odora Hoppers (ed).2002. *Indigenous Knowledge and the Integration of Knowledge Systems: Towards a Philosophy of Articulation.* Cape Town. New Africa Books.

Mudimbe VY (1988). The invention of Africa. Gnosis, Philosophy, and the Order of Knowledge. London: James Currey

Nandy A. (1997): Colonization of the mind. In Rahnema M & Bawtree V. eds. 1997. The Post Development Reader. London, ZED (168-177).

Nandy A. (1998): In Franck F.; Roze J.; Connolly R.; 1998. What Does it Mean to be Human? Circumstantial Productions Publishing. New York, 131-139.

Odora Hoppers C.A. (1998): Structural Violence as a Constraint to African Policy Formulation in the 1990's: Repositionng Education in International Relations. Stockholm University.

Odora Hoppers, C.A. (2001): Towards a Common Understanding of IKS. Submission to COHORT IKS-Champions Group.16th March 2001. Human Sciences Research Council, Pretoria. South Africa.

Odora Hoppers C.A (2001b): IKS and its Implications for Research and Curriculum Transformation in Tertiary Institutions. Keynote address to the University of Venda conference on *IKS: An African Perspective.* September 2001.

Odora Hoppers C.A. (2002): Research on Indigenous Knowledge Systems: The Search for Cognitive Justice as a Fraternal Act. Unisa Annual Faculty Of Education Seminar: *Research in the Faculty of Education.* Senate Hall: 13 September 2002.

Odora Hoppers C.A. (2002): Indigenous Knowledge and the Integration of Knowledge Systems: Towards a Conceptual and Methodological Framework. In Odora Hoppers C.A. ed. 2002. *Indigenous Knowledge and the Integration of Knowledge Systems. Towards a Philosophy of Articulation.* Cape Town. New Africa Books, 2-22.

Saul J.R. (1993): Voltaire's Bastards: the Dictorship of Reason in the West. Toronto Penguin Books.

Saul J.R (2014): the Comeback. Toronto. Penguin Canada books, 7-11.

Shiva V. (1997): Biopiracy: The Plunder of Nature and Knowledge. Boston. South End Press.

Unesco (2000): Science for the Twenty First Century. A New Commitment. The Declaration on Science and the Use of Scientific Knowledge. Paris. UNESCO.

Venter (1997): When Mandela Goes. The Coming of South Africa's Second Revolution. London. Transworld.

Zinn H. (1999): A People's History of the United States: 1492-Present. New York. Colin Harper, 8-9.

11

ETHICAL LEADERSHIP
IN HIGHER EDUCATION
IN THE ERA OF COMPLEXITY

Narend Baijnath

11.1 Introduction

We continue in our time to experience tremendous flux in higher education and in society generally, attributable in part to an ever-widening income and inequality gap in large parts of the world, diminishing opportunities, continued economic uncertainty, and unpredictability about the future. A corollary is social, political and economic volatility manifested in conflicts and protest action as disaffected groups and marginal communities in man societies in the developed and developing world challenge orthodoxy in ever more confrontational ways. This is particularly true for South Africa, which has experienced protracted upheaval in higher education since 2015 over student fees, access and affordability, and the orthodoxy of teaching, learning and curricular content. Leaders of higher education institutions have been drawn into engagement with student leaders and protesters in unprecedented ways, with volatility, latent anger, disruption of the academic programme, destruction of infrastructure, and daily confrontation being the corollaries to the protest movement.

The challenges confronting leadership in all sectors of society have never appeared as complex or more intractable. In the higher education sector, the demand for access has increased exponentially while leaders have had to contend with increasing competition from new organisational forms and delivery platforms made possible by advances in technology. At the same time regulatory mechanisms, reporting and accountability prescripts have rendered the challenges and obligations of leadership ever more onerous. In the developed world, saturation point has been reached with increasing numbers of graduates struggling to find employment, leading to questions about the benefits relative to the costs of higher education. In the developing world, participation rates remain stubbornly low in large parts, with variable degrees of quality and provision to meet burgeoning demands and needs, and unprecedented competition through cross-border delivery that has changed the landscape indelibly, as higher education has increasingly been commodified.

Against this backdrop, higher education leaders are challenged to ensure that their institutions not only survive but thrive in the new international, IT-enabled, volatile and competitive environment now faced (Scott, Coates & Anderson, 2008). And with this has come a significant growth in the complexity and span of responsibilities attendant to their leadership responsibilities. In the South African context, widespread student unrest, increased stakeholder demand for accountability, and pressure from government to deliver more with fewer resources, has made it apparent that universities are unenviably difficult institutions to govern, manage and lead. They have become places where industry, civil society, community and government interests often coalesce or coincide, but increasingly clash. Operating in such a volatile environment impels the need to constantly embrace change and adapt to emerging trends and dynamics (Mabelebele, 2013).

The recognition of the importance and role of universities in the socio-economic development of the country was accompanied by calls for the effective management of the institutions and public accountability to its stakeholders via stringent reporting measures. This development – often referred to as the ideology of managerialism – requires university leaders to develop and implement management systems based on extensive data collection, production of evidence and compliance with elaborate reporting requirements (Cloete & Bunting, 2000). Altbach et al. (2009) argue that one of the biggest challenges affecting the management of universities is the change in the relationship between those responsible for the traditional core functions of academia (teaching and research), and those who are responsible for managing the institution. These roles often diverge and are in tension with each other.

A study on academic leadership in Australia reveals that demands on academic staff and the variety of additional managerial functions have precipitated new tensions and competing priorities where more and more attention is required for administration, compliance and day-to-day-management (Broomhead, 2010). The expectations and demands from within the university, as well as the system, present university leaders with sometimes conflicting or competing priorities. These include the pressure to increase research output, while improving access and success, and generating more third-stream income. A Herculean task when resourcing does not keep pace.

The dominant management and planning model for resourcing traditionally rested on an assumption that the number of hours available for utilisation were finite, and that an individual's efforts could largely be focused on research, a lesser or greater proportion on teaching, and a smaller proportion on generating third stream income. This made possible a comfortable balance and relative freedom to choose the proportions dedicated to each according to an individual's talents and preferences. With burgeoning demands and a raft of new tasks, this kind of proactive planning has all but dissipated completely. As institutions and their leaders are forced increasingly into a reactive mode, proactive planning becomes futile, and demand is piled upon demand, often indiscriminately, and invariably without due regard to impact and practicability as the screws of accountability, transparency, and performance management have tightened inexorably.

In a developing context such as South Africa, added pressures are to promote transformation (even while the concept is not clearly defined or commonly understood). As student demographics have diversified, new challenges are to address the demands of stakeholders with different needs in a highly unequal society stratified by race, class, gender and other divides, the most challenging of which is that of access to technology and the internet. Contemporary politics are still heavily influenced by the dogged legacies of apartheid, while arduous progress is made towards national developmental imperatives. Ideologies and competing aspirations clash within our universities, which have long been the theatre for their articulation and expression. Managing competing demands while fostering the independence of a healthy higher education sector focused on quality in teaching and increasing knowledge production requires extensive skill in negotiation and prioritisation and careful leadership towards a clear vision of the future for the system (CHE, 2015; Kulati & Moja, 2002).

The higher education sector more broadly is in the throes of perpetual change as institutions re-examine their roles in society to be more in tune with the knowledge and human capital needs of their societies, adjust their modes of operation, and respond to or are led by changes in society, economy and technology to remain relevant and sustainable.

11.2 A Context of Perpetual Change

It has been argued that the challenges to higher education leadership have increased as society and institutions have become ever more complex. Contributing to increasing complexity is a range of influences from within and outside the academy. The following analysis illuminates the broad categories of change and their key features, and cites the origin of each. Each change dynamic is described and its influence stated briefly.

SOCIAL PRESSURES		
Demographic shifts	The rise of new demographic groupings/stakeholders/students (digital natives/Generation Z/) will have an impact on academic and enrolment planning. The nature of the student/stakeholder – age, values, learning style, geographic location, mobility – will have a significant influence on the administration of the university.	AIM (2014) Hajkowicz, Reeson, Rudd et al. (2016)
Changing Student Expectations	Student attitudes will change towards 'value for money' and perceived quality propositions. Requires flexibility and responsiveness to students' needs and demands. Evolvement of the view of the 'student as consumer' and the university as 'service provider'.	Ernst & Young (2012)

Multiculturalism and Inclusiveness	Incorporation and legitimisation of non-discriminatory, non-racial, non-western ways of knowing and learning. Promoting the ethics of inclusiveness and rejecting the politics of exclusion. Challenges what is taught, how it is taught and the knowledge categories used in the process.	Soudien (2013) Makoele (2014)
Staffing challenges	Addressing the challenge of ageing academic senior staff members and researchers. Challenge of the slow growth in the number of emerging academics and researchers.	HESA (2011) DHET (2015) CHE (2016) (Staffing chapter)
GLOBALISATION		
Knowledge Economy	Defined as the use of knowledge to generate tangible and intangible value. Knowledge will be used by decision support systems in universities and in various fields and generate economic value. Requires that rules and practices that determined success in the past will need rewriting in an interconnected, globalised economy where knowledge resources and innovation are crucial.	Pew Research Centre (2012) Scott & McKellar (2012) Altbach et al. CHE (2016) – Chapter 1

Democratisation of knowledge and access	The massive increase in the availability of 'knowledge' online and the mass expansion of access to university education in developed and developing markets means a fundamental change in the role of universities as originators and keepers of knowledge.	MacGregor (2014) Scott & McKellar (2012) CHE (2016) Chapter 1
Sustainability as Social Movement	The responsibility of the university towards solving local and national socio-economic problems. The university is seen to have a societal/global purpose.	Green paper (2012) NDP (2012) CHE (2005)
Digitalisation/ Rise of ICTs	Digital technologies will transform higher education and will transform the way education is delivered and accessed, and the way 'value' is created by higher education providers. Includes new forms of delivery i.e. MOOCs and open learning. Movement towards the virtual university.	Duderstadt (2009)
Innovation	Improvement of innovative knowledge production required to survive and thrive in the 21st century. Change in the model of how we think about learning and incorporate innovation. Increased linkages with industry and greater demand for the commercialisation of research.	Jenvey (2014)

Glocalism	Teaching and learning strategies and curriculum development takes into consideration global standards and context – but is based on local learning.	O'Brien & Robertson (2009) Patel & Lynch (2013)
COMPETITIVE PRESSURES		
Contestability of markets and corporatisation of funding	Corporatisation will create opportunities for the entrance of national and multinational players into the educational market. Competition for students will increase. Increase in the provision of private higher education.	Ernst & Young (2012) Altbach et al. 2014
Challenges of funding	Pressure on state funding of higher education will increase significantly. Significant increases in student subsidies are required. Challenges surrounding the decline in government subsidies versus increased access will have to be addressed. Growing pressure to generate more third stream income.	CHE – VitalStats (2014) CHE (2016) Funding chapter
Integration with industry	Universities will need to build and strengthen relationships with industry to support the funding and application of research, and reinforce the role of universities as drivers of innovation and growth. Increasing dependence on business and industry rather than the public purse.	AAU (2013)

Political pressures	Politicisation of the higher education environment. Political interference via policy changes. Greater government reporting and scrutiny. Growing risk of government interference.	HE Amendment Act CHE (2016) Regulation chapter
Differentiation	Movement towards a differentiated higher education system. Differentiation is viewed as a way of ensuring a diverse system that will improve access, improve participation and enable institutions to focus on niche areas that respond to national development needs. This may result in institutional types ranging from largely undergraduate institutions to research intensive institutions.	Cloete (2015) CHET (2013)
INSTITUTIONAL CHANGE CAPACITY		
Maintaining standards	Commitment to assuring the consistency and quality of academic offerings to ensure that programmes are accredited and quality assured on a regular basis.	CHE mandate HE Act 1997 as amended NQF Act
Institutional culture	Nature and influences of local cultures (the way we do things around here), the extent to which the university operates efficiently and in an integrated way. An institution's self-image and its capacity to respond in an agile	Van der Merwe & Suransky (2014)

	manner to a range of stakeholders and social pressures is determined by its culture.	
Transformation – Access, Opportunity and Success	A substantial improvement in undergraduate success and graduate rates required as a central element of transformation. Measures, processes, structures and programmes need to be put in place to ensure student access and success, and as a central precept of transformation.	Badat (2002, 2010)
Transformation – Curriculum, Teaching and Learning	De-colonising, de-racialising, de-masculinising and de-gendering university curricula and knowledge production processes while engaging with related ontological and epistemological issues, including their implications for research methodology, scholarship, teaching and learning, curriculum and pedagogy are vital elements of a broad conceptualisation of transformation.	CHE (2014) 4 year Curriculum CHE (Ogude, Nel & Oosthuizen)

Currie and Vidovich (2009) argue that there are a number of macro pressures that have an impact on the 21st century teaching and learning environment. These include diminished government funding concurrent with the massification of higher education, work intensification, pressures towards privatisation, marketisation and instrumentalism (in learning and teaching), the importation of corporate managerial structures and cultures, increased accountability, new demands associated with accelerated internationalisation, dwindling collegiality and trust, decreased autonomy, and challenges to academic freedom. These add to the mix of pressures and influences which impact upon the university and the challenges of leadership, making proactive and consistent leadership all that more difficult, and more imperative.

11.3 University Leadership in the Era of Complexity

As part of good governance, a university is expected to account to a number of stakeholders with an interest in higher education. These include government, employers, students and industry. Greater public accountability has been a steady feature of public policy and practice for institutions funded by the public purse. The central public concern is whether universities are producing graduates with the necessary knowledge and skills to enter the world of work in the 21st century and become 'good citizens' who can contribute to development and sustainability.

As the relationship between an educated citizenry and a nation's economic prosperity is assumed as trite, universities have been under steady pressure to increase access (especially for students from previously disadvantaged socio-economic backgrounds), to offer quality academic programmes to enable graduates to access job opportunities, while at the same time generating knowledge and research that will assist in resolving national development challenges such as unemployment, health and food security.

The obligation of institutions to transform finds expression in a number of expectations. Universities are required to (a) increase and broaden participation, including greater "access for black, women, disabled and mature students" and "equity of access and fair chances of success to all... while eradicating all forms of unfair discrimination and advancing redress for past inequalities"; (b) "support a democratic ethos and a culture of human rights by educational programmes and practices conducive to critical discourse and creative thinking, cultural tolerance, and a common commitment to a humane, non-racist and non-sexist social order"; and (c) "create an enabling institutional environment and culture that is sensitive to and affirms diversity, promotes reconciliation and respect for human life, protects the dignity of individuals from racial and sexual harassment, and rejects all other forms of violent behaviour" (DoE, 1997).

A shortage of skilful leadership and lack of management capacity have been identified in the last decade by various authors, organisations and governmental agencies as one of the major weaknesses of the South African higher education system (CHE, 2014; CHET, 2002; Herbst, 2007; HESA, 2010; Jansen, 2004; Seale, 2015). There is a widespread recognition of the need for effective leadership to shape institutional transformation and has led to a re-evaluation of leadership practices in higher education (Seale, 2004). Herbst & Conradie (2011) argue that in order to build the leadership capacity for top quality institutions, leaders will have to possess good management and technical skills, as well as well-developed social and emotional skills. In addition, academic leaders must develop the ability to motivate for change and articulate its relevance by establishing an authentic and consistent relationship with stakeholders (Mabelebele, 2013).

Leadership in higher education has become an important topic of discussion during the past decade as new perspectives on academic leadership have emerged along with new ways of organising the decision-making structures in institutions (Aasen & Stensaker, 2007; International Education Association of Australia, 2014). Traditionally, research leaders, with extensive academic capital, have been deemed most appropriate for institutional leadership (Morley, 2013). However, against the background of increasing demands on academic leaders, various researchers and stakeholder groups have expressed concern about the capabilities of current and future university leaders (Jansen, 2004; Mabelebele, 2013; O'Brien & Robertson, 2009). It is clear that a more diverse and onerous compendium of skills is required of higher education leaders in the current ea.

Although a significant amount has been written on leadership in business, much of it might not be applicable to the distinctive operating environment of a university (Bush, 2007; Burns, 2004 & Kulati, 2000). While education can learn from other settings, educational leadership has to be centrally concerned with the purpose or aims of education (Bush & Glover, 2002). Unlike private sector organisations, higher education institutions have diverse goals and objectives (teaching, research and social engagement amongst others) and are organised around the production, preservation and dissemination of an intangible commodity – knowledge. The emphasis on institutional effectiveness, efficiency, and responsiveness within the higher education legislative framework, together with an increase in stakeholder demands, has identified the need for a different approach to academic leadership (Cloete & Bunting, 2000; Green; 1997).

The role of an academic leader in the contemporary context is no doubt complex, and often imbued with ambiguity. One of the fundamental challenges that academic leaders encounter is a lack of clarity about the nature of this context-specific form of leadership that includes both management and leadership functions (Cardno, 2014).

Although academic leaders are required by current accountability systems to focus on a myriad of factors as have been illuminated, they should remain cognisant of the need of staff and students to be motivated, feel valued and respected, and create a teaching and learning environment where communication among all involved is open, honest, frequent, and in good faith (Vogel, 2012).

11.4 Ethical Leadership in the Era of Complexity

For the purposes of the argument here, ethics is understood as "a dynamic and continuing activity rather than an adherence to a system of moral codes and principles enshrined in formal policy statements" (Niesche & Haase, 2010). Leadership on the other hand implies intentional decision-making to enact change, rather than merely to maintain the status quo and support current systemic processes, and such decisions (Vogel, 2012):

A leader's framework of values, belie ̗ ˻ ̗˻ ̗ view, convictions born of deep knowledge and skill, and a strong sense of and dedication to the public interest are what inform his/her ethical framework. From this a leader develops a vision which resonates with the various stakeholders, defines and shapes the change process, and takes actions to make his or her vision a reality. The use of 'ethical frames' provide an opportunity for academic leaders to examine their ways of thinking about complex dilemmas, to consider actions outside the traditional approach and to provide a new perspective to resolving issues and engaging in reflective practice (Shapiro & Gross, 2005).

Multiple frames of reference for ethics can be drawn from the discourse thereon which provide a useful lenses through which to view conduct and practice, or use as measures. Below are distilled five such frames:

- *Ethic of Justice:* Ethical dilemmas are resolved by principles such as fairness, equity, and justice. Decisions are guided through laws, rules, policies, codes and procedures – rules-based decision-making (Beckner, 2004). It implies that pre-established principles, laws and rules will guide leaders' conceptions and perceptions of ethical matters. The ethic of justice is non-consequentialist, where leaders should not consider the consequences of their actions, but make decisions based on predetermined rules and policies.

- *Ethic of Critique*: The ethic of critique is juxtaposed with the ethic of justice in that it "critiques" moral problems caused by the ethic of justice (Nevarez & Wood, 2010). The ethic of critique views laws, rules and procedures as benefitting only specific groups of people – "if the ethic of justice looks towards fairness, the ethic of critique looks toward barriers to fairness" (Starratt, 2004). Shapiro and Gross (2005) defined the ethic of critique as a critical consequentialist perspective that identifies laws, policies, and structures that disadvantage certain groups and the promotion of action to address identified inequities. It involves the in-depth examination of the underlying issues affecting the in (effective) functioning of the university. Who benefits? Who is silenced? How can the university assist in addressing underlying tensions and create a conducive learning environment for all students?

- *Ethic of Care:* This is compassion-oriented and is concerned with and characterised by virtues such as compassion, understanding, and trust. Leaders employing an ethic of care are encouraged to foster understanding of multiple sociocultural realities. The ethic of care reinforces the importance of students and their development, focusing particularly on aiding students in achieving their educational and career goals (Shapiro & Gross, 2005). Leaders operating from this ethic understand the importance of social ties and associations, recognising and being attentive to the manner in which issues have an impact on the institution. Consideration is given to what the long-term effects of decisions and policies are. It requires academic leaders to consider the needs of all stakeholders and to consider "multiple voices."

- *Ethic of Community:* This situates the best interests of the local community as the fundamental principle in decision making that serves the best interests of the community. Consideration is given to what the communities'/country's demands and concerns about the issues facing the institution are, and how these can be mediated through the goals of the university.

- *Ethic of Profession:* This ethic acknowledges that there are guiding values (e.g., principles, codes, assumptions, mores, and expected behaviours) within each profession. According to Shapiro & Stefkovich (2008), leaders operating from this standpoint should view and adhere to professional codes of ethics through the lens of their practical experience in education; be cognisant of their own personal beliefs, convictions, and values in relationship to those within the field; consider the standards and needs of the local community; and place students at the centre of the decision-making process.

Viewed through the foregoing analytical lens, ethical leadership is grounded in a set of competencies that can be strengthened and developed through carefully designed opportunities for reflection, dialogue and practice. Resonant with this, Benoit & Graham (2015) argue that the essence of ethical leadership is the ability to build trusting relationships, based on moral principles of trust, respect, integrity, honesty, fairness, equity and compassion. There is a shared understanding that success depends on a constellation of relationships, both internal and external, not all of which are under the institution's control, but which it can influence through the way it operates from a platform of ethical principles (Berghofer & Swartz, 2012).

Ethical frames such as those illuminated above can enable and empower leaders as they construct and consider alternative courses of action. All decision-making processes would have ethical dimensions to a greater or lesser degree. Using an ethical frame or multiple such frames will assist university leaders to interrogate available courses of action systematically and deeply, ensuring that ultimate decisions are sound and ethically defensible.

11.5 Conclusion

GlobeEthics.net (2015) identifies responsible leadership as a key component in facing the economic, financial, environmental and social challenges of the 21st century. Responsible leadership acknowledges that actions are rooted in value systems and by adhering to these values and aligning actions to them. It acknowledges the relationship between responsible decision-making and responsiveness e.g. responsiveness to the needs of those who are affected by one's decisions and actions.

In the above light, ethical leadership in a higher education context is a social, relational practice concerned with the moral purpose of higher education since ethics is about relationships with others and leadership is a human-centred relational activity (Angus, 2006; Erich & Klenowsky, 2015). Ethical leaders are individuals who act fairly and justly and are viewed as caring, honest and principled persons who make balanced decisions and who communicate the importance of ethics and ethical behaviour to their followers (Brown & Trevino, 2006). Moreover, they promote values such as inclusion, collaboration and social justice when working with all stakeholders.

While it is acknowledged and has been argued that leading higher education institutions has become ever more complex, and the pressures unrelenting, the imperative for attention to the ethical dimensions of leadership and decision-making has never been greater.

Acknowledgement: The research assistance for this article of Dr Marianne Engelbrecht, Office of the CEO, Council on Higher Education, is gratefully acknowledged.

11.6 Chapter References

African Association of Universities (2013): "Perspective of industry's engagement with African universities". Available from: www.aau.org/.../Draft%20Report%20on%20University-Industry%20Lin

AIM (2014): *Speed@work: How Velocity, Turbulence, Fast Growth, Rapid Change and Strategic Agility Affect Business and the Workplace* (Wrightbooks: Australia)

Altbach, P.G., Reisberg, L., Rumbley, L.E. (2009): "Trends in global higher education: Tracking an academic revolution", *UNESCO World Conference on Higher Education Report,* 23-25.

Angus, L. (2006): "Educational leadership and the imperative of including student voices, student interest, and students' lives in the mainstream" in: *International Journal of Leadership in Education,* 9 (4), 369-379.

Avolio, B. J., & Gardner, W. L. (2005): "Authentic leadership development: Getting to the root of positive forms of leadership", in: *Leadership Quarterly* 16, 315–338.

Badat, S. (2002): Transforming South African higher education, 1990–2003: Goals, policy initiatives and critical challenges and issues. Unpublished Paper. African Higher Education Partnership Meeting, 16–18 March 2002, Nigeria.

Badat, S. (2010): *Conceptualising, Strategising and Implementing Higher Education Change: 10 Propositions.* Presentation made at the International Association of Universities Conference, Utrecht.

Bass, B.M. (1995): 'Transformational leadership redux' in *Leadership Quarterly,* 6(4), 463-78.

Beckner, W. (2004): *Ethics for educational leaders.* (Pearson: Boston).

Bennis, W.G. (1990): "Leadership in the 21st century: Managing the dream" in *Training*, 27(1), 43-48.

Berghofer, D. & Schwartz, G. (2012): Ethical leadership: right relationships and the emotional bottom line −the gold standard for success. Available from: http://www.ethicalleadership.com/ BusinessArticle.htm

Broomhead, M., 2010: Leading in time of change. Australian Institute of Management Series. Wiley, Australia.

Brown, M.E. & Trevino, L.K. (2006) "Ethical leadership: A review and future directions" in: The Leadership Quarterly 17, 595-616.

Brown, M. E., Treviño, L. K., & Harrison, D. (2015): "Ethical leadership: A social learning perspective for construct development and testing" in: *Organizational Behavior and Human Decision Processes,* 97, 117−134.

Cardno, C. (2014): "The functions, attributes and challenges of academic leadership in New Zealand" in: *International Journal of Educational Management*, 28(4), 352-364.

Centre for Academic Integrity (1999): *The fundamental values of academic integrity*. Available from: http://www.academicintegrity.org/ icai/assets/FVProject.pdf

Council on Higher Education (CHE), 2000: *Towards A New Higher Education Landscape: Meeting the Equality, Quality and Social Development Imperatives of South Africa in the 21st Century* (CHE: Pretoria).

CHE. (2002): Building relationships between Higher Education and the private and public sectors. Proceedings of the CHE colloquium. Sandton, 27 & 28 June 2002.

CHE (2014 and 2015): *Vital Stats*, Pretoria: CHE.

CHE (2014): Leadership Project – Draft Report. Internal document. Unpublished.

CHE (2016): Issues emerging from CHE's Review of HE: Two decades of democracy, Unpublished.

Ciula, A. (2003): Ethics and Leadership Effectiveness. Available from: http://www.ila-net.org/members/directory/downloads/antonakis-ciulla-13.pdf

Cloete, N & Kulati, T. (2003): *Managerialism within a framework of cooperative Governance.* Report prepared for a chapter in a book on International Perspectives on Managerialism.

Cloete, N. (2015): "Africa needs differentiated higher education systems" in: *University World News.* 6 March 2015. Available from: http://www.universityworldnews.com/article.php?story=201502251427 42928

CIHE (2012): *Ethics matters: Managing ethical issues in higher education.* Available from: http://www.open.ac.uk/ethics-centre/ 0509Ethics.pdf

Cohen, D.V. (2003): "Creating and maintaining ethical work climates: Anomie in the workplace and implications for managing change", in: *Business Ethics Quarterly,* 3(4), 343-358.

CTB (2015): "Chapter 13: Ethical leadership" Available from: http://ctb.ku.edu/en/table-of-contents/leadership/leadership-ideas/ethical-leadership/main

DHET (2012): Green Paper for Post-School Education and Training. http://www.dhet.gov.za

DHET (2015): Staffing South Africa's universities development programme. Available from: http://www.dhet.gov.za/ssauf/Content/ SSAU-DP.pdf

Dion, M. (2012) "Are ethical theories relevant to ethical leadership?" in: *Leadership & Organizational Development Journal,* 33(1), 4-24.

Duderstadt, J. (2009): The future of higher education in the knowledge-driven, global economy of the 21st century (Toronto: Canada).

Erich, L.C, Kimber, M., Cranston, N & Starr, K. (2011): "Ethical tensions and academic leaders" in: *Higher Education Review,* 43(3).

Erich, L.C., Klenowski, H.V. & Smeed, J. (2015): "The centrality of ethical leadership" in: *Journal of Educational Administration,* 53(2), 197-214.

Ernst & Young (2012): *University of the future.* Available from: http://www.ey.com/Publication/vwLUAssets/University_of_the_future/ $FILE/University_of_the_future_2012.pdf

Fukuyama, F. (1995): *Trust: Social Virtues and the Creation of Prosperity.* (Free Press: New York)

Green, M. (1997): *Transforming higher education: Views from leaders around the world.* (American Council on Education: Washington).

Hajkowicz, S. et al. (2016): Tomorrow's digitally enabled workforce: Megatrends and scenarios for jobs and employment in Australia over the coming twenty years. Available from: https://www.acs.org.au/ _data/assets/pdf_file/0018/95103/16-0026_DATA61_REPORT_ TomorrowsDigiallyEnabledWorkforce_WEB_160128.pdf

Hall, M., Symes, A. & Luescher, T. (2002): "Governance in South African Higher Education Research Report". Available from: http://www.che.ac.za/media_and_publications/research/governance-south-african-higher-education-research-report

Haynes, C.C & Pickeral, T. (2008): "Renewing the civic mission of schools" in: *School Administrator,* 65(9), 10-12.

Herbst, H.H. & Conradie, P.D.P. (2011): "Leadership effectiveness in higher education: Managerial self-perceptions versus perceptions of others" in: *SA Journal of Industrial Psychology*, 37(1).

HESA (2010): "Transformation challenges in governance, management and leadership in higher education". Concept document – Commission in the Ministerial Summit on Higher Education – 22-23 April 2010. http://www.hesa.org.za

HESA (2011): *A generation of growth: Proposal for a National Programme to Develop the Next Generation of Academics for South African Higher Education.* Available from: http://www.universitiessa.ac.za/sites/www.universitiessa.ac.za/files/201 1-%20HESA%20Building%20the%20Next%20Generation%20of%20 Academics_0.pdf

Jansen, J., 2002: Seven Major Challenges Facing Higher Education. Keynote Address, Council for Higher Education (CHE) Consultative Conference IV, Johannesburg

Jensen, S.M. and Luthans, F. (2006): "Entrepreneurs as authentic leaders: impact on employees' Attitudes", in: Leadership & *Organization Development Journal*, 27 (8), 646-666.

Jenvey, N. (2014) 'The contribution of universities to the economy' in: *University World News*, 11 April 2014 Issue No: 315. Available from: http://www.universityworldnews.com/article.php?story=201404101732 50629

Karsten, L. (2011): "Ethics and values: The need for student awareness of workplace value systems". Available from: http://www.waceinc.org/ philly2011/conference_proceedings/Refereed%20Papers/New%20Zeala nd/KARSTE~1.PDF

Kotter, J.P. (1990): *A force for change: how leadership differs from management*, (Free Press: New York).

Kouzes, J. M., & Posner, B. Z. (2007): *The leadership challenge.* (Jossey-Bass: California).

Kulati, T. (2000): Governance, Leadership and Institutional Change in South African Higher Education: Grappling with Instability. Tertiary Education and Management. Volume 6, 177–192.

Kulati, T. & Moja, T. (2002): Leadership. Transformation in Higher Education. Global Pressures and Local Realities in South Africa – CHET. (JUTA: Cape Town).

Lichtenstein, S. (2012): 'The role of values in leadership: How leaders' values shape value creation". Available from: http://integralleadershipreview.com/6176-the-role-of-values-in-leadership-how-leaders-values-shape-value-creation/

Mabelebele, J. (2013): Leading and managing higher education institutions in South Africa. Keynote address: HELM LEAD – 13 March 2013. http://hesa.org.za

Mabelebele, J. (2014) "Is public trust in universities declining in South Africa? Dilemmas and paradoxes", Address to a Seminar at the University of the Western Cape; South Africa. 31 July 2014. Available from: https://www.uwc.ac.za/UWCInsight/sholarship@uwc/Pages/Is-Public-Trust-in-Universities-declining-in-South-Africa.aspx

MacGregor, K., 2014. The massification of higher education in South Africa. *University World News.* http://www.universityworldnews.com/article.php?story=2014062015083621

Makoele, T. (2014): Cognitive justice: a road map for equitable inclusive learning environments in the International, *Journal of Education and Research*; 2(7):505-518

Marion, R. (2005): *Leadership in education: Organizational theory for the practitioner* (Cambridge: United Kingdom).

National Development Plan: *Vision for 2030, (2011).* *Chapter 9: Improving Education, Training and Innovation* (National Planning Commission: Pretoria)

Pew Research Centre, 2012. *The future of higher education.* http://www.pewinternet.org

Nagy, J. (2015): "Discretionary behaviour and performance in educational organizations: The missing link in educational management and leadership" in *Chapter 7: Coalface academic leadership in Australian higher education,* 169-196.

National Planning Commission 2011. National Development Plan: Vision for 2030 (Pretoria: NPC)

Nevarez, C., & Wood, J. L. (2010): "Community college leadership and administration: Theory, practice & change", in: *Education Administration,* 4(12).

O'Brien, E. & Robertson, P., (2009): Future leadership competencies: From foresight to current practice. *Journal of European Industrial Training.* Vol. 33(4), 371-380.

Ogude. N., Nel, H. & Oosthuizen, M. (2005): "The challenge of curriculum responsiveness in South African Higher Education". Available from: http://www.che.ac.za/media_and_publications/che-events-presentations/challenge-curriculum-responsiveness-south-african

Pastor, J.C. and Mayo, M. (2008): "Transformational leadership: The role of managerial values and goal orientation" in: Leadership & *Organization Development Journal,* 29 (4), 340-58.

Patel, F. & Lynch, H. (2013): "Glocalization as an alternative to internationalization in higher education: Embedding positive glocal learning perspectives", in: *International Journal of Teaching and*

Learning in Higher Education, 25 (2), 223-230. Available from: http://www.isetl.org/ijtlhe/ ISSN 1812-9129

Princeton University (2015): "Rights, rules and regulations". Available from: http://www.princeton.edu/pub/rrr/index.xml

Rossouw, D. (2015): *Business Ethics.* (Oxford University Press: Cape Town).

Scott, G. Coates, H. & Anderson, M. (2008): "Academic leaders in times of change" from http://research.acer.edu.au/cgi/viewcontent.cgi?article=1001&context=higher_education

Scott, G. & McKellar, L. (2012): Leading professionals in Australian and New Zealand tertiary education. LH Martin Institute, University of Sidney. Available from: http://www.lhmartininstitute.edu.au/professional-development-programs/leadership-programs/69-tertiary-education-leadership

Seale, O. (2004): Rooting for Management Capacity in South African Higher Education. Paper Presented at the HESDA Staff Development Conference. 4 November 2004.

Seale, O. (2015): *Building leadership and management capacity for deans in South African higher education.* PhD thesis, University of the Witwatersrand. Available from: http://wiredspace.wits.ac.za/bitstream/handle/10539/18232/Oliver%20Seale%20PhD%20Thesis%20ver_02-06-15.pdf?sequence=2&isAllowed=y

Shapiro, J. P., & Stefkovich, J. A. (2005): "Ethical leadership and decision making in education: Appling theoretical perspectives to complex dilemmas", available from: http://keithdwalker.ca/wp-content/summaries/d-f/Ethical%20Decision%20Making.Shapiro%20et%20al.EBS.pdf

Shapiro, J. P., & Gross, S. J. (Eds) (2008): E-book: Ethical educational leadership in turbulent times: (Re) solving moral dilemmas (Lawrence Erlbaum: New York)

Starratt, R. J. (2004): *Ethical leadership* (Jossey-Bass: California).

Sweeney, M & Twomey, P. (1997): "Preparing graduates for 2010: The role of cooperative education". Paper presented at the 10th World Conference on Cooperative Education, Cape Town.

Treviño, L. K., Hartman, L. P., & Brown, M. (2000): "Moral person and moral manager: How executives develop a reputation for ethical leadership", in: California Management Review, 42, 128–142.

Treviño, L. K., Brown, M., & Hartman, L. P. (2013) "A qualitative investigation of perceived executive ethical leadership: Perceptions from inside and outside the executive suite" in: *Human Relations,* 55, 5–37.

Van Aswegen, A.S., Engelbrecht, A & Theron, C.C. (2005): The effect of ethical values on transformational leadership and ethical climate in organisations. Available from: http://reference.sabinet.co.za/document/EJC22285

Van der Merwe, J.C. & Suransky, C. (2014): "Transcending apartheid in higher education: Transforming an institutional culture", *Institute for Reconciliation and Social Justice,* University of the Free State. Available from: http://www.tandfonline.com/loi/cree20

Victor, B. & Cullen, J.B. (1988): "The organisational bases of ethical work climates" in: *Administrative Science Quarterly,* 3(1), 101-125.

Vidovich, L. & Currie, J. (2009): "The changing nature of academic work", in: Tight. M., Mok, K.H & Huisman, J (Eds), *The Routledge International Handbook of Higher Education.* (Routledge: New York)

Vogel. L.R. (2012): "Leading with hearts and minds: Ethical orientations of educational leadership doctoral students", in: *Values and ethics   in   educational   administration,*   (10)1.   Available   from: http://static1.1.sqspcdn.com/static/f/275549/17501193/1333636681850/ VEEA+Vol10+No1.pdf?token=T%2FCUWh5d2Il7Ev4r6J7BoLqK%2B qc%3D

Wood, J.L. & Hilton, A.A. (2012): "Five ethical paradigms for community college leaders: Towards constructing and considering alternative courses of action in ethical decision making", in: *Community College Review.* 40.

Zuber-Skerritt, O. (2007): "Leadership development in SA higher education: The heart of the matter", in: *South African Journal of Higher Education,* Volume 21(7), 984-1006.

SECTION 3

Ethical Topics in Higher Education

12

GOVERNANCE FOR SUSTAINABILITY IN HIGHER EDUCATION

Heather Davis and Leo Goedegebuure

"We are in the race between tipping points in nature and our political systems"

Lester R. Brown (in Prugh & Renner, 2014)

12.1 Discussion

One way to consider responsible leadership in higher education is as necessary rapprochement of economic, social and environmental systems in every layer of society. These kinds of dilemmas for the planet and its people are contributing to the complexities for higher education institutions across the world. Responsible leadership in this context aligns with Badaracco (2013) who argues that leading responsibly is crucial in uncertain, high-pressure times where the "new invisible hand" of powerful, pervasive markets touch and shape almost everything. Therefore, becoming attuned to these contexts epitomises responsible leadership and governance for the sector. The aim of this chapter is to unpack and discuss how these kinds of dilemmas affect leadership and governance understandings by reviewing how the sector perceives the idea of sustainability.

Rapprochement of economic, social and environmental systems opens up considerations of accountability within the sector to more than those identified within the narrow bounds of new public management (NPM) (Cox, 2011; Evans, 2008). This expands conceptions for sustainable operations to include human and ecological responsibilities, signalling an epistemological shift towards more expansive and intentional standpoints that see economic obligations in the service of societal responsibilities. If such an epistemological shift is occurring, and we argue that it is, sustainability will likely be its zeitgeist (Davis, 2010). This view is further encouraged by Rotmans (2014) who argues that we no longer "live in an era of change but in a change of eras".

Whilst the idea of sustainability is generally newsworthy, regarding for example, what we can do to recycle or calling on institutions to do more to be sustainable, much of this attention is ad hoc or aimed at 'low hanging fruit'. It is noteworthy therefore in the 30th year of the *State of the World* report, that the focus for sustainability has been elevated to higher order governance responsibilities (Prugh & Renner, 2014). Horwitz (2015:387) succinctly argues why this is so:

> "Using the global addiction to the unsustainable fossil fuel industry and its consequences for climate change and human well-being as the exemplar, the message is clear: we do not have the right decision-making structures, or at least they are not yet influential enough, to alter our global course."

Once past trying to order and tame such "externalities" we can see that taking responsibility for these challenges broadens the scope for responsible leadership and governance in higher education. From this standpoint we can, and must, find ways to work with the kinds of 'super wicked problems' that Levin, Cashore, Bernstein and Auld (2010:2) describe as having:

"...four key features: time is running out; the central authority needed to address it is weak or non-existent; those who cause the problem also seek to create a solution; and hyperbolic discounting occurs that pushes responses irrationally into the future."

Sustainability is an emotive issue that teases out contested and underlying mindsets and values. Such mindsets generally range from denial, to those who think aiming just for sustainability is not going far enough. There are no easy or certain solutions for these complex issues, yet holistic lines of inquiry from the domains of ecologies and the environment are useful sense-making frames to further thinking and actions.

The higher education sector has long been involved in this work shown, for example, through the Talloires Declaration (1990), the recently concluded *Decade for Education for Sustainability Development* (DESD)—2005-2014 (UNESCO, 2005), and ongoing commitments to the 2030 Agenda for Sustainable Development (UN, 2015). Gestures toward leading sustainably and planning for sustainability development are evident in higher education, if not yet mainstream (Adams, Martin & Boom, 2015; Freeman, 2015; Leal Filho, 2011; Leal Filho, Platje, Gerstlberger, Ciegis, Määriä, Klavins & Kliucininkas, 2016; Meek & Goedegebuure, 2008; Shriberg, 2002; Toakley, 2004).

The inherent message for this chapter is to escalate the discourse to the systems level as quickly and in as many ways as possible and consider sustainability as a key governance responsibility for institutions and governments. Within this context, the roles for responsible leadership of higher education institutions are threefold: governing for sustainability commitment; educating the next generation of leaders to take sustainability seriously; and, leading scientific discovery. There are already specific sustainability principles and models to draw upon for this work in higher education (Disterheft, Caeiro, Leal Filho & Azeiteiro, 2016) and more generally (Dunphy, Griffiths & Benn, 2007; Pintér, Hardi, Martinuzzi & Hall, 2012). Given that standpoints about sustainability illuminate underlying mindsets an exploration of sustainability development within higher education is timely. This is a necessary step to make time and space for conversations and actions to elicit commitment to more sustainable and responsible leadership and governance practices for higher education.

One way to explore these concepts is with a case study. The case presented in this chapter uses an Australian lens, in terms of theory and location, to explore the signs of sustainability development in universities. The framework used for sense-making and analysis for this case was developed in Australia by Dunphy et al. (2007). This Corporate Sustainability Development Model (CDSM) was chosen because it was one of the few anywhere to consider sustainability development in both human and ecological terms, using a continuum ranging from rejection, non-responsiveness, compliance, efficiency, strategic proactivity to sustained and integrated positions (pp. 24-28).

The case is drawn from a wider qualitative study exploring university leadership for the knowledge era from which a set of leadership understandings for professional staff were named as worldly, sustaining, "leadingful" (Davis, 2014; Davis & Jones, 2014), relational and "learningful" leadership literacies. This case, unsurprisingly, is drawn from the exploration of the sustaining leadership literacy and is one of the "evidence based images" (Ragin, 1994) derived by the interpretive process as a way to elicit meaning from both the socially complex contexts for tertiary education management and the lived experiences of participants. It makes no claims of generalisation or of statistical significance.

12.2 Case Study: Testing a Corporate Sustainability Development Model (CSDM) in Australian Universities

A study of the lived experience of work and leadership drawn from 226 staff working in Australian universities (Davis, 2012) is drawn upon to present a snapshot of observations about sustainability development in universities. All participants were members of the Association for Tertiary Education Management (ATEM), employed in professional staff roles in administration, management, senior management or executive level appointments, and with representation from all universities in Australia. The CSDM (Dunphy et al., 2007) lens was used as a sense-making for analysis. Given there were no particular models or frameworks developed for higher education that considered both human and ecological sustainability this broader corporate framework developed in Australian was selected.

The details to follow show how respondents viewed their institution's sustainability levels of engagement at that time (and where they wanted their institutions to be five years hence) in relation to human and ecological sustainability. Given that participants were asked as 'lay' observers drawn from a broad range of areas within Australian universities, they were provided with full descriptions of the CSDM[1] for both human and ecological sustainability development indicators. The CDSM is conceptualised in three waves of sustainability development: i) resistance to the notion of sustainability as indicated by rejection or non-responsiveness; ii) that the issue of sustainability is acknowledged as indicated by compliance, efficiency or strategic proactivity; iii) higher order institutional engagement is indicated in a transformative stage

---

[1]See https://leadershipliteraciesresearch.wordpress.com/definitions-of-the-phases-in-the-development-of-corporate-sustainability

called "the sustaining corporation" and shown as sustained and integrated.

12.2.1 Ecological Sustainability

Figure 1 below provides an image of corporate ecological sustainability development levels observed by respondents in 2012 (in blue) and also where they would prefer these levels of engagement to be five years hence (in orange).

Figure 1: Corporate Ecological Sustainability Development Indicators

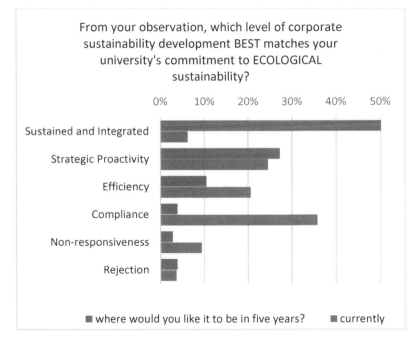

As indicated by these patterns, future engagement preferences for ecological sustainability levels were primarily for "sustaining and integrated" ecologically sustainable commitments, followed by "strategic proactivity". Compared to where respondents identified current practice, these are clearly aspirational goals. Respondents observed that most institutions are currently engaging in second wave levels of "compliance", "strategic proactivity", and "efficiency" stages of development. A small number also recorded observations of third wave "sustaining and integrated" levels of current engagement.

The overwhelming aspirations towards transformation and the sustaining corporation that respondents provided regarding institutional engagement with ecological sustainability has strategic implications for responsible leadership in higher education and provides operational cues for staff recruitment and retainment.

12.2.2 Human Sustainability

The CSDM was also used to elicit observations of institutional engagement with human sustainability development which Dunphy et al (2007) perceive "as engagement with corporate social responsibility" (p. 12). *Figure 2* below shows current corporate human sustainability development levels observed by respondents, as well as preferences for where they would like to see levels of corporate human sustainability development by their institutions five years hence.

Figure 2: Corporate Human Sustainability Development Indicators

Similar to the responses concerning ecological sustainability development, the patterns of responses indicate preferences for future human sustainability development engagement by their institutions primarily at the "sustaining and integrated" development stage, followed by "strategic proactivity" levels of human sustainability engagement.

Compared to where respondents identified their institution's current practice for ecological sustainability, a wider range of indicators was given for human sustainability. This included more observations at the first wave of sustainability development for human sustainability than with ecological sustainability. Like the ecological indicators, current engagement levels with corporate human sustainability development remain at the "compliance" stage, followed by an equal split between "efficiency" and "strategic proactivity". The third wave of the "sustaining and integrated" indicator then followed. More respondents indicated that their institutions were currently engaging in human sustainability at the level of "sustaining and integrated" than they did for ecological sustainability. However, like ecological indicators, there was a wide gap between current practice and where respondents preferred their institutions to be regarding human sustainability development in the future.

This case provides a snapshot of views from professional staff working in Australian universities that indicate that human and ecological sustainability are concerns for them; indeed, they would clearly like to see more done in this area. More importantly for this discussion is that this case suggests that responsible leadership in higher education will need to find ways to explore understandings of the often hard to measure and intangible dilemmas that governance for sustainability elicits. Responsible leaders must pay attention to and encourage critical conversations with stakeholders within and outside the sector, even in the face of contestations and denial by those invested in keeping the status quo.

12.3 Conclusion

There is an increasing body of evidence that our societies are transitioning to a new economy, based on renewable energy and away from fossil fuels. Such an economy differs fundamentally in its principles of decentralisation and radical innovation from the old world order of the industrial era. Indeed, as the history of transitions over many centuries suggest, this kind of economic change will likely come with burst and halts, much like punctuated equilibrium theory as developed by Eldredge and Gould (see, Gould, 2007) that acknowledge these kinds of mindset shifts to be very uncomfortable. Sustainability will be at the heart of such mindset shifts.

Responsible leadership in higher education is vital and has a core three-fold role to play: leading by example through institutional governance, educating and preparing the next generation for the unknown, and making sure we come to terms with sustainable practices for the planet and its people through concerted research efforts. Such responsibilities fit with Wilson's (2016) argument that "creating and implementing indicators of societal and environmental health—the greater good – is central to the work of leadership" (p. 162).

We argue that the idea of ecologies is an appropriate governance and leadership metaphor for higher education so to encompass deeper understandings of sustainability and societal transformation. This is congruent with the necessary privileging of learning, unlearning and relearning in times of rapid change, turbulence and wicked problems. The imperative to do so is articulated by Nobel Laureate, Peter Doherty:

> "the myriad of challenges and problems thrown up by climate change has forced the human race to confront the future [...] humanity never before has been forced to face its long-term future. This is not factored in to how humans think. And it is not immediately clear to me that humanity is as yet up to the challenge. The fact that our very fate depends upon successfully managing a future that is already inconveniently impinging on our present lends a new urgency to the research that will harness the wisdom and unleash the insights necessary to make the future a time of hope rather than fear" (Doherty in Cahill, 2010:1).

Governance for sustainability, like other examples of responsible leadership in higher education, is about hope and taking responsibility for our future in new ways that emphasise participation, collaboration and collectivities. Responsible leadership in these terms, is about being facilitative rather than directive in order to allow everyone, staff *and* students, to take responsibility to lead, accept risk and find ways to innovate. Governance in these terms is setting conditions for agility so that institutions can be clear and firm on ends and more flexible on means.

12.4 Chapter References

Adams, R., Martin, S. & Boom, K. (2015): A preliminary framework for building and assessing university sustainability culture. *Learning from the sharp end: implications for sustainability in higher education international symposium.* Bristol, UK.

Badaracco, J. (2013): *The good struggle: responsible leadership in an unforgiving world,* Boston, Massachusetts, Harvard Business Review Press.

Cahill, S. (2010): Future Fellows show the way. *The Voice,* 6, 1 & 4.

Cox, E. (2011): The next hundred years. *2011 Women's Day Address [transcript]* [Online]. Available: http://www.evacox.com.au/Members/eva/doing-the-right-thing/the-next-hundred-years [Accessed 2-Apr-16].

Davis, H. (2010): The sustainability zeitgeist as a GPS for Worldly Leadership within the discourse of globalisation. *European Academy of Management 10th Annual Conference: Back to the future.* Rome: EURAM.

Davis, H. (2012): *Leadership Literacies for Professional Staff in Universities.* PhD Thesis, RMIT.

Davis, H. (2014): Towards leadingful leadership literacies for higher education management. *Journal of Higher Education Policy and Management,* 36, 371-382.

Davis, H. & Jones, S. (2014): The work of leadership in higher education management. *Journal of Higher Education Policy and Management,* 36, 367-370.

Disterheft, A., Caeiro, S. S., Leal Filho, W. & Azeiteiro, U. M. (2016): The INDICARE-model – measuring and caring about participation in higher education's sustainability assessment. *Ecological Indicators,* 63, 172-186.

Dunphy, D. C., Griffiths, A. & Benn, S. (2007): *Organizational change for corporate sustainability: a guide for leaders and change agents of the future,* New York, Routledge.

Evans, P. (2008): Is an Alternative Globalization Possible? *Politics Society,* 36, 271 - 305.

Freeman, B. (2015): Environment and sustainability plans and policies: Solutions, straightjackets or meaningless drivel? In: DOBSON, I. R. & SHARMA, R. (eds.) *Tertiary Education Management Conference, Leading locally competing globally: Refereed Papers.* Wollongong: ATEM & TEFMA.

Gould, S. J. (2007): *Punctuated equilibrium,* Cambridge, Mass. ; London, Belknap.

Horwitz, P. (2015): Governance for sustainability—How Are We Doing? *EcoHealth,* 12, 387-388.

Leal Filho, W. (2011): About the Role of Universities and Their Contribution to Sustainable Development. *High Educ Policy,* 24, 427-438.

Leal Filho, W., Platje, J., Gerstlberger, W., Ciegis, R., Kaaria, J., Klavins, M. & Kliucininkas, L. (2016): The role of governance in realising the transition towards sustainable societies. *Journal of Cleaner Production.*

Levin, K., Cashore, B., Bernstein, S. & Auld, G. (2010): *Playing it forward: Path dependency, progressive incrementalism, and the "Super Wicked" problem of global climate change [First presented at the International Studies Association Convention Chicago, February 28th – March 3, 2007]*, Yale University.

Meek, V. L. & Goededebuure, L. (eds.) (2008): *Reinventing Higher Education: Toward Participatory and Sustainable Development,* Bangkok: UNESCO.

Pinter, L., Hardi, P., Martinuzzi, A. & Hall, J. (2012): Bellagio STAMP: Principles for sustainability assessment and measurement. *Ecological Indicators,* 17, 20-28.

Prugh, T. & Renner, T. (2014): *State of the world 2014: governing for sustainability*, Worldwatch Institute.

Ragin, C. C. (1994): The process of social research: ideas and evidence. *Constructing social research: the unity and diversity of method.* Thousand Oaks, Calif.: Pine Forge Press.

Rotmans, J. (2014): *Change of era [published in Dutch],* The Netherlands, Aneas Media.

Shriberg, M. (2002): Institutional assessment tools for sustainability in higher education: strength, weaknesses, and implications for practice and theory. *Higher Education Policy,* 15, 153-167.

Talloires Declaration (1990): Talloires Declaration of University Leaders for a Sustainable Future. In: MULTIPLE SIGNATORIES (ed.). France: Association of University Leaders for a Sustainable Future.

Toakley, A. R. (2004): Globalization, sustainable development and universities. *Higher Education Policy,* 17, 311 - 324.

UN 2015. Transforming our world: the 2030 agenda for sustainable development. Geneva: United Nations.

UNESCO 2005. UN Decade of education for sustainable development 2005-2014: The DESD at a glance. Paris: UNESCO.

WILSON, S. G. (2016): Leadership for the greater good: developing indicators of societal and environmental health. In: GOLDMAN SCHUYLER, K., BAUGHER, J. E. & JIRONET, K. (eds.) *Leadership for a healthy world: Creative social change.* Bingley: Emerald.

13

BUILDING UP
A RESEARCH ETHICS SYSTEM:
EXPERIENCE OF A TEACHING
UNIVERSITY

Kam Cheong Li and Billy T. M. Wong

13.1 Overview

Contemporary higher education has witnessed a growing emphasis on research. This trend has shifted academics' work priorities, and teaching institutions have experienced mounting pressure to enhance their research capacity (Cummings and Shin, 2014). Sursock (2015) showed that there are now fewer "primarily teaching-oriented" institutions in Europe, and instead more are "both teaching-oriented and research-based". This trend of placing more stress on research has also been reported in studies on individual institutions in regions such as Malaysia (Latif and Subramaniam, 2016), Vietnam (Nguyen, Klopper and Smith, 2016) and Hong Kong (Lee, 2014). The "publish or perish" syndrome is now more widespread, driving academics to continually deliver research products in refereed journals and other publication venues (Chou, 2014).

With the growth in research activities, research ethics issues have to be better governed and staff awareness and knowledge of research ethics must be further developed. This has been regarded as an integral part of research capacity-building for an institution (ESSENCE on Health Research, 2014; Hyder et al., 2013). As a part of research governance and support, it is necessary for teaching institutions to establish a research ethics system and tackle a wide range of challenges in this area.

This paper presents the experience of a teaching university in Hong Kong in building up a research ethics system while developing its research capacity. It also discusses the emerging issues in research ethics – such as the complexities and tensions between surveillance and privacy, and between transparency and anonymity – that have arisen from advances in research and research methods, and relevant initiatives proposed to address them.

13.2 Research Capacity Development of a Teaching University

The Open University of Hong Kong, which has been a teaching institution since its establishment in 1989, provides flexible education for the diverse needs of students. In the past, our academic staff mainly carried out teaching and administrative duties. After two decades of development, the university has been expanded to provide a wide range of teaching programmes. It also supports engagement in research with the aim of progressively developing its research capacity, in order to transform its teaching expertise into research strengths in disciplines which are highly relevant to the livelihood and economic development of the city. It has achieved significant progress in building up a vibrant research culture and success in obtaining research funding.

In support of the university's endeavours in this regard, relevant preparation has been made for ensuring that research studies are conducted by academics in ethical ways. This paper reviews the major tasks involved in building up a research ethics system.

13.3 Building up a Research Ethics System

The research ethics system was established to support academics in conducting research in a manner that properly protects the rights of human subjects. It is based on relevant laws and ethical frameworks, following which a policy, guidelines and procedures were formulated. The system also involves an institutional committee established to assess ethical issues in the research projects of academics, and enhance academics' awareness of, and familiarity with, the ethical requirements.

13.3.1 Formulation of Policy, Guidelines and Procedures

To support ethical practices in research activities, a policy, guidelines and procedures were formulated with reference to frequently adopted ethical frameworks. For example, the World Medical Association's Declaration of Helsinki (1964) and the Belmont Report (1979) of the United States' National Commission for the Protection of Human Subjects of Biomedical and Behavioural Research provide the underlying ethical principles for research involving human participants or identifiable human materials and data, such as respect for participants, beneficence, justice and informed consent. Despite the fact that the suitability of these frameworks has been raised for research in a digital age (e.g. Aicardi et al., 2016; Pritts, 2008), the ethical principles underlying the frameworks remain the foundation of many contemporary research ethics codes and regulations around the globe (McGinn, 2015).

The research ethics policy formulated should also adhere to the legal system of the country in question. For example, in Hong Kong, the confidentiality of research and personal data related to participants must be maintained at all times, as governed by the Personal Data (Privacy) Ordinance of the Office of the Privacy Commissioner for Personal Data,

Hong Kong.[1] However, a legal system provides only minimum standards that should be adhered to – "it can never be appropriate to defend proposed practice solely on the basis that it is legal" (Masson, 2004, p. 43).

The ethical clearance mechanism should address the potential ethical issues in a research design. The major ones are discussed briefly below.

- *Data Confidentiality and Anonymity:* Based on the principles of privacy and respect for autonomy, research data involving personal information should be kept confidential. This, however, does not apply to situations that may violate legal regulations, such as when a participant reports being a victim of crime or he/she is at risk of physical or psychological harm that presents a moral duty or even legal responsibility for researchers to disclose details to relevant bodies.

- *Informed Consent:* Participants should be adequately informed about the details of a study, and their right to withdraw from it without any negative consequences, before seeking their consent to take part in the research. Attention needs to be paid to vulnerable groups who may lack the capacity or competence to give consent. Such examples include children or young people,[2] and dependency relationships between the researcher and participants (e.g. teacher-student relationships) in which the participants may find it hard to express their wish not to participate in a study. In cases that involve the permission of parents or gatekeepers (e.g. teachers or work-supervisors) in order to reach the participants, their permission should not override the wishes of the participants.

---

[1] Latest version on 25 April 2013, available at: http://www.pcpd.org.hk/english/ data_privacy_law/ordinance_at_a_Glance/ordinance.html
[2] In the case of Hong Kong, those who are below 18 years old are categorized as non-adults and their participation in research requires parental permission.

- *Minimal Risk:* A research design requires a strong justification if it involves more than minimal risks, physical or psychological, to the researcher or participants. The assessment of risks involves taking into consideration both the potential benefits and harm of the research. The possible risks do not arise only during the research process but also from the publication and dissemination of the research findings. For example, participants may be upset by how they are portrayed in publications or disturbed by unwanted media attention (Crow and Wiles, 2008). Relevant procedures should be put in place for managing the risks.

13.3.2 Institutional Regulation and Support

A committee overseeing ethics-related matters in research has been formed in the university for regulating the research activities conducted by academics. This Research Ethics Committee (REC) includes representatives from academic units for processing ethical review applications and ensuring the approved research studies are conducted ethically. Specifically, the REC has to identify the potential ethical issues in a research study before it commences.

Exemption from ethical approval may apply to anonymous surveys when they are for the university's internal use for improving teaching and learning; and this also covers student projects for learning purposes. For degree programmes, only research projects leading to the thesis of a research degree and research publications are subject to ethical review by the REC. Individual academic units have developed their own mechanisms to ensure that ethical issues are handled properly for student projects exempted from review by the committee.

Another area governed by the REC is research integrity, which involves ensuring responsible research practices by academics, following principles such as honesty, rigour, objectivity and openness, and the completeness and accuracy of results in publications. Academics have been made fully aware of their responsibility not to engage in any forms of research misconduct, such as plagiarism, fabrication, falsification or unauthorized use of data, and non-disclosure of potential conflict of interest. Institutional support, such as the provision of software for anti-plagiarism, has also been put in place.

13.3.3 Enhancing Awareness and Familiarity

Efforts have been made to keep academics abreast of the ethical principles and university policy for making justifiable decisions on ethical issues in their research studies. In particular, junior academics and those who have not been actively engaged in research in the past may not be sufficiently aware of, or familiar with, the ethical requirements. Training resources and materials are thus made available for them. Activities such as seminars and roundtable meetings have also been organized periodically, which are useful for enhancing the knowledge of academics in this area, as well as promoting a culture of ethical research practices.

Enhancing the "ethical literacy" of academics helps them to identify and resolve any ethical issues which have not been anticipated and planned for before a study commences. As Wiles (2012, pp. 1–2) explains, this encourages them to "understand and engage with ethical issues as they emerge throughout the process of research and not merely to view research ethics as something that is completed once a favourable opinion on a proposed research project has been granted by a research ethics committee". Maintaining high ethical standards in research is regarded as the responsibility of both individual academics and the institution.

13.4 Tackling Emerging Challenges

Advances in research and research methods have led to the emergence of ethical issues which were not handled in the past. Conventional approaches to ethical issues – such as anonymity and consent, and avoiding any level of risk – have been criticized as being difficult to apply in research using ethnographic methods (Small, Maher and Kerr, 2014), online methods (Roberts and Allen, 2015), visual and creative methods (Riele and Baker, 2016) and covert methods (Roberts, 2015).

For example, the use of content on the Internet for research has led to the difficulty of distinguishing public and private data, e.g. personal and even intimate information shared openly on social networking sites. User-generated content, such as blogs, are often considered publicly published. Yet, users may regard their blogs as a part of their identification rather than simply publicly accessible data (Markham and Buchanan, 2012). The use of online surveys for data collection has also presented the problem of recognizing participants' identity and obtaining their consent. The use of visual data (e.g. photographs and films) usually enables individuals to be identified; and, despite the availability of technology to obscure facial features (Wiles et al., 2008), it may not be possible to obtain consent from all people shown in visual materials. Further consideration is needed when applying the new research methods in compliance with the ethical principles. For instance, Cu, Suarez and Maria (2016) discussed the adaptation of the ethical principles – respect for persons, beneficence and justice – indicated in the Belmont report in the creation of emotion corpora, focusing on the concerns for human subjects from developing countries.

The trend towards open data and open science, for transparency and replication, as well as secondary analysis by other researchers or for knowledge transfer to policy-makers and practitioners, may conflict with the principles of informed consent, confidentiality and anonymity (Neale and Bishop, 2012; Tilley and Woodthorpe, 2011). The latest technology has made partially possible re-identification of de-identified data (Wilbanks, 2014), and so the protection of privacy is not absolutely guaranteed by making data anonymous. For data with personal information or from research participants, consent obtained at the point of data collection is not "once-and-for-all" (Grinyer, 2009). Renewed consent is needed for other research. A practical problem which arises lies in the difficulty of obtaining such consent in terms of reaching the participants and requiring them to give consent repeatedly for research in future.

Such problems have been encountered by the Open University of Hong Kong in supporting academics' research and disseminating research data. For example, research that involves the provision of distance counselling through the Internet has presented difficulties, such as crossing jurisdictions when the subjects are located in other countries, verifying participants' identities, and validating consent. Relevant legal and regulatory requirements have to be reviewed to ensure that none of them are violated. Procedures such as electronic signatures can be considered for obtaining consent online in countries where the use of conventional methods is not available. For ethnographic research that involves photography or videography for recording participants' daily lives, there is a risk that other people are shown in the visual materials collected, and data privacy and informed consent are problems that need to be resolved. The situation became more complicated when visual data were shared online for public access, and anonymising relevant parts of the materials was usually needed. The ethical reviews by the REC thus require looking at each case in detail to analyse the ethical issues and assess whether the proposed measures could be justified.

To address these issues, relevant ethical guidelines and procedures need to be reviewed and updated periodically. The existing literature provides a starting point for this, e.g. Ethics Guidelines for Internet-mediated Research (British Psychological Society, 2013) and the Code of Research Ethics and Guidelines for visual research (International Visual Sociology Association, 2009). Initiatives such as the Participant-Centered Consent (PCC) toolkit[3] and "open consent" (Wilbanks, 2014) have also responded to the needs of data-sharing beyond traditional privacy protection.

13.5 Summary

This paper has outlined the major tasks of a university for establishing a research ethics system, and a number of issues which have emerged in research ethics. The research ethics system does not determine, but informs, decisions to be made systematically, following widely accepted ethical principles.

The latest developments in research and research methods have presented challenges to conventional approaches to research ethics. So that stakeholders of research projects can ensure ethical operations in the studies, both the institution and academics need to keep abreast of emerging ethical issues and their possible resolutions.

Acknowledgement

The work described in this paper was partially supported by a grant from the Research Grants Council of the Hong Kong Special Administrative Region, China (UGC/IDS16/14).

---

[3] http://sagebase.org/e-consent/

13.6 Chapter References

Aicardi, C., Del Savio, L., Dove, E. S., Lucivero, F., Tempini, N. and Prainsack, B. (2016): Emerging ethical issues regarding digital health data. On the World Medical Association draft declaration on ethical considerations regarding health databases and biobanks. *Croatian Medical Journal*, 57, 207–213.

Belmont Report (1979): *The Belmont report: Ethical principles and guidelines for the protection of human subjects of research.* Available at: http://www.hhs.gov/ohrp/humansubjects/guidance/belmont.html

British Psychological Society (2013): Ethics guidelines for internet-mediated research. Available at: http://www.bps.org.uk/system/files/Public%20files/inf206-guidelines-for-internet-mediated-research.pdf

Chou, C. P. (2014): Why the SSCI syndrome is a global phenomenon? In C. P. Chou (Ed.), *The SSCI syndrome in higher education: A local or global phenomenon.* The Netherlands: Sense Publishers, vii–xv.

Crow, G. and Wiles, R. (2008): Managing anonymity and confidentiality in social research: The case of visual data in community research. NCRM Working Paper. ESRC National Centre for Research Methods. Available at: http://eprints.ncrm.ac.uk/459/

Cu, J., Suarez, M. T. and Maria, M. S. (2016): Subscribing to the Belmont report: The case of creating emotion corpora. In *LREC Workshop: ETHics In Corpus Collection, Annotation & Application.* Portoroz, Slovenia, 35–41.

Cummings, W. K. and Shin, J. C. (2014): Teaching and research in contemporary higher education: An overview. In: J. C. Shin, A. Arimoto, W. K. Cummings and U. Teichler (Eds.), *Teaching and research in contemporary higher education: Systems, activities and rewards*. Dordrecht: Springer, 1–14.

Declaration of Helsinki. (1964): Declaration of Helsinki – Ethical principles for medical research involving human subjects. Available at: http://www.wma.net/en/30publications/10policies/b3/index.html

ESSENCE on Health Research. (2014): Seven principles for strengthening research capacity in low- and middle-income countries: Simple ideas in a complex world. Available at: http://www.who.int/tdr/publications/Essence_report2014_OK.pdf

Grinyer, A. (2009): The ethics of the secondary analysis and further use of qualitative data. *Social Research Update*, 56. Available at: http://sru.soc.surrey.ac.uk/SRU56.pdf

Hyder, A. A., Zafar, W., Ali, J., Ssekubugu, R., Ndebele, P. and Kass, N. (2013): Evaluating institutional capacity for research ethics in Africa: A case study from Botswana. *BMC Medical Ethics*, 14:31. Available at: https://bmcmedethics. biomedcentral.com/articles/10.1186/1472-6939-14-31

International Visual Sociology Association (2009): Code of research ethics and guidelines. Available at: http://visualsociology.org/about/ethics-and-guidelines.html

Latif, L. B. A. and Subramaniam, T. T. (2016): Research, publication and funding within the Open University Malaysia: Audit and action. *ASEAN Journal of Open Distance Learning*, 8(1), 24–34.

Lee, M. H. (2014): Hong Kong higher education in the 21st century. *Hong Kong Teachers' Centre Journal*, 13, 15–33.

Markham, A. and Buchanan, E. (2012): Ethical decision-making and internet research: Recommendations from the AoIR Ethics Committee (Version 2.0). Available at: http://www.aoir.org/reports/ethics2.pdf

Masson, J. (2004): The legal context. In S. Fraser, V. Lewis, S. Ding, M. Kellett and C. Robinson (Eds.), *Doing research with children and young people.* London: Sage, 43–58.

McGinn, M. (2015): Considering ethics for social science research. In R. Dingwall and M. B. McDonnell (Eds.), *The SAGE handbook of research management.* Thousand Oaks, CA: Sage, 153–172.

Neale, B., & Bishop, L. (2012): The Timescapes archive: A stakeholder approach to archiving qualitative, longitudinal data. *Qualitative Research*, 12(1), 53–65.

Nguyen, Q., Klopper, C. and Smith, C. (2016): Affordances, barriers, and motivations: Engagement in research activity by academics at the research-oriented university in Vietnam. *Open Review of Educational Research*, 3(1), 68–84.

Pritts, J. L. (2008): The importance and value of protecting the privacy of health information: The roles of the HIPAA privacy rule and the common rule in health research. Available at:
http://www.nationalacademies.org/hmd/~/media/Files/Activity%20
Files/Research/HIPAAandResearch/PrittsPrivacyFinalDraftweb.ashx

Riele, K. and Baker, A. (2016): Ethical challenges in visual educational research. In: J. Moss and B. Pini (Eds.), *Visual research methods in educational research.* New York: Palgrave Macmillan, 231–250.

Roberts, L. D. (2015): Ethical issues in conducting qualitative research in online communities. *Qualitative Research in Psychology*, 12(3), 314–325.

Roberts, L. D. and Allen, P. J. (2015): Exploring ethical issues associated with using online surveys in educational research. *Educational Research and Evaluation*, 21(2), 95–108.

Small, W., Maher, L. and Kerr, T. (2014): Institutional ethical review and ethnographic research involving injection drug users: A case study. *Social Science & Medicine*, 104, 157–162.

Sursock, A. (2015): *Trends 2015: Learning and teaching in European universities.* European University Association. Available at: http://www.eua.be/Libraries/publications-homepage-list/EUA_Trends_2015_web

Tilley, L. and Woodthorpe, K. (2011): Is it the end of anonymity as we know it? A critical examination of the ethical principle of anonymity in the context of 21st century demands on the qualitative researcher. *Qualitative Research*, 11(2), 197–212.

Wilbanks, J. (2014): Portable approaches to informed consent and open data. In J. Lane, V. Stodden, S. Bender and H. Nissenbaum (Eds.), *Privacy, big data, and the public good: Frameworks for engagement.* New York: Cambridge University Press, 234–252.

Wiles, R. (2012): *What are qualitative research ethics?* London: Bloomsbury Academic.

Wiles, R., Prosser, J., Bagnoli, A., Clark, A., Davies, K., Holland, S. and Renold, E. (2008): *Visual ethics: Ethical issues in visual research.* Available at: http://eprints.ncrm.ac.uk/421/

NOWHERE TO HIDE?
ETHICAL SOCIAL MEDIA USE
IN HIGHER EDUCATION INSTITUTIONS

Jeanette C. Botha

14.1 The Social Media Context in South Africa

Social media is firmly established as part of our lives and social fabric. While debates on ethics continue to contest conceptual distinctions between our personal and professional lives and conduct, social media such as Facebook, Linkedin, YouTube, Instagram, Snapchat and Twitter make no such distinction and have crossed these divides to embrace and integrate our personal, professional and social lives for the world to see and respond to in whichever way they choose.

Social media are not private and as such they render the personal, professional, ethical and social distinctions untenable. Any so-called 'privacy settings' are implemented only after the user has relinquished to the owners of the social networking services or search engines, authority and control over certain personal information, as well as a host of other (mainly tracking and marketing) rights: a prerequisite for accessing and using the platform or website. Social media also equalize participants through what Marwick and Boyd (2011) call "context collapse", in which sites group different social networks and histories of friends, family, coworkers and acquaintances within the same category of "friend" or "follower". This levelling of traditional social hierarchies poses a variety of ethical and moral dilemmas for both users and employers.

For example, future employers can and do access the social media profiles of potential job seekers and make judgements on their eligibility for positions based on the content that they encounter (NACE 2012). The same applies to social media "friendships" and "relationships" between professionals that could be, and sometimes are, construed as being in conflict with professional ethos and practice (Madell 2016, cf. Marwick & Boyd 2011). Contractual and business relationships have also been affected. For example, *the Code of ethics and conduct for South African print and online media (2106) and the South African Labour Guide (2106) offer guidelines on ethical social media conduct and practice*, but these remain guidelines, which are difficult to apply consistently and to sanction, if necessary, in a swiftly changing environment.

However, in South Africa, posts on social media have legal effect. Pistorius (2016) cites the case of *Sihlali* v *SA Broadcasting Corporation Ltd [2010] 5 BLLR 542 (LC)* where an SMS was accepted as a letter of resignation and in *Jafta v Ezemvelo KZN Wildlife* [2008] 10 BLLR 954 (LC), the court held that Jafta's email constituted valid acceptance of the job offer, that an SMS is as effective a mode of communication as any written document or e-mail, and that Jafta did communicate his acceptance of a job offer via SMS. Derogatory comments made on Facebook may also provide a fair reason for dismissal, for example *Sedick & another v Krisray* (Pty) Ltd (2011) 8 BLLR 979 (CCMA) and *Fredericks v Jo Barkett Fashions* [2011] JOL 27923 (CCMA).

It is also interesting to note that South Africa courts consider social media and acceptable form of legal service in appropriate circumstances.

Impulsive Twitter postings deserve special mention. In South Africa, Penny Sparrow, who was fired after a racist posting (Wicks 2016); Chris Hart, who resigned from a senior position at a well-known bank for perceived racist utterances (news24); and Gareth Cliff, who resorted to legal action (and won) in the face of accusations of racism (Shange & Herman 2016) demonstrate the power of this medium to destroy reputations, careers and even lives, as is demonstrated in the case of Justine Sacco and others (Robson, J. 2015). Robson explains:

"The furor over Sacco's tweet had become not just an ideological crusade against her perceived bigotry but also a form of idle entertainment... As time passed, though, I watched these shame campaigns multiply, to the point that they targeted not just powerful institutions and public figures but really anyone perceived to have done something offensive. I also began to marvel at the disconnect between the severity of the crime and the gleeful savagery of the punishment. It almost felt as if shamings were now happening for their own sake, as if they were following a script. Eventually I started to wonder about the recipients of our shamings, the real humans who were the virtual targets of these campaigns. So for the past two years, I've been interviewing individuals like Justine Sacco: everyday people pilloried brutally, most often for posting some poorly considered joke on social media. Whenever possible, I have met them in person, to truly grasp the emotional toll at the other end of our screens. The people I met were mostly unemployed, fired for their transgressions, and they seemed broken somehow — deeply confused and traumatized."

The simplicity, speed and accessibility of Twitter, as well as limited number of characters of tweets both inhibit meaningfully contextualized communication on the one hand and, seemingly, attract snap judgements and comments on the other. Furthermore, the interpretation of tweets is globally subjective and susceptible to the whimsical moods of *twitterati*, rendering the tweeter open to unbridled adulation or vitriolic abuse.

In the higher education environment, the most pernicious problems around social media include rampant copyright infringement and plagiarism by both staff and students (Czerniewics 2016; Thomas, A 2015); abuse of working hours to surf the net and social media sites, run own businesses, access pornography, engage in personal self-promotion, (for example, academics posing as consultants and openly advertising their expertise on a variety of social platforms), and veiled or overt criticism of colleagues, managers and/or the institution on social platforms. All of these raise serious ethical quandaries for higher education institutions and their staff.

 While most social networkers are fairly passive observers, a study on Social Networkers in America, conducted by the Ethics Resource Centre (ERC) identified a group which they called "Creators" who actively post commentary, write blogs and share ideas (often about work).

"More than one in ten employees are active social networkers (ASNs) who spend at least 30 percent of their workday linked up to one or more networks...... very little of the online time is work related. One third of those (33 percent) who spend an hour or more of the workday on social networking say that none of the activity is related to work. Another 28 percent say just a small fraction (10 percent) of their online time has something to do with their job. In other words a growing number of workers are getting paid for time spent on their interests [...] Social networkers and ASNs in particular, do air company linen in public. Six of ten ASNs would comment on their personal sites about their company if it was in the news, 53 percent say they share information about work projects once a week or more, and more than a third say they often comment, on their personal sites, about managers, co-workers and even clients. As a result, workplace secrets are no longer secret and management must assume that anything that happens at work; any new policy, product or problem, could become publicly know at almost any time [...]" (ERC 2013: 8-9)

In South Africa, social media are also being used to mobilise groups, engender solidarity and support and in an increasing number of cases, effect personal, reputational, professional and institutional damage and destruction. Much of this is currently ascribed to the need for accelerated transformation and/or political agendas, both in the public and private domains. One thus finds higher education being drawn via social media, into a highly-charged socio-political environment and being used as a vehicle for socio-economic transformation via agendas which have sometimes tenuous links to traditionally mandated university business. For higher education institutions this has, for example, meant an unanticipated onslaught of issues ranging from unprecedented student and labour demands; demands for the inclusion of a wider range of stakeholders in all university decision making and operations; serious disruptions to institutional meeting, planning and budgeting cycles (and finances); and significantly disruptive impacts on core business in terms of management and staff's time, that has been diverted to addressing these mostly ad hoc issues, which have often assumed crisis proportions.

An example of this dynamic is the #MustFall movement. On 10 March 2015 a group of University of Cape Town students flung human faeces on the statue of Cecil John Rhodes calling for the monument to be taken down and asserting their disgust and protest at this ever-present reminder of continued white supremacy and colonial oppression at the university. The #RhodesMustFall movement found its echoes in campuses across the country, generating a momentum that contributed to the #FeesMustFall movement, which soon engulfed many higher education institutions. What started as resistance to fee increases for 2016 subsequently morphed into a massive campaign against any form of university fee payment. The energy generated by these movements was then harnessed in pursuit of the #OutsourcingMustFall campaign, which demanded that general workers employed by external companies and "outsourced" to universities, be absorbed into the staff complements of universities, along with significantly increased salaries and conditions of service. More recently the Afrikaans language has been targeted for abolition at some universities, under the slogan '*Afrikaans-must-fall*' (Nkosi 2016).

This rapid, volatile and unpredictable turn of events has caught most of the higher education institutions off-guard resulting in serious disruptions to university operations and administration. Shutdowns have been the order of the day as university leadership has scrambled to make sense of protesting students' ever-changing demands and their opaque *modus operandi*. In many instances purposeful intellectual engagement and attempts at pragmatic discourse have given way to vitriolic rhetoric, emotional outpourings, outright racism, mudslinging, reputational havoc and disruption of normal business, as well as costly violence and destruction[1] both publicly[2], and in all forms of the media, especially the social media[3].

14.2 The Higher Education Response

Two observations emerge from this scenario. Firstly, one discerns a failure of existing higher education leadership and governance models to accommodate this new dynamic. Secondly, one discerns a total disregard for the *social mores*, the ethics, around communication that have traditionally prevailed in civil society. One notes, for example, instances of deliberate public humiliation of various vice chancellors who have quite literally been forced to submit to the will of students and who have had their humiliation filmed and commented on in the news and social media (Nkosi, B. 2015). Similarly eminent politicians have had mocking songs sung about them in public or commanded to kneel upon receiving student demands (SAPA, 2012). All of these instances exhibit a total disregard for traditional mores.

The 'hashtag' (#) symbol and the aligned sloganeering speak to the centrality and prevalence of social media in these movements, both as a means of engendering solidarity for the cause(s) and their accretive power as vehicles for garnering support, disseminating opinion, organizing and planning logistical operations and mobilizing supporters (Ojigho 2014). What began as a social expression of solidarity swiftly

---

[1] The Citizen. 22.11.2015, Emily Cork. TUT exam hall torched. http://citizen.co.za/878027/tut-exam-hall-torched/
[2] Eyewitness News. Ziyanda Ncgobo. 1 March 2016. NWU & WSU REMAIN CLOSED, UFS RESUMES CLASSES. http://ewn.co.za/2016/02/29/NWU-WSU-remain-closed-UFS-resumes-classes
[3] EYEWITNESS NEWS. 17/02/2016. #UCT: VICE-CHANCELLOR'S OFFICE PETROL BOMBED IN OVERNIGHT PROTESTS. Siyabonga Sesant & Lauren Isaacs. http://ewn.co.za/2016/02/17/Protesting-students-arrested-as-UCT-vice-chancellor-condemns-violence.

morphed into overt activism. Universities themselves, have similarly (albeit reactively) used social media to defend their positions and communicate with staff and students. Clearly, social networking is "wiping out old boundaries, exposing the workplace to greater public scrutiny and creating risks that never existed before." (ERC 2013b:11)

Few institutional policies and processes seem to be in place to empower leadership and management to deal with the raft of new stakeholders who reside outside of recognized governance structures and have negligible experience in higher education leadership, management and policy, but who are increasingly shaping university agendas and impacting on their financial sustainability. It is an invidious position for affected higher education institutions, which is exacerbated by an absence of ethics as a guiding principle.

Risks to the institutions (especially reputational risk) posed by the cumulative impact of social media use and abuse in promoting these various agendas have prompted a small number of higher education institutions to develop social media policies that provide guidelines (and sanctions) for social media use. However, it seems the impact and risk for universities posed by social media, is not yet being taken seriously enough by most universities.

Struwig and Van der Berg (2016) assert:

"We have conducted research – due to be published soon – that shows South Africa's higher education institutions should take this issue more seriously. Most universities don't have formal social media policies. Some don't seem to have considered social media as a potential risk to their reputation at all.....Our research involved 23 of South Africa's 25 public universities. The aim was to investigate whether they had social media policies at all and how they generally managed social media. The results show that:

- 91% of universities don't have formal social media policies;
- four universities were in the process of approving draft social media policies. These were not available for us to examine at the time of the study; and
- 61% don't have any formal document that manages social media [...]
- [...] We were able to obtain nine documents – social media policies, guidelines or strategies – for analysis.
- 44% focus on social media only as a risk to the institution. 33% focus on it as both a risk and a relationship-building tool, while 22% focus on it only as a tool for building relationships;
- most of the documents refer to "brand" and "image". Just 22% focus on brand, image and reputation;
- 56% referred directly to disciplinary action for those who transgress the guidelines within the document; and
- 67% offered both professional and personal guidelines in the use of social media.
- Universities need to understand the important role played by social media in their corporate strategies to obtain optimal results for sustained growth and development."

Given the dearth of current research on these newly emerging dynamics and their impact on higher education institutions, this research and its findings of these researchers are apposite, confirming both the unpreparedness of leadership and management, and existing institutional governance structures, to deal with their current multi-stakeholder context and the unpredictable role and impact of social media in higher education leadership, management and operations.

14.3 Looking Ahead: The Ethical Use of Social Media

Disconcertingly, there is no explicit mention in these findings of the *ethical* use of social media. Perhaps that is because ethical conduct is values-based, which implies that discretionary decisions are grounded in values, which generally refer to standards and norms that encompass what is good, right and fair conduct. Virtually all higher education institutions assert values in their institutional strategies, to date most of these have not been embedded in ethical codes of conduct or in social media policies (where they exist) at our universities.

Fairness and accountability are invoked in some social media policies. For example Harvard University's *Guidelines for Using Social Media* (2014) exhorts:

> "*Do No Harm* – ... You must ensure that your authorized use of social media does not harm or otherwise injure the University, its faculty, its students, its alumni, or its employees."

The University of Pretoria's Policy on Social Media (2016) asserts the following:

> "Users of the University's social media channels are required to demonstrate high standards of ethics and conduct and to act responsibly when they exchange ideas and information on the University's social media networks. [However] ... 3.2.1 Personal use of social media must be conducted in a manner that indicates no link or association with the University. *For this reason personal use is not covered in this policy*" [my italics].

Both of these examples fail to acknowledge the interconnectedness of social media and the inability of our institutions to monitor effectively and apply appropriate sanctions, where abuses occur, especially in instances of personal use. Exhorting people to "do no harm" or forbidding the use of social media for personal purposes at work, will not stop them from doing so, especially at home (cf. ERC 2013). It is therefore suggested that a values-based ethical commitment in regard to the use of social media on the part of every staff member, and collectively as an institution, would contribute more meaningfully and effectively to its appropriate use and management in higher education institutions.

King III (2009, 22: 19) asserts that "Responsible corporate citizenship implies an ethical relationship between the company and the *society* in which it operates (my italics)." It is this intra and inter-ethical relationship between staff, students and stakeholders of the institution, the institution itself, and the society within which it functions, that is deserving of urgent and more concerted attention in the use of social media.

A number of omissions can be identified at higher education institutions when it comes to managing ethical social media use in their institutions. These include:

- Appreciating the holistic extent and nature of the risks to the institution and its staff and students, of untrammelled social media access and usage.
- A lack of understanding of the role of social media in the institution, as being inclusive of ethical, professional and socially responsible dimensions that traverses the public and private domains.
- A dearth of information around, and training available for, staff and students on the nature, potential and pitfalls of the social media, and the do's and don'ts in regard to its use in relation to the institution
- No holistic social media polices in place to offer guidance and provide a framework for monitoring, evaluation, updating and redress. This has the effect of further disempowering institutions

when it comes to responding with acumen and agility to emerging threats and opportunities.

- A lack around the identification and monitoring of current and emerging trends in social media, which militates against the proactive management thereof.

14.4 Conclusion

Social Media is a newly developing area of law, yet to be tested comprehensively and conclusively in South Africa's courts. This needs to happen within the context of freedom of expression which a cornerstone of South African democracy and higher education practice in South Africa. Universities and other institutions in South Africa are thus caught squarely in the middle, having to grapple with the tension between regulating social media versus the right to free expression, which by its very nature includes robust, critical and sometimes uncomfortable contestation. While these are still nascent challenges in South Africa, they are being dealt with around the world to a greater or lesser extent. It therefore makes sense to pre-emptively put in place measures such as clear, ethically-grounded social media policies, which will promote and embed ethical social media conduct and practice. Bearing in mind that social media also provides higher education with the opportunity to communicate effectively and share information with students (and for students to share information with each other) on a hitherto unprecedented scale, responsible leadership in higher education institutions in South Africa would be well served in the current context, to revisit their governance and sustainability policies and processes to ensure that this critical aspect of higher education leadership, management and governance is embedded in every aspect of their operations,

14.5 Chapter References

Czerniewicz, L. (2016): Student practices in copyright culture: accessing learning resources, Learning, Media and Technology, DOI: 10.1080/17439884.2016.1160928.

Code of ethics and conduct for South African print and online media (2106), http://www.presscouncil.org.za/ContentPage?code=PRESS CODE

CMC Woodworking Machinery (Pty) Ltd v Pieter Odndaal Kitchens (2006), http://www.safli.org/za/cases/ZAKZDHC/2012/44.pdf

Ethics Research Centre (2013): *National Business Ethics Survey of Social Networkers*: New Risks and Opportunities at Work. United States of America, www.ethics.org

Harvard University, *Guidelines for Using Social Media*, version 2 effective 08/18/2014, p. 3, http://provost.harvard.edu/files/provost/files/social_media_guidelines_vers_2_0_eff_081814.pdf

King III Report (2009): *The King Report on Corporate Governance for South Africa* (The Institute of Directors in Southern Africa).

Law Society of South Africa (LSSA) (2015): *Guidelines on the use of Internet-based Technologies in Legal Practice*, http://www.lssa.org.za/upload/documents/LSSA%20Guidelines%20on%20the%20Use%20of%20Internet%20Based%20Technologies%20in%20Legal%20Practice%2 0March%202015.pdf Viewed 9 March 2016.

Madell, R. (2016): *Should You "Friend" Your Boss?* Workplace Relationships: To friend or not to "friend" your boss, http://career-intelligence.com/friend-boss, viewed 10 March 2016.

Marwick, A., Boyd, D. (2011): I tweet honestly, I tweet passionately: Twitter users, context collapse, and the imagined audience. *New Media and Society*, 13, 96–113.

NACE (2012): *The Use of Facebook in the Talent Acquisition Process.* National Association of Colleges and Employees. Pennsylvania, USA. From http://www.naceweb.org/uploadedfiles/naceweb/connections/ social-jobs-partnership-executive-summary.pdf, viewed 15 March 2016.

News 24 (2016): *Standard Bank's Chris Hart resigns after 'racist' Twitter row*, http://www.news24.com/SouthAfrica/News/standard-banks-chris-hart-resigns-after-racist-twitter-row-20160314

Ngoepe, K. (2016): Tuks social media rules limit freedom of expression – SRC.2016-03-04 06:05. News 24. http://www.news24.com/South Africa/News/tuks-social-media-rules-limit-freedom-of-expression-src-20160304

Nkosi, N. (2016): IOL News. Charges to be laid over Tuks scrap Afrikaans call. 18 February 2016 at 09:22am, http://www.iol.co.za/ news/crime-courts/charges-to-be-laid-over-tuks-scrap-afrikaans-call-1986171, viewed 18 March 2016.

Nkosi,B. (2015): *Wits protest: Habib forced to hear student demands*, http://mg.co.za/article/2015-10-17-wits-protest-habib-forced-to-hear-student-demands

Pistorius,T. (2016): Quoted in Thebe, M: Beware of Social Media Pitfalls. Law Society of South Africa. De Rebus. January 27th 2016, http://wwwderebus.org.za, viewed 12 March 2016.

Robson, J. (2015): *How One Stupid Tweet Blew Up Justine Sacco's Life,* http://www.nytimes.com/2015/02/15/magazine/how-one-stupid-tweet-ruined-justine-saccos-life.html

South Africa Press Association (2012): *Stop insulting ANC Leaders: Mantashe,*.http://www.sabc.co.za/news/a/5489850049d07e1c8a69ae424 1 895f18/Stop-insulting-ANC-leaders:-Mantashe-20121601

Shange, N. and Herman, P. (2016): *Angry Twitter mob hijacked racism debate - Gareth Cliff,* News24.com, http://www.news24.com/South Africa/News/racism-debate-hijacked-by-angry-twitter-mob-gareth-cliff-20160107

South African Labour Guide (2016): http://www.labourguide.co.za/ most-recent/1358-social-media-guidelines-on-the-policy-for-employees-using-social-media-for-non-business-purposes

Struwig, M and van der Berg, A. (2016): *Why universities should start taking social media far more seriously,* The Conversation. Africa Pilot, January 18 2016. https://theconversation.com/africa

Thomas, A. (2015): South Africa: *Dishonest Academics May Make Students Think Plagiarism Is Acceptable.* http://allafrica.com/stories/ 201508071614.html

University of Pretoria. Office of the Registrar (2014): Policy on Social Media, http://www.up.ac.za/media/shared/409/social-media-policy.zp84971.pdf

Wicks, J. (2016): *Twitter erupts after KZN estate agent calls black people 'monkeys'.* 04 JAN 2016 08:50 JEFF WICKS. Mail & Guardian. http://mg.co.za/article/2016-01-04-twitter-erupts-after-kzn-estate-agent-calls-black-people-monkeys

Universities in Transformation: The Ethics of Preparing Graduates for Global Citizenship

Mandla Makhanya

15.1 Introduction

The concept of a responsible and critical citizenry is acknowledged globally as a foundational responsibility of the university (Unesco 1998; Ahier, J, Beck, J, and Moore, R: 2003; Robbins, A: 1963; Dearing. 1997; DoE 1997). Such citizenship is not an axiomatic "by-product" or outcome of higher education, but involves a process of "socialization" which assumes that graduates, in the course their studies, will develop an ability to think critically and analytically, that they will have a thorough understanding of their societies both nationally and internationally, as well as a mature knowledge of ethical and responsible citizenship, and its practice.

This may be demonstrated in forward-thinking, "enlightened" reflection, in the evaluation, analysis and renewal of current knowledges and the production of new tributaries of innovation, and in an environment of tolerance for the public good (DoE, 1997: 1.2 – 1.4). The *World Declaration on Higher Education for the Twenty-First Century: Vision and Action* confirms that students should "(b) be able to speak out on ethical, cultural and social problems completely independently and in full awareness of their responsibilities, exercising a kind of intellectual authority that society needs to help it to reflect, understand and act" and that "(f) they must play a role in helping identify and address issues that affect the well-being of communities, nations and global society." (Unesco 1998a: 2(b), 2(f)).

Institutions of higher education also need to ensure that they are producing graduates who are competent in their disciplines and fields of study, as well as well-rounded global citizens, cognizant of the changing international employment environment and employer expectations, while meeting the demands of the professional labour market (Bridgstock 2009; McIlveen 2010; Archer & Chetty 2013; Knight & Yorke 2004). These demands are by no means novel, but have received much attention in research on employability and graduateness, with the idea of citizenship often linked to the idea of transferable skills, aimed at equipping graduates to adapt to a dynamic work-environment (Bridgstock 2009; Glover et al. 2002; Institute for the Future 2011; UK Comission for Employment and Skills 2014).

Citizenship, as such, has thus not enjoyed particular emphasis in higher education as it is often seen as part of a growing list of demands placed on universities, especially in emerging economies. The emphasis on this particular concept, and the responsibility of higher education to inculcate citizenship, is however growing and is increasingly assuming prominence in the corporate university (Unesco 1998; Ahier, J, Beck, J, and Moore, R: 2003; Robbins, A: 1963; Dearing. 1997; DoE 1997).

15.2 Discussion

15.2.1 Global Citizenship

There is relatively little clarity on the transmission of *citizenship,* in particular, to the student, be it via curricular content or pedagogical (andragogical) process, or both (DoE, 1997, Robbins, A, 1963; Dearing,

1997; Nussbaum, M, 2006). Globally, universities are charged to contribute to the production of responsible and critical citizens by virtue of education being "a foundation for human fulfilment, peace, sustainable development, economic growth, decent work, gender equality and responsible *global* [my emphasis] citizenship", as well as "a key contributor to the reduction of inequalities and poverty" by creating the conditions and generating the opportunities for better, sustainable societies (Unesco Position Paper ED 2015a: 13,3).

In this way, quality and equality are closely linked to education for discerning citizenship. In 1997, South Africa's Department of Education (DoE 1997: 1.4) acknowledged the inadequacy of higher education in carrying out this particular mandate, when it asserted:

> "Higher education has an unmatched obligation, which has not been adequately fulfilled, to help lay the foundations of a critical civil society, with a culture of public debate and tolerance which accommodates differences and competing interests. It has much more to do, both within its own institutions and in its influence on the broader community, to strengthen the democratic ethos, the sense of common citizenship and commitment to a common good."

The difficulty in nurturing global citizenship as part of graduateness is a well-documented phenomenon (Sawahel 2014; Steur et al. 2012). Although there is some Northern research, such as that conducted by Ahier *et al* (2003:135) in British universities, which has shown that while university life in itself contributes to a sense of society and community among students, which is underpinned by values such as fairness, respect, responsibility and altruism, such values do not constitute a holistic expression of a "critical citizen" discussed above. Moreover, it does not indicate how this would be realized in an Open Distance Learning environment.

The conceptualization of citizenship in this scholarship is also somewhat leaner than the overarching view of "responsible *global* citizenship" referred to in the Unesco position paper (1998: 2(a) and 2(f)) above. It is therefore possible that the corporate approach to global citizenship has contributed to the re-conceptualization and understanding of citizenship in higher education (cf. Madge *et al*, 2015), especially in the era of *new managerialism*.

15.2.2 Global Citizenship and Corporate Governance

When we turn to King III principles in the world of corporate governance to expand our view of global citizenship (King III, CH 2.1.4), they assert that: "Good corporate citizenship is the establishment of an ethical relationship of responsibility between the company [*university* (my parenthesis)] and the society in which it operates. As good corporate citizens of the societies in which they do business, companies [*universities*] have, apart from rights, also legal and moral obligations in respect of their social and natural environments. The company [*university*] as a good corporate citizen should protect, enhance and invest in the wellbeing of society and the natural ecology", and King IV (King IV, 2016:4) states: "Ethics considerations are part of the rationale for regarding the organization as an integral part of society, for corporate citizenship, sustainable development and stakeholder inclusivity."

Responsible *global* citizenship enriched in the corporate environment can influence the conventional understanding of a responsible and critical citizenry advocated by universities and reflects a broad economic, social and environmental responsibility, (the *Profit-People-Planet* approach). This approach places a more deliberate focus on quality of life for all people and the ethical stewardship of the environment *in addition to* and *as part of* the core function of scholarship and research.

It is this emphasis on sustaining the environment, with its concomitant moral and ethical underpinnings, which we wish to instil in higher education's understanding of responsible, critical citizenship. Given our acknowledged "ability to change and to induce change and progress in society" (Unesco, 1998b), universities are in a position to sensitize students to our own triple bottom-line approach of *Pedagogy, People and Planet.* Leadership should however guard against simply transposing corporate governance principles on academia, practising the same *critical consciousness* (Freire, 2007) of responsible global citizenry by examining how tertiary education may benefit from a corporate approach. Debate about this has been intense as academics have critiqued marketization and managerialism, so a thorough epistemological grounding is required, recognizing the inherent diversity of higher education across the world (Deem and Brehony, 2005; Horncastle, 2011).

15.2.3 Global Citizenship, Corporate Governance, and Universities

Any attempt to embed a corporatized conceptualization of global citizenship, or one distinct from that of more traditional notions of critical citizenship in universities, is likely to be met with resistance and will not deliver the desired results. The contestation is most intense when (academic) citizenship insists on epistemic justice, curricular reform, intellectual dissent and social equality. It is therefore critical that Universities advocate an understanding of *global* citizenship as consonant with, and complementary to (academic) citizenship, irrespective of its epistemic location.

There is, in addition, growing evidence from the internationalization of higher education that the changing geopolitical landscape requires Northern scholarship to respond differently to challenges emerging from the Global South, which is producing new governance and curricular alignments, as well as a growing resistance to what is construed as knowledge (and technological) hegemony (Mbembe, 2016). Subaltern, postcolonial and decolonial perspectives are growing and asserting local knowledges in order to ensure relevance in developing societies, whose constructions of citizenship are contingent upon different social forces and conceptions of nation, identity and belonging (Giroux, 2016). The ethics of leadership and the role of higher education and technological innovation in such circumstances are also contested, and skills and characteristics associated with *graduateness* tend to be ranked differently (*Horizon Report*, 2016). In this context, ethical and responsible global citizenship becomes increasingly relevant, as a characteristic of the successful 21st century graduate.

15.3 Conclusion

While higher education institutions are unambiguously tasked by global sentiment, policy and commitment to be [the] "foundation for human fulfilment, peace, sustainable development, economic growth, decent work, gender equality and responsible global citizenship" and "a key contributor to the reduction of inequalities and poverty by bequeathing the conditions and generating the opportunities for better, sustainable societies" (Unesco *Position Paper ED* 2015b: 13,3), these expectations present a number of complex challenges, given the cultural diversity that exists at national and global levels, and the strategic, administrative, logistical and policy barriers that need to be navigated.

The emphasis on ethical leadership in respect of global citizenship is not merely about imposing the concept through governance, imitation of business ethics, or superficial re-curriculation, but will require a far greater immersion in, and appreciation of, how the corporate notion of global citizenship and the academic notion of critical citizenship, may be harmonized to produce the best possible model for the university environment and the academic project.

15.4 Chapter References

Accreditation. CAA Quality Series no.2. Ministry of Higher Education and Scientific Research United Arab Emirates, www.caa.ae

Ahier, J, Beck, J, and Moore, R. (2003): *Graduate Citizens? Issues of Citizenship and Higher Education*, London. New York. Routledge Falmer.

Archer, E. & Chetty, Y. (2013): Graduate Employability : Conceptualisation and findings from the University of South Africa. *Progressio*, 35(1), 134–165.

Bridgstock, R., (2009): The graduate attributes we've overlooked: enhancing graduate employability through career management skills, Higher Education Research & Development, 28 (1), 31-44.

Council on Higher Education (2016): *South African Higher Education Reviewed: Two Decades of Democracy*, Pretoria, Eight Task Team Reports, Chap. 3: Governance, 105-141.

CHEA/CIQG (2015): CHEA International Quality Group International Quality Principles, www.chea.org/pdf/Quality%20Principles.pdf. Accessed 2016/03/20

Dearing (1997): The Dearing Report, www.educationengland.org.uk/documents/dearing1997/dearing1997.html, accessed 04/03/2016

Deem, R. and Brehony, K.J. (2005): "Management as ideology: the case of "new managerialism" in higher education", *Oxford Review of Education* 31(2), 217-235.

Department of Education (1997) *Education White Paper 3: A Programme for the Transformation of Higher Education*. Pretoria, Department of Education.

Kigotho, Wachira (2015): *Producing unemployable graduates wastes time and money.* University World News, 20 March 2015, Issue No. 359, http://www.universityworldnews.com/article.php?story= 20150319130200274, accessed 20/04/2016

Freire, P. (2007): *Education for Critical Consciousness.* Sheed and Ward Ltd. Continuum. London, New York.

Giroux, H.A. (2016): "Beyond pedagogies of repression", *Monthly Review*, vol. 67(10), March, pp.57-71.

Glover, D., Sue Law & Youngman, A. (2002): Graduateness and Employability: student perceptions of the personal outcomes of university education. *Research in Post-Compulsory Education*, 7, (February 2015), 293–306.

Horncastle, J. (2011): "Taking Care in Academia: The Critical Thinker, Ethics and Cuts", *Graduate Journal of Social Science* 8(2), 41-57.

Institute for the Future (2011): Future Work Skills, Available at: http://apolloresearchinstitute.com/research-studies/workforce-preparedness/future-work-skills-2020.

The Institute of Directors in Southern Africa (2016): King IV Report on Corporate Governance for South Africa 2016, www.adamsadams.com/wp-content/uploads/2016/11/King-IV-Report.pdf, accessed 09/11/2016

—— (2009): King III Report on Corporate Governance 2009, http://c.ymcdn.com/sites/www.iodsa.co.za/resource/collection/94445006-4F18-4335-B7FB-7F5A8B23FB3F/King_III_Code_for_Governance_Principles_.pdf

Knight, P. & Yorke, M. (2004): *Learning, curriculum and employability in higher education*, London: Routledge Falmer.

Madge, C, Raghuram, P, and Noxolo, P. (2015): "Conceptualizing international education: From international student to international study", *Progress in Human Geography*, vol. 39(6), 681-701.

Mbembe, A.J. (2016): "Decolonizing the university: New directions". *Arts & Humanities in Higher Education*, vol. 51(1), 29-45.

McIlveen, P. (2010): No Title. *HECSI*, www.hecsu.ac.uk/graduate_ market_trends_summer_2010_theaussie_blueprint_for _employability.htm, accessed May 20, 2011.

Nussbaum, M. (2006): *Education for Democratic Citizenship*. Institute of Social Studies Public Lecture Series 2006, No. 1. The Hague: Institute of Social Studies.

Pace, L.A. (2007): "The Ethical Implications of Quality", The electronic *Journal of Business Ethics and Organisation Studies*, Vol. 12, No.2, Business and Organisation Ethics Network, available at: http://ejbo.jyu.fi/articles/0401_2.html, accessed 19/04/2016

Robbins, A: (1963). Higher Education. Report of the Prime Minister's Committee. London. HMSO, www.education england.org.uk/ documents/robbins/robbins1963.htm

Sawahel, W. (2014): New EU initiative to boost graduate employability. *University World News*, March 9.

Steur, J.M., Jansen, E.P.W.A. & Hofman, W.H.A, (2012): Graduateness: An empirical examination of the formative function of university education. *Higher Education*, 64, 861–874.

The NMC Horizon Report: 2016 Higher Education Edition. 2016. New Media Consortium.

UK Commission for Employment and Skills, 2014. The Future of Work : Jobs and skills in 2030. *Evidence Report*, 84, February.

https://www.gov.uk/government/uploads/system/uploads/
attachment_data/file/303334/er84-the-future-of-work-evidence-
report.pdf.

UNESCO (1998): *World Declaration on Higher Education for the
Twenty-First Century: Vision and Action.*
www.Unesco.org/education/educprog/wche/declaration_eng.htm,
accessed: 2016/04/22

UNESCO (2015): Position Paper on Education. ED-14/EFA/POST-
2015/1. http://hdr.undp.org/en/statistics/hdi, accessed: 2016/04/20

UNESCO (2015): Sustainable Development Goals, http://www.un.org/
sustainabledevelopment/sustainable-development-goals/. Accessed:
2016/04/20

Van Damme, D. (2001): "Quality Issues in the Internationalisation of
Higher Education", Higher Education, Vol. 41, No. 4 (Jun., 2001), 415-
441, published by Springer, http://www.jstor.org/stable/3448132,
accessed: 09/07/2008 03:55

Woodhouse, D. (1999): Quality and Quality Assurance in Organisation
for Economic Co-Operation and Development (OECD) 1999, *Quality
and Internationalisation in Higher Education* (IMHE). Paris, OECD.

SECTION 4

Open and Distance Education

16

SOME EXPLORATORY THOUGHTS ON *OPENNESS* AND AN ETHICS OF CARE

Elizabeth Archer & Paul Prinsloo

16.1 Introduction

Amidst the different claims and counter-claims of disruption, innovation and revolutions facing higher education, the notion of *Openness* is, on the one hand deeply embedded in the evolution of distance education, and on the other hand, one of the key characteristics of more recent phenomena such as Open Educational Resources (OER) and Massive Open Online Courses (MOOCs). Key to these three phenomena is the claim that they aim *to widen access*, and while the statistics do support this claim with regard to number of registrations or users, widening access is much larger than just providing access and it raises a number of *ethical* issues and concerns.

Openness has become one of the "corporate buzzwords" (Birnbaum 2001: 3) and is "presented as universally applicable quick-fix solutions – along with the obligatory and explicit caution that their recommendations are *not* quick fixes and will require substantial management understanding and commitment" (Birnbaum 2001:4). *Openness* is much more buzzword or fad and is deeply political, embedded in our epistemologies and ontologies, and reflecting and often perpetuating inequalities and injustices.

While there are many possibly ways to engage with exploring the ethical issues and implications of widening access and opening up opportunity, one possible heuristic lens is to explore these is through the claim that with opening up or widening access comes certain *responsibilities*. But having said that, determining the scope of these responsibilities is more complex and more nuanced than perceived at a first glance.

Considering the scope, definition and ethical implications of *Openness* and responsibility in these three phenomena, it is important to consider a number of questions such as: Is widening access enough? What are the fiduciary duties of the one who widens access or does widening access cancel or change the inherent fiduciary duty?

In this chapter we briefly explore ethics, responsibility and care while mapping the notion of *Openness* in three different, but overlapping phenomena namely Open Distance and Distributed education, OER and MOOCs. We then propose the need to move towards an ethics of care which acknowledges the need for leadership in Higher Education to take a teleological approach to *Openness* in order to truly leverage its potential.

16.2 Ethics, Responsibility and Care

In general parlance, ethical practice is often equated with doing good or doing no harm, at least not intentionally. This is where the complexity in defining the term and scope of ethical implications in *Openness* lies. There is ample evidence that even the best intentions to do good often have harmful effects or unintended negative consequences that could not have been foreseen at the outset of the action.

Traditionally, one way to disentangle the definition and scope of ethics in particular contexts was to distinguish between deontological and teleological approaches (Marshall 2014). *Deontological* approaches to ethics, are rule-based and form the foundation of legal and regulatory frameworks, as well as the Terms and Conditions (T&Cs) stipulating rights and responsibilities in a particular context. As can be expected, deontological approaches work best in relatively stable environments. We acknowledge that even when there is agreement to follow a deontological approach, agreement will still have to be reached regarding the type of rule, for example contract-based, consent-based, informed by legal principles in a particular context, or based on a rule consequentialism.

A *teleological* approach to defining ethics focuses on consultative, discursive spaces where the potential for harm and the scope of consent, and recourses in cases of unintended harm are negotiated and agreed upon. An ethics of justice or a teleological approach is therefore based on the decisions of an "autonomous, objective and impartial agent" (Edwards as cited in Botes 2000: 1072) formulating and applying universal rules and principles to "ensure the fair and equitable treatment of all people". An ethics of care or a teleological approach focuses on fulfilling "the needs of others and to maintain harmonious relations" (Botes 2000: 1072). An ethics of care has at its foundation the consideration of potential vulnerabilities of those affected by the intervention or opportunity.

Approaching the notion of *Openness* through the lenses of ethics, responsibility and care raises some interesting questions in the context where the discourses of widening access are often based on relaxing admission or access requirements. In this chapter we propose the need to consider widening access through the lens of an ethics of care. We now will briefly explore and map the notion of *Openness* in the contexts of distance education, OER and MOOCs before contesting some of the claims regarding *Openness* in these contexts.

16.3 *Openness* in Distance Education

The history of distance education provides ample evidence that opening up opportunities for previously excluded populations was an integral part of distance education from its very early beginnings. This can also be seen in the development and varying degrees of *Openness* to libraries and knowledge as documented by Latimer (2011), from monastic libraries, to chained libraries, to university readers and now we are losing even more chains through e-resources. Germane to distance education is the optimising of technologies of the day to offer educational opportunities for those who could not attend face-to-face education whether due to, inter alia, cost, admission requirements, the need to relocate or studying whilst working.

It is crucial also to understand that not all distance education institutions are open, while all open distance learning institutions are also distance learning institutions. Having said that, it is equally important to note that not all open distance learning institutions are equally open, and that an institution's *Openness* is dependent on national regulatory and funding arrangements and frameworks. *Openness* is, however, also a concept that is much wider than just admission requirements or the recognition of prior learning, but also refers to flexibility with regard to registration periods, curricula, pedagogy, affordability, re-admission and rules of progression, to mention but a few (Lockwood 2013).

In broad terms, *Openness* in the context of distance education therefore foremost points to opening up opportunities to individuals and/or populations who would have been excluded from educational opportunities. Closer inspection, however reveal that while increasing access to education is but one aspect of *Openness*, providing access does not, per se, signify a more ethical stance than, for example, limiting access.

In terms of an ethics of justice, *Openness* in distance education contexts mean providing equal opportunities for all, regardless of race, gender, income or class. The principles and defining characteristics underlying an ethics of justice cannot, however, sufficiently address and accommodate the complexities, intersectionality and multi-dimensional nature of individuals and different relations in different contexts. In a certain sense, ODL as moral practice and public good is already a counter-narrative to the question of desert, which proposes that some students deserve access to higher education, while many prospective students may have to accept that they do not have access. An ethics of care will move beyond just widening access, but consider seriously the fact that providing access is but a start. Actually, an ethics of care proposes that providing access without providing reasonable care to ensure success is actually justice denied.

16.4 Openness in OER

It is commonly acknowledged that OER represents tools to facilitate change by amongst others: decreasing cost of replication of materials, reducing cost and time in curriculum development, increasing the audience for research and making it easier to ensure the recency of the resources employed in our offerings (De Hart et al. 2015; Butcher & Hoosen 2012; Glennie et al. 2012; Anderson 2008). These are but a few of the beneficial natural outflows of the advent of OER and attributed to its *Openness*.

The revolutionary power of OER, however, lies in the opportunities it provides to re-examine, interrogate and shift the entrenched paradigms held in higher education. It provides the opportunity for ethical and epistemological change pertaining to the role of higher education, sustainable business models in higher education, research, as well as teaching and learning. In this approach to *Openness* however we need to move beyond just OER to OEP:

> "Open Educational Practices (OEP) are defined as practices which support the production, use and reuse of high quality open educational resources (OER) through institutional policies, which promote innovative pedagogical models, and respect and empower learners as co-producers on their lifelong learning path. OEP address the whole OER governance community: policy makers, managers and administrators of organizations, educational professionals and learners." (International Council for Open and Distance Education, n.d.)

With this approach higher education leaderships ethical responsibility does not only lie in opening of access (for whatever given value attributed to *Openness*), but in an acknowledgment that these new technologies require an ethics of caring. An ethic that recognises that the change brought about by OER, as technology, not only represents a disruption in access to knowledge, but is also a product of a changing society. It places an ethical burden on us to ensure that the disruptive technology does not dictate the change, but that the technology is harnessed in a responsible manner towards a praxis of pedagogy and leadership for new generation of graduates equipped to be responsive in an increasingly dynamic Knowledge Economy and Academe (Archer & Chetty 2013).

16.6 *Openness* in MOOCs

Ethics in the context of MOOCs is, "like MOOCs themselves, something of a moving target" (Robbins 2013 para. 2). Adding a layer of complexity to considering the ethics in one aspect of MOOCs, namely *Openness*, is the wide variety of pedagogies in MOOCs, and the seemingly proliferation of forms of MOOCs, often changing one of the key traditional elements of MOOCs such as the size (massive), *Openness* (open), online (by adding blended or hybrid elements) and courses (with a plethora of opinions regarding the criteria for an offering to be considered a course) (See Clark 2013; Conole 2013). Clark (2013), for example, refers to eight types of pedagogical models in MOOCs for example synchMOOCs that have a fixed start date, fixed dates for assignments and assessments and a fixed end date, while asynchMOOCs that have no or frequent start dates, have no or looser dates set for the handing in of assignments and not end date. (See Clark 2013 for a full discussion of each of these types of MOOCs). Each of the different types of MOOCs – whether as described based on their pedagogies (Clark 2013), or on the more traditional differentiation between connectivist MOOCs (cMOOCs) and MOOCs primarily using interactive media (xMOOCs) (Conole 2013) – will have their own ethical issues. Due to the huge variety in the phenomenon, we therefore briefly refer to some general elements regarding the ethical implications specific to the notion of *Openness* in MOOCs.

It is clear that the claims that MOOCs are democratising education and making education accessible for all need to be scrutinised and contested. There is evidence that these claims overestimate who actually has access to MOOCs, and that having access does not equate an ethics of care where there is an indifference about admission requirements, credentialising, often no oversight over the quality of course materials, and importantly, no oversight regarding how users' data are used and shared (Prinsloo & Slade 2015; Prinsloo & Slade 2016; Robbins 2013). There is furthermore no oversight regarding the ethical issues in the research on the participants as required by Ethical Review Boards (Robbins 2013; Willis, Slade & Prinsloo 2016).

Often overlooked are the ethical issues in the *design* of MOOCs as illustrated in the research by Millet and Luo (2014). There are, for example, the ethical issues with regard to the knowledge-claims and the fact that most MOOCs are presenting epistemologies and ontologies originating from North-Atlantic contexts, often presented as universal truths devoid of contextual sensitivities, and the possibility that there may be different ways of seeing knowledge and being. The choice of language of tuition also has implications for how *open* a MOOC is, as are the recognition of the rich diversity in student profiles and their different aspirations, goals, and available time and resources. Other questions in the context of the ethical dimensions of the *Openness* of MOOCs are, for example, how open are the resources or are they copyrighted and commercialised? How open are the pedagogies and assessment regimes (see for example, Clark 2013)? How *open* are MOOCs with regard to the *hidden* costs such as data and resources to be downloaded, etc.? And, how *open* or tolerant will the MOOC provider be with regard to inflammatory or abusive comments and harassment?

While we agree that ethics in MOOCs is a "moving target" (Robbins 2013 para. 2), we cannot avoid thinking through the ethical implications of the notion of *Openness* in MOOCs. Mapping out the ethical issues may assist us in opening up *Openness* and discovering the different nuances and varying degrees of *Openness* that contest the simple binary of open vs closed.

16.7 The Fallacy of *Openness* (Moving Beyond Binaries)

Much of the opposition to *Openness* resides in fallacies surrounding how *Openness* is understood. *Openness* has somehow become to be perceived as having descriptive value beyond claims pertaining to barriers to access. This was optimised in the study conducted by John Bohannon, a science journalist at Harvard University (Guardian, 2013) who submitted hundreds of fake articles to Open Access journals of which many accepted the paper. The design of this study was of course in and of itself flawed as there was no control group where the fake article was submitted to traditional closed access journals. As has been seen recently the results may well have been more of an indication of the rise of predatory journals (Scholarly Open Access 2015) and the problematic nature peer review (Mulligan & Hall 2013; Resnik & Elmore 2016) endemic to both open and closed access publication.

In the same vein the word *Open* does not in any way relate to the quality of material, ethical nature of the material, whether the material is accredited and recognised, the contextualization of the knowledge, whether or not employers seek employees with such knowledge, whether the production and reproduction of such knowledge is cost free, sustainability, etc. It merely indicates that the degree of accessibility is higher and more flexible than traditional access to knowledge.

If we then move beyond a mere deontological to a teleological approach to ethics, leaderships' responsibility lies in embracing an ethics of care which in broad terms includes, the (1) considering the intellectual integrity of the offering or resource; (2) a commitment to prevent harm; (3) transparency regarding the *limitations* of the offering or resource (e.g. accreditation by other providers, etc.); (4) a declaration of costs (hidden but also opportunity costs for students or users); (5) a clear and accessible declaration of the Terms and Conditions (T&Cs) of use; (6) a commitment not to exploit users' data outside of the scope of the T&Cs; and (7) seeing students and users of resources in terms of inherently vulnerable human beings and not (just?) as users of services/products and/or customers.

In effect, this is true for any type of material whether open or closed access. The disruption brought about by *Openness* as a technology has however re-sensitised us to these ethical considerations. We should not fall into the trap that these ethical responsibilities and ethics of caring is only important for leadership when addressing *Openness*, but recognise that the same ethics is applicable, required when dealing with less open resources.

Openness has a number of implications such as the scalability and cost (to the institution) of the care and support provided. As higher education in general, and specifically distance and distributed learning providers increasingly face funding constraints and serious concerns about their sustainability, implementing a more ethical approach to widening access does have cost, operational and resource implications. Concomitantly, *Openness* and cost to students is something which cannot be ignored as students around the world demand a lowering of cost surrounding access to education as is seen in the recent #feesmustfall movement. Higher Education Leadership is facing increasing pressure to produce more, of a higher quality, whilst decreasing cost, *Openness* may provide some tools in dealing with these contrasting challenges if approached with an ethics of caring.

16.8 Conclusion

In this chapter we aimed to contest the notion of Openness as used as 'buzzword' in distance and distributed learning, OER and MOOCs. Widening or opening access is not a "universally applicable quick-fix solution" (Birnbaum 2001 par 4) and requires careful consideration. We therefore need to move beyond a *simple* or *deontological* understanding of *Openness* and the comfort of binaries of open vs. closed. In this chapter we proposed moving to a teleological understanding of the ethical implications of Openness and to move beyond an ethics of justice or a rule-based understanding to an ethics of care.

16.9 Chapter References

Anderson, T. (2008) "Open Educational Resources plus social software: Threat or opportunity for Canadian higher education?" In: *Conference at UBC.* Vancouver: OER Knowledge Cloud.

Archer, E. & Chetty, Y. (2013): "Graduate Employability : Conceptualisation and findings from the University of South Africa", *Progressio,* 35(1), 134–165.

Birnbaum, R. (2001): *Management fads in higher education. Where they come from, what they do, why they fail.* San Francisco, CA: Jossey-Bass.

Botes, A. (2000): "A comparison between the ethics of justice and the ethics of care", *Journal of Advanced Nursing,* 32, 1071–1075. DOI: 10.1046/j.1365-2648.2000.01576.x

Butcher, N. & Hoosen, S. (2012): *Exploring the Business Case for Open Educational Resources,* https://www.col.org/resources/exploring-business-case-open-educational-resources, accessed March 25, 2016.

Clark, D. (2013, April): *MOOCs: Taxonomy of 8 types of MOOCs.* http://donaldclarkplanb.blogspot.co.za/2013/04/moocs-taxonomy-of-8-types-of-mooc.html, accessed March 25, 2016.

Conole, G. (2013): *MOOCs as disruptive technologies: strategies for enhancing the learner experience and quality of MOOCs.* http://www.um.es/ead/red/39/conole.pdf, accessed March 25, 2016.

De Hart, K., Chetty, Y. & Archer, E. (2015): "Uptake of OER by Staff in Distance Education in South Africa", *International Review of Research in Open and Distributed Learning,* 16(2), 18–45, http://www.irrodl.org/ index.php/irrodl/article/view/2047/3272.

Glennie, J., Harley, K., Butcher, N., & Van Wyk, T. (2012): "Open Educational Resources and change in higher education : Reflections from practice". Perspectives on open and distance learning, Commonwealth of Learning: Vancouver.

International Council for Open and Distance Education, n.d. *Definition of Open Educational Practices*, http://www.icde.org/en/resources/open_ educational_quality_inititiative/definition_of_open_educational_ practices, accessed March 25, 2016.

Latimer, K. (2011): "Collections to Connections: Changing Spaces and New Challenges in Academic Library Buildings". *Library Trends*, 60(1), 112–133.

Lockwood, F. (2013): *Open and distance learning today.* New York: Routledge.

Marshall, S. (2014): Exploring the ethical implications of MOOCs. *Distance Education*, 35(2), 250-262.

Millet, A., & Luo, H. (2014): "Ethical considerations in MOOC design and delivery: a case study", *Online Learning Consortium International Conference*, http://olc.onlinelearningconsortium.org/conference/2014/ aln/ethical-considerations-mooc-design-and-delivery-case-study, accessed March 25, 2016.

Mulligan, A., & Hall, L. (2013): "Peer review in a changing world : An international study measuring the attitudes of researchers". *Journal of the American Society for Information Science & Technology,* 64(1), 132–161.

Prinsloo, P., & Slade, S. (2015): "Student privacy self-management: implications for learning analytics", *Proceedings of the Fifth International Learning Analytics & Knowledge Conference (LAK15)*, 83-92. http://dl.acm.org/citation.cfm?id=2723585, accessed March 25, 2016.

Prinsloo, P., & Slade, S. (2016): "Student vulnerability, agency and learning analytics: an exploration", *Journal of Learning Analytics* (In press).

Resnik, D.B. & Elmore, S.A. (2016): "Peer Review : A Possible Role of Editors", *Science and Engineering Ethics*, 22, 169–188, http://dx.doi.org/10.1007/s11948-015-9625-5.

Robins, J. (2013, March): "The ethics of MOOCs", *InsideHigherEd.* https://www.insidehighered.com/blogs/sounding-board/ethics-moocs, accessed March 25, 2016.

Scholarly Open Access (2015): Scholarly Open Access: Beall's List of Predatory Publishers 2015. https://scholarlyoa.com/2015/01/02/bealls-list-of-predatory-publishers-2015, accessed March 25, 2016.

Shaw, C. (2013): "Hundreds of open access journals accept fake science paper", The Guardian, http://www.theguardian.com/higher-education-network/2013/oct/04/open-access-journals-fake-paper, accessed March 25, 2016.

Willis, J. E., Slade, S., & Prinsloo, P. (2016): Ethical oversight of student data in learning analytics: A typology derived from a cross-continental, cross-institutional perspective. Submitted to special issue of *Educational Technology Research and Development* (Exploring the Relationship of Ethics in Design and Learning Analytics: Implications for the Field of Instructional Design and Technology), guest edited by M. Tracey and D. Ifenthaler, (in press).

17

OPEN EDUCATIONAL PRACTICE: CAVEAT EMPTOR

Som Naidu

17.1 Introduction

The case for *open educational resources* and *massive open online courses* is clearest and strongest when seen within the broader conversation around *open educational practice*. This comprises open access to educational opportunity, and alternative modes of learning as well as engagement with open scholarship. While the case for access to educational opportunity and approaches to various modes of open learning are now widely recognized and accepted, the case for engagement with open scholarship is not entirely clear and convincing. This chapter explores the major confounds around the case for open scholarship to separate the hype from the facts, and shed light on ethical and moral issues surrounding engagement with open educational practices. Implications of these practices for the roles, responsibilities and commitments of universities as well as other educational institutions in society, and the framing of a values driven and future-proofed curriculum for them are outlined and discussed.

17.2 The Case for Open Educational Resources

Few developments in the open and online education space have rattled the Zeitgeist of educational practice and caused as much interest in, as well as controversy over its form and function, as has been the case for *open educational resources* (OER) and *massive, open and online courses* (MOOCs) (see Jona & Naidu, 2014). Among other things, these developments highlight issues to do with the roles and responsibilities of educational institutions around equity and access to educational opportunity, as well as opportunities and challenges for change and innovation in educational curricula and its pedagogy.

The socio-political imperatives for the adoption of OER by educational institutions are clearly justifiable and defensible, especially as a credible response to meeting relevant targets of the United Nations Sustainable Development Goals agenda around reducing inequality, and in providing an inclusive and equitable quality education, and lifelong learning opportunities for all. But the educational and economic arguments for their widespread adoption are still not entirely clear and convincing (see Naidu, 2016).

Let's consider the assumptions of the educational argument first. The educational imperative suggests that content ought to be released and with permissions to enable them to be used and manipulated in ways that are not possible with conventional proprietary material. There can be advantages for users in being able to do this (i.e., revise, remix, and redistribute educational resources) with freedom and impunity. But it is not always necessary to revise and remix a resource before it is usable (see Naidu, 2016). Neither learners nor teachers want to always rip apart an educational resource before it is of any use to them (see Allen, & Seaman, 2014; see also Wiley, 2016). Besides, this may not be always advisable. Most educational resources will have a level of integrity that is determined by its authors or developers which they would want to protect and for good reason. Altering this in different ways can run the risk of misinterpretation and misrepresentation of the essence of the original resource (Baggaley & James, 2016).

Educational resources are often selected for their overall suitability and relevance for a set of learning outcomes, and not for their exposure to being able to be modified by users. Some will be more suitable than others, and few will ever come exactly fit for purpose. The imperative for educational resources to be able to be revised and remixed for effective use suggests furthermore, a perspective on teaching that is subject matter content-focused, suggesting that the content is the primary object of an educational transaction and it is that which needs to be taught and learned. Whereas conventional wisdom plus a growing body of literature on learning experience design suggests that the focus of the learning and teaching transaction ought to be, not on teaching the subject matter content, but squarely on the design of appropriate and relevant learning experiences for learners (i.e., the learning activities) and only then selecting appropriate and relevant educational resources, or parts of them to fuel this learning engine (see Goodyear & Carvalho, 2013; Naidu, & Karunanayaka, 2014).

Given this perspective on learning and teaching, being able to revise and remix an educational resource is not that important. What is important is how an educational resource or parts of it are used and integrated in a learning activity or experience. If a user of a resource were to have a significant contribution to make on a subject, there is always the opportunity of being able to do it without having to infuse it into an existing resource. The adoption of OER will improve access to educational resources of course, but OER by themselves, no matter how modifiable, will not necessarily improve educational practice any more than any other comparable educational resource (see Smith, 2016). For it to be educationally effective and efficient, OER like any other educational resource will require careful integration into the learning and teaching transactions. For attempts at demonstrating how this kind of integration of OER in educational practice is achievable see Naidu and Karunanayaka (2014).

Let's now consider the assumptions of the economic arguments in favor of OER. These are based on the premise that educational resources or outputs developed with the support of the public purse ought to be released free of cost, and with permissions for their retention, reuse, revision, repurposing and redistribution (see http://opencontent.org/blog/archives/3221). The reasons why one should be able to reuse, revise, remix and repurpose a resource at no cost are contentious at least in two significant ways.

First it posits an *a priori* condition of what is meant by cost free (i.e., that which is supported with public funds), and with a range of permissions (i.e., from most to least open). But it does not make clear for whom and where. Does it mean that educational resources published with funding from a particular jurisdiction is made available cost free to all other jurisdictions? If so, then how is this justifiable and implemented across jurisdictions, other than relying on the goodwill and reciprocity of participants in the process, as there will surely be a few who will very likely want to opt out of such an arrangement? Moreover, there will be always costs associated with the development, production and distribution of content such as textbooks and peer-reviewed journal articles that are not usually supported by the public purse. How this expense is met under a cost-free regime is still unclear.

The second significant sticking point with the economic arguments for open content has to do with the derivatives of the permissions being sought by proponents (see https://creativecommons.org/licenses/). How was the creative commons licensing scheme and its attendant permissions structure developed to serve as an alternative to the conventional proprietary system (i.e., what processes or research methods were followed in the development of the scheme)? How were these categories derived? And furthermore, how does the new licensing scheme propose to protect the integrity of the original piece of work from misinterpretation, misrepresentation, plagiarism and poaching if they were to be subjected to revision and remixing by anyone with freedom and impunity. Surely, a good place to start such a conversation would have been to examine how resources are often and best used in educational settings, and only then embarking on developing a model of permissions for such use (see Smith, 2016).

17.3 The Case for Massive Open Online Courses (MOOCs)

MOOCs appeared on our radar in much the same way, rather incidentally, and without foremost, a careful consideration of what a massive open online course might look like, let alone why we might need and want to develop such courses (Naidu, 2013a). Around 2008 two educators, George Siemens and Stephen Downes were offering a graduate seminar online on "connectivism and connective knowledge" for about 25 students at University of Manitoba in Saskatchewan, Canada, when it dawned upon them to open up this course to anyone and everyone with an internet connection. So they did, lo and behold, around 2,200 others from the general public took up the invitation to join without having to pay anything for the experience (see Siemens & Downes, 2011). What do you call such a course that has suddenly gone from attracting 25 to 2,000 participants and is open to anyone at no cost, and without any prior knowledge of the subject matter? Their collaborators, Dave Cormier and Bryan Alexander, called it a "massive, open, online course". The term stuck and an idea was born (see http://bit.ly/1k50ijB).

Incidentally, the subject matter of the online seminar that George Siemens and Stephen Downes were offering was about knowledge building in a connected world (see Downes, 2008; Siemens, 2008). Therefore the first round of MOOCs were propelled by the belief that knowledge and understanding was best developed by participants engaging in an open discussion, debate and exploration of the subject matter content and its context to arrive at their own individual and collective understandings. This reflected a constructivist approach to learning and teaching (although Siemens and Downes would suggest a *connectivist* approach), and these courses were dubbed cMOOCs. Another category of MOOCs mostly emanating from Ivy League colleges in the USA, were more heavily reliant on presentation of the subject matter content and its discussion in short video clips which was supported by multiple choice type quizzes that were moderated and marked by graduate teaching assistants reflecting the learning and teaching *modus operandi* of these campus-based operations. These variants began to be called xMOOCs (see Daniel, 2012; Adams, Yin, Madriz, & Mullen, 2014).

Type of MOOCs notwithstanding, *educators* saw in this development benefits for attracting large numbers of students, especially to graduate seminars with dwindling intakes (Baggaley, 2014). At the operational level, educators saw benefits for them in the anytime, any pace and anywhere flexibility afforded by the approach in terms of scheduling their teaching, research and other commitments (Naidu, 2013a; Peach & Bieber, 2015). Moreover, the use of online learning technologies which were now robust enough could be adopted to support *participatory pedagogies* which promoted a view of learning and teaching that suggested that knowledge and understanding is best developed through *connection, collaboration, cooperation* and *co-creation* among relevant participants (Andersen, & Ponti, 2014; Downes, 2008).

Educational administrators saw in this initiative, an opportunity to showcase and promote their brand with the help of star performers such as Nobel Laureates or high profile teachers and researchers if they had them on staff, on subjects of their particular strengths, and in specialist areas. Much like a bargain sale, or one for the price of two used by entrepreneurs to lure shoppers through their doors, these slim pickings from an organization's course offering served as digital shopfronts, or taster courses as pathways and forays into the global market for potential highly motivated and high achieving students who might want to consider joining the organization for fulltime study (Jona, & Naidu, 2014; Yuan, & Powell, 2013).

Entrepreneurs and venture capitalists saw in this initiative a golden opportunity for profiteering in the education industry (Wolfson, 2013). The technology was now available and reliable enough to be used to offer a high standard of education (a product from a largely English speaking and more developed world) to the masses of students (mostly resident in the less developed world where the market was for this kind of education), and who were hungry for any such educational opportunity, no matter how poor in quality. Anything was better than nothing for students in such educational settings who were eager for further education, and better still, if it came with a foreign and western educational badge or qualification. And if it were from an Ivy League institution, then no questions were asked (see Wolfson, 2013).

17.4 The Case for Open Educational Practices

Despite their rather chequered trajectory, as outlined in the above, the case for *open educational resources* and *massive open online courses* has a solid pedigree in the tradition of *open educational practice*. There are three critical attributes to the concept of open educational practice: 1) *open* access which means inclusive and equal access to educational opportunities without barriers such as prior knowledge and entry qualifications, and ability to pay; 2) *open learning* which is the opportunity to study and learn at anytime, anywhere and at any pace, as well as anyhow irrespective of one's physical location; and 3) *open scholarship* which means the release of educational resources under an open license scheme which permits no-cost access, use, reuse, adaptation, retention and redistribution to others.

The concept of *open access* is deeply grounded in a socio-economic and political agenda which seeks education for all as the path to real freedom and justice (see Sen, 1999). For without education, as Sen argues, one cannot really be part of the mainstream conversation and therefore unable to compete equitably. At the operational level this means not just equal, but equitable access from a position of disadvantage to educational opportunities without having to meet the usual barriers such as prior knowledge and qualifications and ability to pay. In the absence of this, there can be no real freedom and therefore no justice (i.e., not simply political freedom, but freedom to choose as one wishes to).

The concept of *open access* is perhaps best embodied in the development of opportunities for *open, flexible and distance learning* which enables learning at anytime, anywhere and at any pace, as well as anyhow. The classic case for this has been the establishment of the United Kingdom Open University and many similar organizations world over subsequently (The Open University, http://bit.ly/1n2w72l). This type of educational opportunity also involved making available educational resources at no, or a reduced cost to learners especially in resource poor and developing regions of the world. This could be considered a precursor to the current conceptions of *open scholarship* which is regulated release of educational resources under an open license scheme that permits no-cost access, and allows permissions to adopt, adapt, retain and redistribute such resources freely and with appropriate restrictions.

The case for *open, flexible and distance learning* provision has clearly been won as is clear from the growth of open and distance learning educational institutions, as well as practices all over the world and in relation to the value they are adding to socio-economic and political development of societies especially in the developing regions. However, the case for *open scholarship* which comprises the adoption and use of artefacts such as open educational resources and the provision of massive open online courses is not all that clear, and actually far from won (see Weller, 2014).

The key sticking points in relation to this battle have to do with the ethical and moral implications of open educational practices especially in relation to assuring quality of educational provision with integrity, and a duty of care of students as well as staff. And this is the focus of the rest of this chapter.

17.5 Assuring Quality of Educational Provision

But before we explore any of that, let's make clear upfront that open educational practice is a good thing. And there are many good reasons for it which are adequately articulated in this chapter as well as others in this volume. It's good for the students, the teachers and educational organizations. But let's make clear also that engagement with open educational practices (and especially the adoption of OER and MOOCs) will not necessarily improve or assure a high quality of educational provision without careful thought to their integration into educational practice (see Smith, 2016). Furthermore, open educational resources may not be necessarily of any better quality than any other educational resource, just as MOOCs may not be inherently any better than any other type of course (Lowenthal & Hodges, 2015). How a high quality learning experience can be assured in an open educational context needs careful consideration.

Let's think through the confounding issues. In most educational settings, the educational organization assumes a responsibility for providing the best, or at least a high quality educational experience to students who choose to join it. In most cases this responsibility is articulated in a variety of ways including organizational mission and goals, strategic plans and processes, and commitments to teaching and the provision of related academic as well as administrative support services. Students and their parents will often make their choices to enrol and undertake to pay for these services based on these promises. And upon registration, they will be right to expect these services and all other commitments that were made, just as educational organizations would expect from students their best foot forward (Hil, 2016).

A problem arises when either party fails to keep its promise without due cause. For instance, students will run the risk of failure and expulsion from the organization expeditiously in the case of their inability to meet and fulfil the requirements of their academic program or in the case of academic or any other kind of misconduct. But while educational institutions will make all manner of claims about their international reputation and ranking, the high quality of their research staff, and the quality of teaching and related resources, repercussions for failure to deliver on these claims and promises are never as clearly articulated.

There are many reasons for this lack of clarity on the implications of failure to deliver on its promises by educational institutions. For instance, the levels of recruitment and retention of popular or highly qualified staff are never as explicitly linked to the promises the organization will have made to its students about the strength and reputation of its staffing. More often than not, and especially in higher education, the curriculum and its pedagogy is often determined and influenced by individual faculty members or a few people and arbitrary processes including political influences (e.g., State Government of

Victoria, Australia, http://bit.ly/1UW5acZ). Students will have little prior knowledge of what they are going to get in a course and what exactly they will be paying for. In their defence, organizations will argue that the determination of the curriculum and its pedagogy is the domain of experts, and that they are the experts, not novice students who are there to learn. And even though organizations will insist that they have processes in place for it to occur, attempts to seek student feedback on teaching is often so flawed that most efforts fail to allow any meaningful student input into what is included in the curriculum, let alone how it is taught and learned. It is arguable that such below par educational practices amount to a failure on the part of educational institutions to meet their commitments to their students, and as such a neglect of duty of care (see Marshall, 2014).

17.6 Assuring Quality in the Adoption of OER

The case for the adoption of open educational resources at the institutional level is a good example of this kind of arbitrary posturing and the failure of its protagonists and educational institutions to keep their promises about the quality of educational provision. The key point made in favor of the adoption of OER is the ability to mitigate the rising costs of commercially published textbooks and similar educational materials. Yet providing educational resources cheaply to students is rarely proposed as an institutional imperative, and how are open educational resources going to make a student's learning experience any better apart from reducing costs is never made really clear (DeRosa, 2015). Besides, if the reduction of the costs of education for the student were the endgame for an institution, then surely there are many more expedient ways of achieving this like closing down recreational and other non-essential services.

Yet teachers and students are expected to be hunting for and adopting open educational resources, which are valid and reliable without any clear help and assistance with what they are looking for in the first place, or how to be able to recognize them, and evaluate their quality and educational potential before using them. Besides, the implications of this expectation for students and teachers without access to the Internet are not questioned, and those in the non-English speaking world are rarely considered. As most of the OER, currently, seems to be in the English language and most easily portable over the Internet. Protagonists of OER and educational institutions are quite happy to pass this role on to novice teachers and students, after having argued vehemently that the determination of the content of a curriculum was their role and responsibility, and not that of students who are there to learn.

But none of this may be inherently a bad thing as there is much learning going on, on the part of students as well as teachers when they are being encouraged and expected to search for and evaluate educational resources that they can adopt and adapt for their respective needs. The contentious issue has to do with the ethics of these expectations for students and teachers. Placing students and teachers into an uncharted and unsupported learning and teaching environment amounts to a serious dereliction of responsibility by the institution in relation to the quality of educational provision, and as such a neglect of the duty of care of both the students and the staff (see Marshall, 2014). Open content, nor more and more content, in and of itself, will not make for good teaching. What will make for good teaching is the design of relevant, suitable and authentic learning experiences and then selecting appropriate (open) content to support these learning experiences (see Naidu, & Karunanayaka, 2014).

17.7 Assuring Quality in the Adoption of MOOCs

The case for MOOCs is just as problematic if not more, in relation to the quality of educational provision (see Bates, 2012). The strongest points in favour of MOOCs are that they open up access to learning opportunities for a much larger audience, in fact an indefinite number of takers. That is certainly true. MOOCs make it possible for any number of learners from the remotest regions of the world to access content from the best educational organizations without leaving their home or workplace, and listen and learn from the most reputable of experts at no real cost except for their own access to the Internet. Yet these are the key sticking points with MOOCs (see Granger, 2013).

MOOCs are only accessible to those with reliable access to the Internet. And MOOC protagonists will be quick to argue that the goal of MOOCs is to make education openly and freely accessible and furthermore, that this is the future of higher education and indeed education more generally (see Adams, Yin, Madriz, & Mullen, 2014; Coursera, 2013; Koller, & Ng, 2013; Wolfson, 2013; Universities UK, 2013). But what kind and quality of education they are talking about is never made clear? Just because the current crop of MOOCs are emerging from research intensive and Ivy League institutions does not mean that they come with a high quality curriculum and pedagogy (Granger, 2013). In fact, most of the current iterations of MOOCs simply replicate what happens in face-to-face classrooms generally, and many are actually rather poor reflections of common classroom pedagogy, despite Siemens' and Downes' exhortations of MOOCs as participatory learning spaces (see Anderson, 2013). Most contemporary MOOCs tend to simply record a live lecture *in situ* (without much attention to sound quality and movement of the presenter), chunk it and post it online, along with short quizzes to assess learning achievement.

Surely this amounts to a serious neglect of academic responsibility in relation to quality of educational provision. But doing any more, and especially for an infinite number of potential students would obviously require a lot more time, effort, resources, as well as systems and processes for course design and development. In most cases, these implications have not been thought through or made available and were not taken into account. And not because this kind of knowledge and expertise is rare but because the starting point of the development of MOOCs has been the delivery technology which is supposed to carry it through. The long history of learning and teaching in the open, flexible, distance and online mode using a wide range and mixture of media by open and distance learning institutions world over wasn't even considered as a possible source of inspiration and guidance on best practices.

And some of the weakest links in relation to contemporary MOOC pedagogy are *assessment, feedback* and *accreditation* (see Naidu, 2013b; Naidu, & Barberà, 2015). Assessment of learning achievement in most MOOCs is undertaken with the help of multiple choice type questions. Of course there can be robust multiple choice type questions for assessing all types and levels of knowledge and understanding, but they are surely inadequate as the only or primary approach. Moreover, timely and relevant feedback is essential in supporting and promoting learning. There are no shortcuts to this. Good feedback will always require time and effort. Relegating this to a few automated comments on the right or wrong response to multiple choice type questions is inadequate and grossly unfair to students. Furthermore passing this responsibility on to student peers, especially without much supervision and guidance including accreditation and award of badges based on this kind of limited-overs pedagogy, is even more problematic (Norton, 2013, p.27).

Contemporary approaches to MOOC pedagogy may be defensible on the grounds that they serve a variety of purposes and students (see Kizilcec, Piech, & Schneider, 2013). For some takers they offer a top-up on relevant concepts or subject matter, and an uncomplicated quick and easy refresher course might be all they are looking for. For others, it might fulfil the professional development requirements of their workplace and employment (Laurillard, 2016). So a scant offering might not be such a bad thing if it meets its purpose. It is also arguable that the quality of a MOOC is really irrelevant as long as learners on the other end of the line have access to opportunities, that they will never be able to access or afford, and which have the potential to help improve their situation somewhat, never mind by how much. Having access to something is clearly better than having nothing at all. And institutions could rightly argue that if this kind of work is worth doing, then it is worth doing however poorly (see Chesterton, 2007).

But if this were the true motivation and intentions of MOOCs, then one would have expected that the adoption of the print medium (which can be made truly accessible to all) would have been the medium of choice as opposed to the internet and the web. Ah but the print medium is not as nearly as attractive. Therefore, there is no doubt that the technology is a key driver of developments, yet few MOOC promoters are acknowledging the real drivers of MOOC mania. And that's where the purported rationale for MOOCs as a liberating force comes unstuck and the real hidden agenda is revealed.

So what is the real agenda? Organizations see MOOCs as a shop front where potential students can browse at no cost, but if they wanted to buy (i.e., acquire the credit), then either they would have to register, pay for it and take the course of study, or pay to take the assessment and achieve the credit. In this manner MOOCs offer a new pathway to student recruitment. And for that reason, it doesn't matter how many students do not start or drop out from a MOOC, just as it does not matter how many shoppers walk into the store after watching the window display, as even a few more than the usual would be a good outcome (Granger, 2013). MOOCs also offer institutions an avenue to promote their brand, which is why most MOOCs are originating from reputable and research-intensive universities as they are the ones who have something to showcase. However, very few of these institutions are acknowledging the real drivers and motivations of their interest in, and engagement with offering MOOCs on their campuses.

17.8 Integrity and Duty of Care of Students and Staff

Another very important factor that research-intensive and Ivy League institutions are compromising on in their dogged pursuit of even greater prominence and visibility in a globalized economy is research integrity which is a cornerstone of their existence (see Marshall, 2014). While purporting to provide open and free access to educational content and the expertise of publically funded organizations for the common good is laudable, many of these organizations will also acknowledge the use of MOOCs as a way of testing the student market and learning about the business of online education without adopting the usual safeguards such as seeking ethics clearance in order to do so (see Granger, 2013).

Universities will go on *ad nauseam* about their insistence on academic and research integrity, yet they are themselves grossly out of line and guilty of failing to pursue the same high levels of rigor in using real students, real courses, in the name of learning analytics for research and experimentation with their approaches to teaching and learning. Informed consent from students as key stakeholders regarding educational provision, and in this case their use for commercial exploitation is rarely sought, if not ignored (Norton, 2013). Surely, there is a duty of care of the student by the institution that is being compromised here. A student, and especially the freshman type, is a lot more than a client of a product or service. It is arguable that when an institution accepts a student, it undertakes a commitment to educate, nurture and care for that individual both academically and socially. And many institutions, especially those with religious foundations, rightly commit to offering this kind of pastoral care in their mission and goals.

The treatment of staff and institutional expectations for them to engage in open educational practices, including open scholarship, is equally unreasonable and unfair. Like all credible educational resources, there are costs associated with their development and dissemination, and someone has to cover these costs. Passing on these costs to the creators of the content in case of open access publishing for instance, runs the risk of once again, perpetuating inequality by setting up barriers against those without the required funding (usually junior researchers and faculty members), to be able to participate equitably in such open educational practices.

Moreover, many who are asked to, or those who put up their hand to develop MOOCs have no prior experience with the development of such courses, let alone online courses or even components of these courses. Many will be expected to work with no support with online learning experience design, nor any help with the effective and efficient use of the technology that will be used to carry the course (see Bolliger, & Wasilik, 2009). It is no surprise then that most MOOCs mirror what happens in the face-to-face classroom because that is what most MOOC developers are familiar with and know best despite knowing, that teaching online and in the face-to-face mode is not simply about old wine in new bottles. What works in the face-to-face mode will not necessarily work well in the online learning space (Inglis, 2005).

Furthermore, with the adoption of open educational practices, teaching at universities today has become a lot about being able to work with a wide range of technologies in and outside of the classroom as opposed to simply barking from a lectern. It is about supporting learning in a media and an information-rich learning environment, and it is also about coordinating the work of casual teachers and tutors who will be teaching in a course. So it is about managing and coordinating teams. Yet the requirements for the preparation of staff for teaching at the university has not kept pace with these developments in the workplace. Recent reports are suggesting that a PhD is no longer an adequate preparation for teaching at a university (see Ross, 2016). It will be for doing research, but not for teaching because the contemporary teaching environment has moved along so much from when teaching was about communicating one's research. Yet the conventional PhD, which is an increasingly inadequate qualification for teaching at a university, remains an essential criteria for appointment to academe (Group of Eight, 2013). Universities have commitments and responsibilities towards the professional development of their staff in relation to teaching quality enhancement, but few address this responsibility rigorously and systemically.

17.9 Concluding Remarks

Education is a public good. For without education there is no real freedom to be able to make informed decisions, to take advantage of learning opportunities and make meaningful choices that impact our daily lives. In the absence of money or some such privilege, education is the greatest leveler, for it affords us the wherewithal to be able to compete equitably, especially from a position of disadvantage. And without being able to compete openly and fairly, there can be no real justice. So the more widely and openly accessible education is, the better are our chances for meeting goals such as those set by the United Nations in relation to its millennium development and sustainable development agenda, particularly in relation to providing an inclusive and a high quality education and lifelong learning opportunities for all.

The adoption for *open educational practices* is integral to meeting these agenda. It includes access to learning opportunities, anytime, anywhere and at any pace, as well as the release of educational resources at no cost to the user, and with permissions for adaptation to local conditions. Apart from these preconditions, open educational resources and learning opportunities such as MOOCs are not inherently any different from any other educational resource or practice. And educational resources and learning opportunities, however open and flexible, will not, by themselves ensure a high quality learning experience. So regardless of the hype and hysteria around the case for all things open and cost free, open educational resources and MOOCs will not save the day for us. What will save the day for us and ensure a high quality learning experience is the effective, and efficient integration of open educational practices (as well as open educational practices) in the design of productive pedagogies and learning experiences for our students (see Gore, Griffiths, & Ladwig, 2004; Naidu, 2013c).

17.10 Chapter References

Adams, C., Yin, Y., Madriz, L. F. V., & Mullen, C. S. (2014): A phenomenology of learning large: the tutorial sphere of xMOOC video lectures, *Distance Education, 35*(2), 1-15. doi: 10.1080/01587919.2014.917701.

Allen, I. E., & Seaman, J. (2014): *Opening the curriculum: Open educational resources in U.S. higher education, 2014.* Oakland, CA: Babson Survey Research Group. Retrieved from http://www.online learningsurvey.com/oer.html.

Andersen, R., & Ponti, M. (2014): Participatory pedagogy in an open educational course: challenges and opportunities, *Distance Education, 35*(2), 1-16. doi: 10.1080/01587919.2014.917703.

Anderson, T. (2013): Promise and/or peril: MOOCs and open and distance education. *Commonwealth of Learning.* Retrieved from http://www.ethicalforum.be/sites/default/files/MOOCsPromisePeril.pdf

Baggaley, J. (2014): MOOCS: digesting the facts, *Distance Education, 35*(2), 1-5. doi: 10.1080/01587919.2014.919710.

Baggaley, J., & James, S. (2016): The fog of online learning, *Distance Education (37)*1, 121-129, doi: 10.1080/01587919.2016.1153962.

Bates, T. (2012): What's right and what's wrong about Coursera-style MOOCs. Online learning and distance education resources moderated by Tony Bates, August 5, 2012, http://www.tonybates.ca/2012/08/05/whats-right-and-whats-wrong-about-coursera-style-moocs/.

Bolliger, D.U., & Wasilik, O. (2009): Factors influencing faculty satisfaction with online teaching and learning in higher education. *Distance Education, 30*(1), 103-116, doi: 10.1080/01587910902845949.

Coursera (2013): About Coursera, https://www.coursera.org/about.

Chesterton, G. K. (2007): What's Wrong with the World? Dover Publications (first published 1900).

Daniel, J. S. (2012): Making Sense of MOOCs: Musings in a maze of myth, paradox and possibility, *Journal of Interactive Media in Education,* http://jime.open.ac.uk/articles/10.5334/2012-18/.

DeRosa, R. (2015, January 9): Beyond the buck: An expanded vision of open access, http://bit.ly/1VhZVET.

Downes, S. (2008): Places to Go: Connectivism & Connective Knowledge, http://bit.ly/1iyM0I0.

Goodyear, P., Carvalho, L. (2013): The Analysis of Complex Learning Environments, in H. Beetham & R. Sharpe (Eds.), *Rethinking Pedagogy for a Digital Age: Designing for 21st Century Learning 2nd Edition*, New York: Routledge, 49-63.

Gore, J. M., Griffiths, T., & Ladwig, J. G. (2004): Towards better teaching: productive pedagogy as a framework for teacher education. *Teaching and Teacher Education*, (20)4, 375–387.

Granger, B. (2013): *Introduction to MOOCs: Avalanche, Illusion or Augmentation?* Policy Briefs published by the UNESCO Institute for Information Technologies in Education, 8 Kedrova St., Bldg. 3, Moscow, 117292, Russian Federation.

Group of Eight (2013, March): The Changing PhD: Discussion paper. The Group of Eight Group of Eight House Level 2, 101 Northbourne Avenue Turner ACT 2612 www.go8.edu.au. https://go8.edu.au/sites/default/files/docs/the-changing-phd_final.pdf

Hil, R. (2016): Against the Neoliberal University. *Arena: The Australian Magazine of Left Political, Social and Cultural Commentary, No. 140*, 12-14. Arena Printing and Publishing Pty Ltd. Fitzroy, Melbourne, Australia.

History of the Open University, The Open University, http://bit.ly/1n2w72l.

Inglis, A. (2005): Quality improvement, quality assurance, and benchmarking: comparing two frameworks for managing quality processes in open and distance learning. *The International Review of Research in Open and Distributed Learning, 6* (1), 1-13, http://www.irrodl.org/index.php/irrodl/article/view/221/867.

Jona, K., & Naidu, S. (2014*): MOOCs: emerging research. Distance Education,* 35(2), 141-144. doi:10.1080/01587919.2014.928970.

Kizilcec, R. F., Piech, C. & Schneider, E. (2013): Deconstructing Disengagement: Analyzing Learner Subpopulations in Massive Open

Online Courses, http://rene.kizilcec.com/wp-content/uploads/
2013/02/Kizilcec-Piech-Schneider-2013-

Koller, D., & Ng, A. (2013): The Online Revolution: Report from Year 1, presented at Coursera Partners' Conference, University of Pennsylvania.

Laurillard, D. (2016): The educational problem that MOOCs could solve: professional development for teachers of disadvantaged students, *Research in Learning Technology* 2016, 24, http://dx.doi.org/10.3402/rlt.v24.

Lowenthal, P. R., & Hodges, C. B. (2015): In Search of Quality: Using Quality Matters to Analyze the Quality of Massive, Open, Online Courses (MOOCs). *International Review of Research in Open and Distributed Learning,* Volume 16(5), 83-101, http://www.irrodl.org/index.php/irrodl/article/view/2348/3435.

Marshall, S. (2014): Exploring the ethical implications of MOOCs, *Distance Education,* 35(2), 1-13. doi: 10.1080/01587919.2014.917706.

Naidu, S. & Karunanayaka, S. (2014): Engines of Education: Integrating OER in Learning and Teaching. In: S. Karunanayaka & S. Naidu (Eds.). *Integrating OER in Educational Practice: Practitioner Stories.* The Open University of Sri Lanka, 3-22.

Naidu, S. (2013a): Transforming MOOCs and MOORFAPs into MOOLOs, *Distance Education,* 34(3), 253-255, doi: 10.1080/01587919.2013.842524.

Naidu, S. (2013b): *Foreword.* In Assessment *and evaluation of time factors in online teaching and learning,* edited by Elena Barberà and Peter Reimann, New York, Idea Group.

Naidu, S. (2013c): Instructional design models for optimal learning. In Moore, M.G. (Ed.), *The Handbook of Distance Education*, 3rd edition, New York, Routledge, 268-281.

Naidu, S. (2016): The case for open educational practice, *Distance Education, 37*(1), 1-3. DOI: 10.1080/01587919.2016.1157010.

Naidu, S., & Barberà, E. (2015): Editorial: The Weakest Link -- Assessment and Accreditation in MOOCs, *Special Themed Issue: Assessment and Accreditation in MOOCs*. Digital Education Review - Number 25, June 2014- http://greav.ub.edu/der/.

Norton, A. (April 2013). *The online evolution: when technology meets tradition in higher education*, Grattan Institute, Melbourne, Victoria, Australia, http://grattan.edu.au/wp-content/uploads/2014/04/186_online_higher_education.pdf.

Peach, H.G., & Bieber, J.P. (2015). Faculty and Online Education as a Mechanism of Power. Distance Education, 36(1), 26-40. doi: 10.1080/01587919.2015.1019971.

Ross, J. (2016): PhDs failing to make the grade with uni employers. *The Australian (Higher Education Segment).* March 30th.

Sen, A. (1999): *Development as Freedom.* Oxford: Oxford University Press.

Siemens, G. (2008): Learning and knowing in networks: Changing roles for educators and designers, http://bit.ly/1hJynVC.

Siemens, G., & Downes S. (2011): Connectivism and connective knowledge (course: CCK11). University of Manitoba, http://cck11.mooc.ca/.

Smith, M. (2016): *Feature: open is as open does*, http://roer4d.org/wp-content/uploads/2014/01/ROER4D-Newsletter-February-March-2016.pdf.

State Government of Victoria, Australia, Gender Identity, http://bit.ly/1UW5acZ.

Universities UK (2013): Massive Open Online Courses: Higher education's digital moment?, London, UK, http://www.universitiesuk. ac.uk/policy-and-analysis/reports/Pages/massive-open-online-courses.aspx.

Weller, M. (2014): The *battle for open: How openness won and why it doesn't feel like victory*. London: Ubiquity Press. doi: 10.5334/bam.

Wikipedia, Massive Open Online Course, http://bit.ly/1k50ijB.

Wiley, D. (2014): Iterating towards openness: pragmatism over zeal, Retrieved from http://opencontent.org/blog/archives/3221.

Wiley, D. (2016, January 29). The concensus around "openness", Blog post. *Iterating toward openness*, http://opencontent.org/blog/archives/ 4397.

Wolfson, L. (2013, June 18): Venture capital needed for 'broken' U.S. education, Thrun says. *Bloomberg News*, http://buswk.co/PJS58G.

Yuan, L., & Powell, S., (2013): "MOOCs and Open Education: Implications for Higher Education", http://publications.cetis.ac.uk/2013/ 667.

UNIVERSITAS TERBUKA INDONESIA OPEN POLICY: SECURING THE RIGHTS TO KNOWLEDGE AND HIGHER EDUCATION

Daryono & Sri Sedyainingsih

18.1 Background

Indonesia has been preoccupied by long lasting issues related to access, equity and quality of higher education. Just in a recent decade, higher education access has improved substantially by the increased higher education participation rate. This becomes possible due to the progressive educational policy to allocate twenty percent of state budget into education sector as it was only five percent. The progressive policy, however, has not yet resolved the problem of quality and equity issues between Java where major quality higher education institutions are located and out of Java where the scarcity of quality higher educational resources are present. This is also worsened by the geographical conditions in which they are not well distributed. As the only Open University in Indonesia, Universitas Terbuka (UT) has been mandated to open access to higher education and reduce knowledge gaps by producing quality of educational materials available to public. Since its establishment, UT utilizes open and flexible learning to enable learner studying on their needs. In 2012, UT established its open policy for educational materials produced by UT. This policy aims at users of

Open Educational Resources in Indonesia and respectively reduce knowledge divide. This article articulates the ethical dimension of UT open policy.

18.2 Introduction

Human development index (HDI) is currently serving as an important indicator to reveal the level of welfare and equal access to education. The HDI shows that higher HDI is associated with the higher level of human development and welfare. One of the important indicators is the access to knowledge and education to enable community optimally developing themselves on their own purposes and virtues (UNDP, 2012). Indonesia HDI has been progressing slowly since the last ten years. The slow progress of HDI is caused in particular by the low percentage of secondary and post-secondary educational attainment. The low educational attainment is also shown by disparity of the number and the quality of educational institutions between Java and out of Java.

Considering the wide geographical condition of Indonesia which consists of more than seventeen thousand island, the educational infrastructure and human resource capacity gaps are indispensable. Most higher educations with good quality is located in Java. Accordingly, the quality of human resources is also centered in Java Island. However, the Internet infrastructures have been fast-growing, covering major islands of Indonesia. It is predicted that in the next five years, the number of internet access increases rapidly. This is also supported by the Indonesia Master Plan on Internet Infrastructure Development to promote Indonesia into new digital era in 2025 (MP3EI, 2014).

Asian Higher education in general still faces great challenges of access, equity and quality (Dhanarajan and Abeywardena, 2010). The large number of higher education providers throughout the country has facilitated access, and the Universitas Terbuka (UT) has easier access to higher education from the remote areas of th. has been increased substantially in the last ten years as the go committed to allocate twenty percent of state budget into edu However, there are still issues relating to equity and quality that ha. be addressed, such as tuition, flexibility, resource availability, standa. and legal infrastructure. Equity issues continue to challenge policy makers as they try to ease participation disparities between the rich, the middle class and the poor as well between rural and urban populations (Dhanarajan, 2014). Similarly, quality concerns also preoccupy both central and local governments as education sector has been decentralised to local government. The challenges of access, equity and quality in one hand and the promising digital development in the future on the other may reveal different higher educational landscape in particular the role of open and flexible university in the near future. This article discusses two consecutive impacts of UT Open Policy in addressing the long concurrent issues of access, equity and quality in higher education: first, democratization of higher education and secondly, eradicating the knowledge divide.

18.3 Democratisation of Higher Education

Indonesia higher education access and quality have still been challenging due to demographic and geographic constraints. Prior to local autonomy policy in 2000s, higher education policy was extremely centralized under central government. Currently higher education policies are being restructured by providing greater roles of local government to contribute on the development of local higher education institution. In line with local autonomy, the progressive higher educational policy has also been introduced by allocating more authorities and roles of the local government. Within five-year period successfully increased higher education participation rate one percent to thirty two percent accordingly (OECD/Asian ment Bank, 2015).

vever quality divide of higher education between Java and out of is still continuously presence. Out of 122 public universities, there e only 20% of them located out of Java island and only one of them is listed on the top-ten public universities. In addition, among more than 3900 private universities, only less than 10% private universities have been accredited as a good performance and most of them are in Java as well (http://forlap.dikti.go.id/perguruantinggi/homegraphpt). Yet, a good part of human resources is centred in Java island. Along with colonial legacy of Java as a centre of administration and industrialization, the migration of high skilled graduates into Java island has also been indispensable until now. Currently Java island is inhabited by about 60% of Indonesia population (National Statistics Bureau, 2012). Considering the higher education quality divide and the outflow human resources from out of Java island, there need an education system to enable students to receive a quality higher education from their domicile. It is only open and distance education system that would be able to serve these purposes.

The establishment of Universitas Terbuka (UT) in 1984, that utilizes open and distance modes, was primarily to scale up higher education participation and to continuously upgrade the teacher competence and qualification. These two missions were set to be accomplished during the UT first mission. Considering the massive amount of high school graduates who were unable to be accommodated in face to face (f2f) university, and the limited funding and infrastructure to establish new f2f university, only the Open University system may overcome these two major constrains. In addition, considering geographic conditions of Indonesia, the distance higher education which highly relies on educational media enable the need to reach student living in very remote area.

In the 32 years of serving the nation UT has transformed itself into the only higher education in Indonesia promoting flexible and inclusive higher education by adopting open policy (UT, 2012). The open policy consists of three major principles of open enrolment, open admission and open content (licensing). The open enrolment ensures the flexibility of students to enrol in the program on their needs that is open during the year around. This in the future may adopts self-pace pedagogy to enable student learning on their pace. Respectively the open admission allows students admission without any restrictions of demographic variables, geographic location and their primary identity. To promote equity, UT is currently producing the audio digital learning materials to serve students with visual impairment. Furthermore, as part of public higher education institution's obligation UT owned digital learning material in the format of text, audio and video are now dedicated to public by adopting Creative Common license. This open content or license is very important to eradicate knowledge divide between Java island where the major universities are located and out of Java Islands where a shortage of quality educational resources.

By adopting open policy, UT is best fit to serve the Indonesia with the world's largest archipelago with over 17,000 islands and over 80% of nation comprised of water. With the large and heterogeneous demographic condition of over 245 million people in 2014, and consisting of various ethnic and regional cultures with over 1,000 local languages and dialects spoken among different ethnic groups, UT may serve politically as a tool to promote Indonesia's unity and prosperity (UT, 2015). Considering these conditions UT has been designed to be both flexible and inexpensive, by focusing on serving potential students who, due to various constraints, including lack of funding, living in isolated and rural areas and working, lack the opportunity to attend the face-to-face mode of higher education.

In 2014, over 400,000 students, residing in different parts of the country and some living overseas, enrolled in UT. Over 95% of these students are working adults. UT has major roles to play in developing quality human resources needed for the nation's sustainable development. Since its establishment, UT has enrolled over 1.5 million students and has produced over 1 million alumni, working in various professional fields. As an open and distance teaching university, UT depends on the advancement of Information and Communication Technology (ICT) (UT, 2015). Since each establishment, UT has use ICT to provide Internet based information services for general academic and administrative information services. UT's innovation in the use of internet-based teaching and learning can be seen as a pioneering initiative in the Indonesian higher education system. UT has implemented and continually improved its online services, including those designed for tutorials, web-based supplementary materials, self-assessment, examination results dissemination, online counselling, information dissemination, and online examination. Other online services are being developed to improve teaching and learning as well as administrative services for students. However UT's conventional delivery system through printed learning materials is also preserved to serve students' preference and those who live in very remote area of Indonesia where the ICT infrastructures have not yet been certain.

UT students cover various demographic and geographic conditions that ensure the inclusivity of services. Among major islands in Indonesia, students resided in Java Island are still predominant. This is due to the fact that Java Island contributes to about 65% of Indonesia population. However UT student located in other islands are comparable in term of the proportion of the population. It currently becomes important when UT enables to serve the Indonesia's workers, majority as a domestic (informal) worker, living overseas where they unable to be served by Indonesia higher education to secure their rights to education. UT' students living overseas are growing steadily in 30 countries accounted for 2% of UT's student body. The distribution of student's geographic location is presented in the following figure:

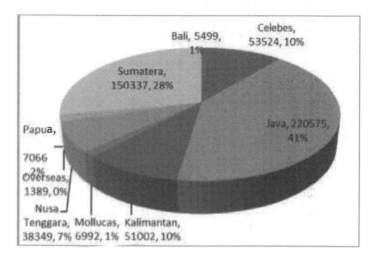

Source: UT Annual Report 2014.

In terms of gender and age UT students are predominantly by female middle age students. This may reflect current Indonesia demographic features that the fast growing numbers of women enter into labour market. These features may also represent UT major student body who are teachers.

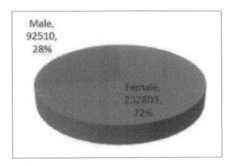

Source: UT Annual Report 2014.

It is interesting that the distribution of students in term of their age currently varies across ages. The age of students which were previously dominated by adult learner is currently also dominated by growing number of fresh high school graduates --accounted for 27% of student body. This shifting figure of student age reveals that Open Education has been perceived to fulfil the need of young age student. Those features are shown in the following figure.

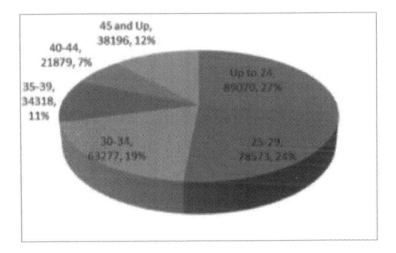

Source: UT Annual Report 2014.

As part of the national mission to ascertain access to higher education, UT reaches students with financial burden who are living in very remote areas. Through special scholarship program UT provides free tuition and living expenses to enable those potential students fulfil their dream to attain higher education degree. This program has successfully implemented for about five years and the success of rate of those students are remarkably high (UT 2014). This has proven that UT's Open and Inclusive Policy enables to democratize higher education and in the future is expected to eradicate inequality and injustice and ensure the increased prosperity and welfare for the disadvantage community living in remote area of Indonesia.

18.4 Eradicating the Knowledge Divide

UT's open content policy serves an important role for the success of Open Educational Resources (OER) implementation in Indonesia. As having the importance of OER to reduce knowledge and educational resource divide among educational institutions, UT developed learning materials to be open to public (Daryono and Belawati, 2010). Since the beginning, UT's learning materials have been widely used by students and lecturer from other universities. The limited availability of quality learning materials in many parts of Indonesia in particular out of Java Island has made them to use UT printed learning materials which are written by nation-wide scale experts. Based on the printed learning materials UT develops multimedia learning materials including video lecture, audio broadcast, web based learning supplement, and dry laboratory (virtual laboratory). The UT's owned learning materials are now declared to public and adopt Creative Common License to enable re-use and repurpose them.

Considering the needs of teachers across Indonesia in particular out of Java Island to quality learning materials, UT developed online teacher forum in 2008 administered by Faculty of Teacher Training and Education. A number of teaching resources were developed by the USAID project on the development of primary education infrastructures. Parallel to the online teacher forum (*Guru Portal Online*), the other departments have similarly opened up the educational material including the video streaming resources, course curricula, research articles and other digital resources. Having considered the importance of OER in the future in 2012 UT enacted the decree to adopt Creative Common Licenses for major learning resources. This policy aims at providing necessary legal basis of intellectual property right governance in UT. This policy has not been applicable to printed learning materials as the writers of UT learning materials come from other universities which still lack of OER awareness.

In line with the Open Policy, Indonesia government has made exclusionary provision of the production and reproduction of knowledge in the Indonesian Copy Right Law as it is used for educational and research purposes and for disadvantage community (Law Number 19 of 2012). These provisions allow for the development of a Commons environment especially in promoting OER. Parallel to the principles of fair use and fair dealing to educational materials are also adopted by Copy Right Law 19 of 2002. Following the exclusionary clauses of copy right exemption, the Law No. 12 of 2012 on Higher Education was enacted and stipulated that the government shall develop open educational resources. This law serves as a foundation of the Higher Education Institution to implement the provision of OER in Indonesia.

Along with the open content policy the substantial growing of Internet users in Indonesia, the need of quality content is indispensable. The culture of knowledge sharing becomes the backbone of information society (Castle, 2010). As information becomes overwhelmed over the internet there need a content management system (CMS) to enable filtering and selecting the quality of information and knowledge to be used for common goods and university role becomes important to develop CMS. In Indonesia the internet user grows substantially since the last five years and it is predicted that it steadily grows in the near future. The growing Internet users show a promising future to transform into digital era even though Indonesia network readiness is still considered low compared to other ASEAN countries. In 2013 Indonesia networked readiness index is 3.7, at same level as Viet Nam but It is lower compared to Malaysia 4.8, Brunei Darussalam 4.4 and Singapore 5.8 respectively (APEC, 2015). The government however has committed to accelerate the development of Internet infrastructure by developing National Plan on Accelerating and Widening Economic Development through the use of Internet and Communication Technology (Kominfo, 2015). About 63 thousand of Mobile Internet Broadband are currently installed in sub district/county to enable village inter-connectivity program. This program aims at amplifying and extending the information and knowledge exchange and sharing. The growing internet user and penetration are predicted in the following figures.

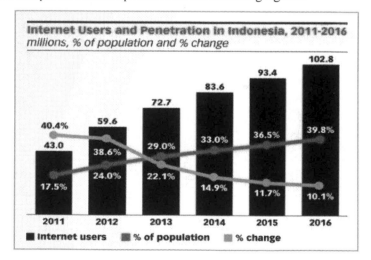

Source: Bayu S.R. (2013) Digital Landscape in Indonesia: Population, Mobile and eCommerce. eMarketer 2012.

The UT OER policy provides a legal basis of OER development by adopting Creative Common licenses. The number of UT's academics to use OER in their online learning is steadily increasing as they may perceive benefits. There are various modus of the adopting and localizing the OER. Many academics prefer the attribution license and localize them into Indonesian situation. The increased UT's academics awareness of OER may provide positive signal on the culture of knowledge sharing. The following figure reveals the growing awareness of academics toward the benefit OER to be integrated into their online learning.

18.5 OER Integration into UT Online-Learning

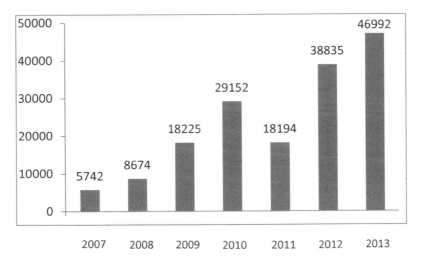

Source: Hewindati (2014) The Spirit of UT Openness, paper presented in seminar: Positioning e-Learning in An Open and Global Education Arena, UT, 13 March 2014.

Along with the movement of open content, OERs seem to have been increasingly received as highly recognizable references by both learner and educator. The OER have also substantially helped educator and learner to locate the best available educational resources and been adopted into various learning activities (Daryono and Tian Belawati, 2010). The flexibility and openness of OER are among the preferred features to enable user to adjust it in any learning situation and to support UT's open policy.

Having been a success of the OER's adoption, UT launched massive open online course as UT's community services in 2014. These courses are designed as OER based courses to serve community who is willing to upgrade their knowledge and understanding. As part of the UT's mission to populate the open online course, this program aims at providing quality online learning experience to the community at large. The learner's participation is steadily increasing but it requires more promotion and advocacy as the MOOCs has not yet been popular to the general people. The UT's MOOCs participation is presented in the following figure.

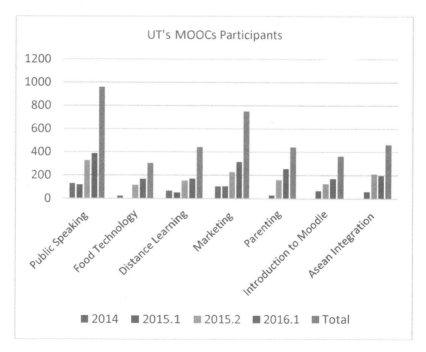

18.6 Conclusion

Major roles of Open University to address access, equity and quality have still encountered a gap between the "is" and the "ought". Open university, in which its major mission is to promote inclusive higher education, faces great challenges due to the perceived quality as a second-class university and lack of self-independent learning culture. However in line with increasing awareness of the Open Education system and the rapid changes of the Information and Communication technology, the UT's Open Policy may have contributed to reduce this gap and enabled to promote equal access to higher education and to decrease knowledge divide in Indonesia. Furthermore the fast growing ICT infrastructures require progressive open higher education to response the fast changing higher education landscape in the future. The adoption of Open Policy need to be guaranteed to ensure the university governance addressing ethical issues of access, equity and quality as part of the inclusive higher education policy.

18.7 Chapter References

Asia Pacific Economic Cooperation (APEC) (2014) https://www.kominfo.go.id/content/detail/5296/rencana-strategis-kementerian-kominfo-2015-2019/0/program_prioritas, accessed by 6 October 2014.

Bayu S.R. (2013): *Digital Landscape in Indonesia: Population, Mobile and eCommerce.* eMarketer 2012.

Belawati T. (2014): *Toward Open Movement*, Jakarta: Universitas Terbuka.

Castle, M (2010): *The Rise of Network Society: Information Age: Economy, Society and Culture.*

Daryono and Tian Belawati (2010): Prospects and Challenges for Introducing Open Educational Resources in Indonesia, in: *Open Education Resources: An Asian Perspectives*, Dhanarajan and Porter ed. Canada: Commonwealth of Learning.

Dhanarajan, G (2014): OER Educational Resources in Indonesia – A Review (unpublished).

Dhanarajan G and Ishan Abeywardena, (2010): Higher Education and Open Educational Resources in Asia: An Overview, in *Open Educational Resources: An Asian Perspectives*, Dhanarajan and David Porter ed. Canada: Commonwealth of Learning.

Hewindati (2014): The Spirit of UT Openness, paper presented in seminar: Positioning e-Learning in An Open and Global Education Arena, UT, 13 March 2014.

Indonesian Statistics Bureau (2012) Indonesian Population Report, https://www.bps.go.id/

Kementerian Konunikasi dan Informasi (2014): https://www.kominfo.go.id/content/detail/5296/rencana-strategis-kementerian-kominfo-2015-2019/0/program_prioritas, accessed by 6 October 2014.

Master Plan Percepatan dan Perluasan Pembangunan Ekoniomi Indonesia (2014): http://www.indonesia-investments.com/projects/government-development-plans/masterplan-for-acceleration-and-expansion-of-indonesias-economic-development-mp3ei/item306. Accessed by 16 October 2014

OECD/Asian Development Bank (2015): *Education in Indonesia: Rising to the Challenge*, Paris: OECD Publishing,

UNDP (2012): *The Rise of the South: Human Progress in a Diverse World*, UNDP.

United Nation (2015): Sustainable Development Goals clearly determine on the 4th objective to promote equitable and inclusive education which may be only achieved by flexible and open education, http://www.un.org/sustainabledevelopment/ sustainable-development-goals/, accessed by 2015.

Universitas Tebuka (2012): UT Decree on Open License.

Universitas Terbuka (2014): UT Annual Report, Jakarta: Universitas Terbuka.

Wicaksono, T.Y. and Friawan, D. (2011): Recent development in Higher Education in Indonesia: Issues and Challenges *in Financing Higher Education & Economic Development in East Asia*, Armstrong S. and Chapman B. (Eds.), Australian National University E Press. Canberra, Australia.

19

THE ADVANTAGES
OF DISTANCE LEARNING

Brad Huddleston

The concept of distance learning is not as new as one might think. Its roots go all the way back to 1892 when the first university-level distance learning program was developed by the University of Chicago. The United States Postal Service was used for course correspondence. Distance education then took advantage of radio in 1923 and television by 1963.[1]

Just to be clear on our definitions, distance learning "is a way of learning remotely without being in regular face-to-face contact with a teacher in the classroom".[2] Distance learning is synonymous with *distance education*. "Hybrid" or "blended" education seeks "to take advantage of the best features of both face-to-face and online learning."[3]

By the 1980's, classrooms around the world were beginning to be introduced to personal computers. The first personal computer appeared

---

[1] Distance Learning Has Been Around Since 1892, You Big MOOC. James Marshall Crotty, 14 Nov 2012 http://www.forbes.com/sites/jamesmarshallcrotty/2012/11/14/distance-learning-has-been-around-since-1892-you-big-mooc/#4e65861c5bf7

[2] What is Distance Learning? Simon Midgley. The Complete University Guide. http://www.thecompleteuniversityguide.co.uk/distance-learning/what-is-distance-learning/

[3] About Hybrid. University of Wisconsin. http://www4.uwm.edu/ltc/hybrid/about_hybrid/

in 1981 and weighed in at a whopping 10.8 kg (24 lb).[4] Sometimes excitement overrides practicality, but there was a sense that "the future is now" and down that path they went. Contrary to some modern notions, each student being required to have their own computing device is not all that new. The very first school one-to-one laptop program was introduced in 1990 to grade 5 girls at Methodist Ladies' College in Melbourne, Australia.[5] At this point you might be guessing that each 10-year-old girl received an Apple computer. Not so. It was a Toshiba T1000SE.[6]

These are very exciting times in the world of education. Ever since computer scientist Tim Berners-Lee invented the modern version of the World Wide Web back in 1990,[7] educators saw the incredible potential to enhance and accelerate distance learning in ways that could not have been previously imagined. Because of this new technology of interconnectedness, these computers could now be networked globally. Combine that with technology advancing at an exponential pace and prices decreasing in many cases, distance learning could now take advantage of information sharing far beyond the local classroom and be made available to everyone.

19.1 Creative Engineering to Expand the Internet

Although the internet is also referred to as the World Wide Web, there are still large swaths of the world without access. Some very

---

[4] The Evolution of Technology in the Classroom. Purdue University Online. http://online.purdue.edu/ldt/learning-design-technology/resources/evolution-technology-classroom
[5] (25 Years Ago) The First School One-to-One Laptop Program. Audrey Watters. 12 Feb 2015. http://hackeducation.com/2015/02/12/first-one-to-one-laptop-program
[6] Ibid.
[7] Who Invented the Internet? History. Ask History. Evan Andrews. 18 Dec 2013. www.history.com/news/ask-history/who-invented-the-internet

creative engineering attempts are being made to make the internet available in the most remote regions on earth. For example, in the summer of 2016, Google's *Project Loon* experimented with launching internet-beaming balloons into the stratosphere over areas such as Sri Lanka[8] and Peru. Google managed to keep a balloon over Peru for 98 days.[9] Facebook co-founder Mark Zuckerberg has announced that his company will be making web access available from space. A satellite named *Amos-6* will take aim at large parts of sub-Saharan Africa.[10] Facebook is also experimenting with a high-altitude solar-powered drone named *Aquila* to bring the internet to faraway parts of the world.[11]

The motives for bringing the internet to isolated regions of the planet are, no doubt, many. Distance education stands to be one of the beneficiaries of such mind-boggling engineering.

19.2 Unintended Consequences

Almost no one disputes the potential efficacy of computer-aided, distance and blended learning. However, there have been a number of unintended consequences due to the overuse and misuse of ever-invasive technology. When the modern technology revolution hit in the 1990's, we did not have terms such as:

- Sexting
- Video game addiction

---

[8] Google's Project Loon: Now its internet-beaming balloon tests take off in Sri Lanka. Liam Tung. 16 Feb 2016. http://www.zdnet.com/article/googles-project-loon-now-its-internet-beaming-balloon-tests-take-off-in-sri-lanka/

[9] Google's Inernet-Beaming Ballon Gets a New Pilot: AI. Cade Metz. 23 Sept 2016. https://www.wired.com/2016/09/project-loon-google-brings-ai-skies/

[10] Facebook satellite to beam internet to remote regions of Africa. Sam Thielman. 6 Oct 2015. https://www.theguardian.com/technology/2015/oct/05/facebook-mark-zuckerberg-internet-access-africa

[11] Facebook's solar-powered internet plane takes flight. Sean Farrell. 21 July 2016. https://www.theguardian.com/business/2016/jul/21/facebook-solar-powered-internet-plane-test-flight-aquila

- Cyber-bullying
- Digital Addiction
- Internet Addiction Disorder
- Facebook Depression
- Nomophobia (fear of going without your phone)
- FOMO (Fear Of Missing Out)
- Text Neck[12]
- Revenge Porn
- Phantom Ringing Syndrome[13]
- Cybersickness[14]
- Cyberchondria[15]
- The Google Effect[16]
- Digital Detox

Not only is this list far from complete, it is ever-growing. What has become apparent to those of us who study these issues is that the scales of technology have been tipping in favor of the negative side for a very long time, and if we were to be honest, since the beginning. If we are going to be able to use technology to its maximum positive benefit, much self-discipline will be required to steer clear of what we now know, thanks to neuroscience, is clearly negatively affecting our brains.

---

[12] A Modern Spine Ailment: Text Neck. Stephen Shoshany, DC, CCEP. Spine-health , 6 Nov 2015. http://www.spine-health.com/blog/modern-spine-ailment-text-neck

[13] Eight new mental illnesses brought to you by the Internet. Evan Dashevsky. PCWorld. 16 Oct 2013. http://www.pcworld.com/article/2054386/eight-new-mental-illnesses-brought-to-you-by-wait-for-it-the-internet.html

[14] Ibid.

[15] Ibid.

[16] Ibid.

19.3 Neuroscience and Ethics

As the negative psychological and emotional side effects of an over-saturated technology culture continued to raise alarm bells, neuroscience took note and has stepped in to attempt to help us better understand what is going on in the brain. A 2012 article in *The Atlantic* titled "Exploiting the Neuroscience of Internet Addiction" described the ethical dilemma this way:

> "The leaders of internet companies face an interesting, if also morally questionable, imperative: either they hijack neuroscience to gain market share and make large profits, or they let competitors do that and run away with the market."[17]

The article goes on to give an example from the video game industry:

> "Gaming companies talk openly about creating a "compulsion loop", which works roughly as follows: the player plays the game; the player achieves the goal; the player is awarded new content; which causes the player to want to continue playing with the new content and re-enters the loop."[18]

You can also think of the compulsion loop as a dopamine loop. Although dopamine has many functions in the brain, it is most commonly associated with the pleasure system and produces feelings of enjoyment.[19] Dopamine causes us to seek out pleasurable activities such

---

[17] Exploiting the Neuroscience of Internet Addiction. The Atlantic. Bill Davidow. 18 July 2012.
[18] Ibid.
[19] Dopamine Neurotransmitter: The role of neurotransmitter dopamine in movement and cognition, Psychologist World. https://www.psychologistworld.com/biological/neurotransmitters/dopamine.php

as sex, food, drugs,[20] video games,[21] social media,[22] and pornography.[23] Dopamine is not necessarily our enemy. In fact, dopamine is necessary for learning.[24] The issue is when we get *too much* dopamine. In an article titled *Why Limit Screen Time? Reasons You Should Limit Screen Time*, Sherrelle Walker writes:

> "Screen time causes the release of dopamine, a chemical that contributes to learning and concentration. As a result, our brains may become desensitized to the effects of normal levels of dopamine, making it hard to concentrate and focus on non-screen-based stimuli."[25]

19.4 I No Longer Feel Anything - Anhedonia

Clinical psychologist Dr. Archibald Hart describes a condition known as *Anhedonia* in his excellent book titled *Thrilled to Death: How the Endless Pursuit of Pleasure is Leaving Us Numb*. Anhedonia refers to the reduced ability to experience pleasure. And it is a phenomenon

---

[20] Why We're All Addicted to Texts, Twitter and Google. Susan Weinschenk, Ph.D. Psychology Today. 12 Sep 2012. https://www.psychologytoday.com/blog/brain-wise/201209/why-were-all-addicted-texts-twitter-and-google
[21] Brains of Excessive Gamers Similar to Addicts. Jennifer Walsh. LIVESCIENCE. 15 Nov 2011. http://www.livescience.com/17033-gamer-brain-reward-system.html
[22] Social Media Triggers a Dopamine High. Molly Soat. American Marketing Association. https://www.ama.org/publications/MarketingNews/Pages/feeding-the-addiction.aspx
[23] Brain scans of porn addicts: what's wrong with this picture? Norman Doidge. The Guardian. 26 Sep 2013. https://www.theguardian.com/commentisfree/2013/sep/26/brain-scans-porn-addicts-sexual-tastes
[24] Dopamine and Learning: What the Brain's Reward Center Can Teach Educators. Martha Burns, Ph.D. The Science of Learning Blog. 18 Sep 2012. http://www.scilearn.com/blog/dopamine-learning-brains-reward-center-teach-educators
[25] Why Limit Screen Time? Reasons You Should Limit Screen Time. Sherrelle Walker, M.A. The Science of Learning Blog. 18 Nov 2010. http://www.scilearn.com/blog/5-reasons-you-should-limit-screen-time

that is growing by leaps and bounds. Scientists are adamant that as we push our stress level and exciting stimulation higher and higher, we are literally overloading the pathways to the pleasure centre of the brain. This overload causes our brain's pleasure centre to demand a further increase in the level of stimulation before delivering more feelings of pleasure. This results in a decline in our pleasure system's ability to deliver enjoyment out of ordinary, simple things.[26]

More and more I hear young people say, "I'm bored." With such a fast paced culture, I often think *"how can anyone be bored in this day and age?"* But it's true. Young people, despite all of the digital stimulation they experience, still manage to get bored very easily. Once the brain enters into an anhedonic state, the numbing effect causes us to be bored until we can get our next "digital fix" and the problem only grows worse the more we stimulate ourselves with our devices. What ends up happening is that children find slower-paced activities, including education activities, boring and if they have a smart phone nearby, they will opt for that.

On a regular basis, grandparents tell me that their grandchildren come to visit with digital devices in tow, and that they quickly disappear somewhere in the house opting for screen time. How sad that an entire generation of children are more stimulated by devices than they are by grandma and granddad. What have we done to these children? Fortunately, neuroscience is offering scientific insight into this dilemma. Hopefully, we will do something about it.

19.5 The Addictive Process

Digital addiction is just as real as any other drug addiction. Dr. Sylvia Frejd and Dr. Archibald Hart provide an example of the

---

[26] Dr. Hart, Archibald D. Thrilled to Death: How the Endless Pursuit of Pleasure is Leaving Us Numb. Tennessee. Thomas Nelson, Inc. 2007. Page 3

addictive process in their book *The Digital Invasion: How Technology is Shaping You and Your Relationships*.

> "As an example, let us imagine you are playing a video game. You initially spend half an hour playing the game, and it gives you a lot of pleasure. If you keep playing the game, however, the pleasure system becomes overloaded and starts to diminish the pleasure you experience. Now it demands even more game playing just to give a little pleasure. Therefore, you have to give increasing amounts of time to game playing just to keep the pleasure flowing. To put it simply, overloading the pleasure system gradually raises the bar so that you have to increase the level of stimulation to maintain the pleasure. This phenomenon is called the *addictive process*. It is the basic cause of all addictions.
>
> Dopamine is the basic neurotransmitter (chemical messenger) that carries the signal to your pleasure center from different parts of the brain. As you go for more and more pleasure, you push the dopamine level higher and higher. This is called *dopamine flooding*, and it creates a spiraling effect that results in compulsive drug or behavior abuse"[27].

19.6 Multitasking Is a Myth

When speaking to audiences around the world, I will often ask, "Who in this audience has the ability to multitask very well?" Of course many hands instantly go up. The truth is, no one on earth can multitask. As it turns out, the brain is a sequential processor. In an article titled *Students can't resist distraction for two minutes ... and neither can you*, columnist Bob Sullivan writes:

---

[27] Excerpt From: Dr. Archibald D. Hart & Sylvia Hart Frejd. "Digital Invasion." iBooks. https://itunes.apple.com/us/book/the-digital-invasion/id598305287?mt=11. Pages 126 and 127.

"Multitasking has been the subject of popular debate, but among neuroscientists, there is very little of that. Brain researchers say that what many people call multitasking should really be called "rapid toggling" between tasks, as the brain focuses quickly on one topic, then switches to another, and another."[28]

All of this switching between tasks, as it turns out, is bad for grades. Nicholas Carr, in his book, *The Shallows: What the Internet is Doing to Our Brains*, writes, "Many studies have shown that switching between just two tasks can add substantially to our cognitive load, impeding our thinking and increasing the likelihood that we'll overlook or misinterpret important information."[29]

Dr. John Medina, a developmental molecular biologist who focuses on brain development, explains:

The brain is a sequential processor, unable to pay attention to two things at the same time. Businesses and schools praise multitasking, but research clearly shows that it reduces productivity and increases mistakes.[30]

19.7 Multitasking, Depression and Anger

In the past quarter century, the mental health of teenagers has been declining at an alarming rate. Problems such as depression and anxiety

---

[28] Students can't resist distraction for two minutes … and neither can you. Bob Sullivan. 18 May 2013 http://www.nbcnews.com/technology/students-cant-resist-distraction-two-minutes-neither-can-you-1C9984270

[29] Excerpt From: Nicholas Carr. The Shallows: What the Internet is Doing to Our Brains. https://itunes.apple.com/us/book/shallows-what-internet-is/id380556044?mt=11

[30] Medina, John J. Brain Rules: 12 Principles for Surviving and Thriving at Work, Home and School. Pear Press. Copyright © 2008 by John J. Medina. iBooks Page 133.

have increased by 70% among adolescents.[31] I find it interesting that this 25-year time frame corresponds with the popularization of the internet. My experience tells me there is a link.

According to a study from Michigan State University in an article titled: *Multimedia Use Tied to Depression, Anxiety*: "Using multiple forms of media at the same time – such as playing a computer game while watching TV – is linked to symptoms of anxiety and depression, scientists have found for the first time."[32]

Even though we can get an emotional high from task switching, there is a price to pay. The brain undergoes chemical changes that include the release of stress hormones and adrenaline. The release of the stress hormone cortisol has the potential of making us more aggressive and impulsive, not to mention raising our risk for cardiovascular disease[33] and weight gain.[34]

Dr. Alan Keen, a behavioural scientist at Australia's Central Queensland University, says that multitasking is a significant reason "we are witnessing epidemics of rage." He adds, "If I'm living in a big city with a busy job and I'm multitasking and I'm a busy parent, all that translates into chemical changes in the brain."[35]

---

[31] Today's youth: anxious, depressed, antisocial. Madeleine Buntin. The Guardian. 13 Sep 2004. http://www.theguardian.com/society/2004/sep/13/childrensservices.mentalhealth
[32] Multiple Media Use Tied to Depression, Anxiety. Michigan State University. MSUTODAY. 4 Dec 2012. http://msutoday.msu.edu/news/2012/multiple-media-use-tied-to-depression-anxiety/
[33] Is multi-tasking bad for your brain? Experts reveal the hidden perils of juggling too many jobs. John Naish. Daily Mail. 11 Aug 2009. http://www.dailymail.co.uk/health/article-1205669/Is-multitasking-bad-brain-Experts-reveal-hidden-perils juggling-jobs.html
[34] Stress, Hormones, and Weight Gain. Medical Author: Melissa Conrad Stöppler, MD. Medical Editor: William C. Shiel Jr., MD, FACP, FACR. MedicineNet.com. http://www.medicinenet.com/script/main/art.asp?articlekey=53304
[35] Is multi-tasking bad for your brain? Experts reveal the hidden perils of juggling too many jobs. John Naish. Daily Mail. 11 Aug 2009.

19.8 Digital Education Content Causes the Same Reaction in the Brain

When many parents first observe the mesmerisation that occurs when their children stare intently and quietly at a television, tablet, phone, or computer screen, they feel a miracle is occurring right before their eyes. They sense relief that there is finally an activity that will hold their child's attention for long periods of time so they can do other things. These digital devices understandably become a very reliable and consistent babysitter. For many parents, digital devices such as tablets and video games end up becoming the bane of their existence when it comes time to take the device away. The tantrums often grow in intensity, and parents often relent and give the device back just to calm the child and restore peace. A short-term solution to peace often grows into an out-of-control monster.

During and after my seminars, it is not uncommon for well-meaning parents to say something to me like, "I agree with you. Regular video games are bad, so I only allow my child to play with education apps and games." With as much grace as I can muster, I explain to them that the brain does not distinguish content. In other words, when we are interacting with digital content, the brain is not working in the background on our behalf assessing educational versus non-educational content and then deciding what it will get addicted to and what it will not. It is simply responding to the stimulation that is generated by interacting with the digital device. Full stop.

In an article titled "This is Your Child's Brain on Video Games" that appeared in *Psychology Today*, Dr. Victoria Dunckley described the chronic brain stress that video games can cause:

---

http://www.dailymail.co.uk/health/article-1205669/Is-multitasking-bad-brain-Experts-reveal-hidden-perils juggling-jobs.html

"It's easy to imagine how an exciting video game can cause hyperarousal. But in fact, numerous mechanisms act synergistically to raise arousal levels with all types of interactive screen-time. And contrary to popular belief, many of them occur *irrespective of content.*"[36]

19.9 The Ramifications for Distance Learning

Distance learning curricula designers, educators, facilitators and students would benefit by understanding that brain health is affected by interacting with digital devices, regardless of content, and the clock starts ticking the moment our eyes lock on a screen. As good as distance learning can be, we must recognize that it has the potential to contribute to brain stress. If we place too much repetitive stress on our median nerve, carpal tunnel syndrome is likely to result with all of the associated painful symptoms in our hands and wrists.[37] Similarly, if we place too much repetitive stress on our brains by excessive interactivity and multitasking with digital devices, we will suffer the associated mental, emotional, psychological and cognitive consequences.

This calls for a conscientious strategy to assist our students in managing the manner and length of time in which they interact with digital media. A course on brain health management would be a recommended prerequisite to any course of study that utilizes digital media, and that of course includes distance learning.

---

[36] This is Your Child's Brain on Video Games. Victoria L. Dunckley M.D. Psychology Today. 25 Sep 2016. https://www.psychologytoday.com/ blog/mental-wealth/201609/is-your-childs-brain-video-games
[37] Carpal Tunnel Syndrome Face Sheet. National Institute of Neurologival Disorders and Stroke. http://www.ninds.nih.gov/disorders/carpal_tunnel/ detail_carpal_tunnel.htm

The remainder of this chapter will contain solutions and recommendations that I hope will get a larger conversation started and also inspire additional research in this area.

19.10 Solutions

Although more research is needed, we know enough from neuroscience and psychology to certainly get started with a workable strategy and tip the scales of brain health, and all that is associated with it, in our favour.

If digital addiction has already set in, implementing these strategies will prove to be difficult until digital detox is achieved. If the addiction is particularly severe, professional assistance might be required for a season, but change *is* possible. When parents discover these principles on their own or implement the applicable solutions that I propose, it is very gratifying to hear some of them say something like, "It's so good to have my child back."

19.11 It All Begins at Home

In general, I sometimes notice a trend among parents when a school first introduces technology, such as computer-aided learning or a one-to-one laptop or tablet program. Well-meaning parents assume this is a good thing, believing that in order for their children to be successful later in life, they must learn computer skills at the earliest age possible. After a year or two of technology implementation, things don't always go so well and parents start to become weary of their children not wanting anything but screen time. After hearing me speak about the preceding issues, it is common for parents and students to raise concerns that the school is requiring too much homework on a tablet or laptop. While that might be true in a handful of cases, I find that the real culprit is the large amount of screen time spent on activities that have nothing to do with the academic work the school is requiring on a tablet.

It appears to me that some parents and students assume that the *pleasurable* digital activities such as social media and YouTube are not harming their brains but instead, the problems are stemming from the intensive concentration on school work on a tablet. The truth is, *all* screen time affects the brain. Common Sense Media has reported that on any given day, teenagers in the U.S. spend nearly nine hours using media for enjoyment.[38] My experience is that this is true anywhere in the world where there is a penetration of broadband internet and smart phones. Notice, the bulk of students' screen time is spent on *enjoyable* activities such as watching television, playing video games, watching videos and movies and listening to music,[39] and not on academic pursuits. Any educators worth their salt always hope their students find learning as enjoyable as any other activity, but this is generally not the case once digital addiction has set in. Once this occurs, enjoyment can only be found in activities that produce very large quantities of dopamine.

Knowing this, I always challenge young parents to first be honest about their own digital addiction before criticizing their children and their children's school. Nearly four in ten (39%) of them admit they interact more with their smart phones than they do with their children, friends, or co-workers.[40] Now that we have two simultaneous generations struggling with digital addition, it makes it particularly difficult to deal with. Anyone who has worked in the mental health field

---

[38] Teens spend a 'mind-boggling' 9 hours a day using media, report says. Kelly Wallace, CNN. 3 Nov 2015. http://www.cnn.com/2015/11/03/health/teens-tweens-media-screen-use-report/

[39] Ibid.

[40] Millennials engage with their smartphones more than they do actual humans. Catey Hill, Editor. MarketWatch. 21 June 2016. http://www.marketwatch.com/story/millennials-engage-with-their-smartphones-more-than-they-do-actual-humans-2016-06-21

will tell you that *denial* is the first and most difficult hurdle that an addict has to get over. Another layer of complexity is added with so many young teachers addicted to digital activities as well.

What I recommend to parents is that they severely limit all activities that involve technology and save their child's brain reserves for digital activities that are truly important, such as school work. Even then, a strategy for brain health management needs to be put firmly and consistently in place.

19.12 Remove All Technology from Bedrooms and Sleep

The average person now spends more time on their phone than they do sleeping.[41] The lack of sleep around world where technology has deep penetration is shocking and its devastating psychological, emotional, cognitive, and academic effects are well documented. Every parent should remove all technology, including televisions, from every bedroom in the house. The bedroom should be a dark, quiet place to sleep (without music).

The average amount of sleep that teenagers get is between seven and 7 1/4 hours. Studies show that they require 9 1/4 hours of sleep.[42] It is not uncommon for me to encounter teenagers who sleep far less than seven hours per night, especially those who are addicted to video games, social media and pornography.

In addition, all technology should be turned off at least an hour before bedtime as the blue light exposure from the devices sends a signal to our brains that it is still daylight and inhibits of release of the

---

[41] Average person now spends more time on their phone and laptop than sleeping, study claims. Madlen Davies. Daily Mail. 11 Mar 2015. http://www.dailymail.co.uk/health/article-2989952/How-technology-taking-lives-spend-time-phones-laptops-SLEEPING.html

[42] Sleep in Adolescents (13 - 18 Years). Nationwide Children's. http://www.nationwidechildrens.org/sleep-in-adolescents

sleepy hormone melatonin.[43] One study found that "two hours of exposure to a bright tablet screen reduced melatonin about 22 percent."[44]

19.13 Work Sequentially

Understanding that multitasking is harmful to the brain, we must learn to work the way the brain functions, and that is in a sequential manner. This is also called unitasking and monotasking. Our grandparents worked more this way because they were not distracted by technology.

Curricula designers should consider structuring courses in such a way that students work on one learning task at a time as much as possible. Following is a partial list of recommendations for unitasking successfully.

- Parents and teachers must first model and then instruct young people to monotask.

- Parents and teachers must gently *force* students to work sequentially. Simply explaining these principles is important, but not enough. An underdeveloped prefrontal cortex will prohibit young people from being able to fully understand the ramifications of their actions.[45] This also means that children are

---

[43] Sleepless in America: How Digital Devices Keep Us Up All Night. NBC News. Hallie Jackson. 24 Jun 2015. http://www.nbcnews.com/nightly-news/sleepless-america-how-digital-devices-keep-us-all-night-n381251
[44] Really? Using a Computer Before Bed Can Disrupt Sleep. Anahad O'Connor. The New York Times: Well. 10 Sept 2012. http://well.blogs.nytimes.com/2012/09/10/really-using-a-computer-before-bed-can-disrupt-sleep/?smid=tw-nytimes&_r=0
[45] Barry Corbin, "Unleashing the Potential of the Teenage Brain: Ten Powerful Ideas." Victoria, Australia. Hawker Bownlow, 2008, 20.

not able to self-regulate[46] very well and are in need of constant policing.

- Do not allow students to listen to music while reading, studying and doing homework. This is a form of multitasking[47] and cognition will be hampered (among other things).

- When doing homework, physically remove all technology that is not germane to the work at hand.

- Do one subject at a time. When "brain breaks" are needed, do not do digital activities such as check email or social media. Instead, do analog activities such as taking a brief walk, power nap, etc.

19.14 Combine Analog When Possible

Remember the word analog? In this context, it simply means activities that do not involve digital technology. It is clear that if we are going to protect our brain health, mental and emotional well-being, and cognitive abilities, we are going to have to tip the scales in favor of analog activities in a day's time. Following are some suggestions to get the creative juices flowing as we seek ways to integrate more analog back into our lives:

- Offer printed textbooks and supplemental materials when possible.
- Offer audio versions of lectures and teachings when possible as audio does not require the learner to look at a screen.
- Encourage students to take notes on paper instead of typing.

---

[46] What is Self Regulation and How To Help a Child to Learn Self Regulation. Day 2 Day Parenting. 7 Nov 2013. http://day2dayparenting.com/help-child-learn-self-regulation/
[47] Neuroscientist Daniel Levitin Explains Why Multitasking Is a Harmful Addiction. David Hershkovits.

- When doing research, encourage students to print their research and work off of paper as much as possible.
- Instead of education video games, encourage education board games.
- Use traditional flash cards.

At this point, some might be thinking, "What?!?! It sounds like we're going to have to go back to the Stone Age." Not so. I'm simply being honest regarding the limitations the brain has with digital technology and work within those limits.

19.15 Dramatically Reduce Screen Time

One of the most frequent questions I am asked is, "How much screen time per day do you recommend for children?" While there is a fairly large and growing pool of research related to media's negative effect on the brain, very little exists on appropriate time limits for each age group. There are plenty of answers floating around, but they are all over the map and are rarely based in science.

Much research still needs to be done to more accurately answer this most crucial and valid question. Nevertheless, I will do my best with the little information we have.

The brain is resilient but it is also fragile. That's why honest scientific scales must be developed to determine what balance looks like for each age group.

According to Dr. Archibald Hart, any digital activity that goes beyond one hour is going to push the adrenal system beyond its normal limits.[48] How much beyond that before the brain begins to suffer damage is not fully known, although we know it does eventually occur.

---

[48] Focus on the Family Weekend Magazine radio program. February 21, 2009

For an adult, working within an hour time limit, say 50 minutes, and then giving the brain an analog rest seems logical and wise.

As for children, many have understandably looked to the American Academy of Pediatrics for guidance. However, the AAP has recently relaxed their screen time rules for some kids.[49] This is very disturbing to me. With Virtual Reality and Augmented Reality now here, the brain stimulation will no doubt sky rocket.

Until more scientific study can be done, I think it would be good to get some parenting guidance from the tech industry itself. The New York Times ran a story titled *A Silicon Valley School That Doesn't Compute* that reported:

> "The chief technology officer of eBay sends his children to a nine classroom school here. So do employees of Silicon Valley giants like Google, Apple, Yahoo and Hewlett-Packard.
>
> But the school's chief teaching tools are anything but high tech: pens and paper, knitting needles and, occasionally, mud. Not a computer to be found. No screens at all. They are not allowed in the classroom, and the school even frowns on their use at home."[50]

The school that is being referred to is a Waldorf School, which has a teaching philosophy of using physical activity and learning through creative, hands-on tasks. There are 160 Waldorf schools in the United States, 40 of which are in California. Those who believe in this non-

---

[49] A major update relaxes screen time rules for some kids. Ariana Eunjung Cha. The Washington Post. 21 Oct 2016. https://www.washingtonpost.com/news/to-your-health/wp/2016/10/21/big-updates-new-screen-time-rules-by-age-from-the-american-academy-for-pediatrics/?utm_term=.77755dbfc7fe
[50] A Silicon Valley School That Doesn't Compute. Matt Richter. The New York Times. 22 Oct 2011. http://www.nytimes.com/2011/10/23/technology/at-waldorf-school-in-silicon-valley-technology-can-wait.html

digital, analog form of learning say that computers interfere with attention spans, creative thinking, movement and human interaction.[51]

Why would a chief technology officer and Silicon Valley tech employees send their children to a non-tech school and even agree to limit it at home? What do they know that we don't? As one with a computer science degree, I think they are just being honest, from experience, about just how much brain stress technology causes, and they want to protect their children.

To further bolster the case, Technology Columnist Nick Bolton, writing for the *New York Times,* must have been shocked by Steve Job's answer to his question, "So, your kids must love the iPad?"

Job's reply was, "They haven't used it... We limit how much technology our kids use at home."[52]

After all of my research and experience, I recommend an 80/20 rule for adults: 80% analog in a day's time, and 20% digital. For children under the age of 12, I would conduct a simple test. I would give them some form of digital technology for 30 minutes and then ask for it back. If you get any response other than peaceful compliance, I would begin backing the time up until you do.

19.16 What We Would NOT Say to a Cocaine Addict

Time and again, scientists compare digital addiction to cocaine addiction. For example, consider this article titled *Internet addiction changes brain similar to cocaine*:

"The researchers found more patterns of "abnormal white matter" on brain scans of internet addicts, compared with scans of non-

---

[51] Ibid.
[52] Steve Jobs Was a Low-Tech Parent. Nick Bolton. The New York Times. 10 Sep 2014. http://www.nytimes.com/2014/09/11/fashion/steve-jobs-apple-was-a-low-tech-parent.html

addicts. White matter areas in the brain contain nerve fibres that transmit signals to other parts of the brain.

These changes showed evidence of disrupting pathways related to emotions, decision-making, and self-control.

The researchers said earlier studies have found similar white matter changes in the brain scans of people addicted to alcohol, cocaine, heroin, marijuana, meth, and ketamine (also known as "Special K")."[53]

In order to prevent digital addiction and to facilitate properly designed digital curricula, we have to first think about the issue correctly.

Here is what you would *not* say to someone seeking help for cocaine addiction: "You know, you just need *balance*. You know what they say, '*moderation* in all things'".

And yet, that is how we tend to treat addiction to technology. We tell ourselves and others that we just need to keep our technology use in balance. There is truth to that statement but please understand that a cocaine addict will not be free of the addiction by simply backing off some. Neither will a digital addict. South Korea is the most wired nation on this planet. As a result of their supersaturation if interconnected technology, they have set up approximately 200 counseling centers and hospitals with more than 1,000 trained internet-addiction counselors. South Korea is not the only country struggling. China has more than 300 of these digital detox rehabilitation centers.[54] When digital addicts check in for detox, no "drugs" in the form of technology are allowed.

---

[53] Internet changes brain similar to cocaine: Study. Ryan Jaslow. CBS News. 12 Jan 2012. http://www.cbsnews.com/news/internet-addiction-changes-brain-similar-to-cocaine-study/

[54] Internet Rescue Camp. Frontline, digital_nation, PBS. 21 Mar 2009. http://www.pbs.org/wgbh/pages/frontline/digitalnation/virtual-worlds/internet-addiction/internet-rescue-camp.html

There is a difference, however, between technology and cocaine. There is no redeeming value in illicit drug use. Technology on the other hand, has the potential to be used for very productive purposes. Understanding technology's efficacy and addictive nature will help designers of digital curricula and students stand a much better chance of attaining true iBalance.

CONTRIBUTING AUTHORS

C. STÜCKELBERGER, Switzerland

"The significant role of higher education in developing a global ethical culture"

Prof. Dr. Dr. h.c. Christoph Stückelberger is a Theologian, and Founder and President of the Globethics.net Foundation. He has been Executive Director of the Geneva Agape Foundation since 2016 and is Professor of Ethics at universities in Switzerland, Nigeria, Russia and China.

O. IKE, Nigeria

"Ethics in higher education as a tool for discovering our ultimate destiny"

Reverend Monsignor Professor Dr Obiora Francis Ike is the Executive Director of Globethics.net. He holds degrees in philosophy, theology, economics, journalism and political science. His doctorate is from Bonn University with a specialisation in Ethics and he is Professor of Ethics and Intercultural Studies, Godfrey Okoye University, Nigeria. Ike has held several professorial posts as well as positions of service in Church, Society and State within Africa and in Europe. He founded of a number of educational and development organisations in Nigeria and served as founder and Chairman of the Umuchinemere Procredit Microfinance Bank Ltd in Nigeria and is Chairman of the Enugu State Government Economic Advisory Committee.

P. KOCHAPPILLY, India
"Harmony as the horizon of higher education"

Prof. Dr Paulachan Kochappilly holds a Doctorate in Moral Theology from Accademia Alfonsiana, Rome. He is a member of Bijnor Mission Province of the Carmelites of Mary Immaculate. He is a Professor of Moral Theology at Dharmaram Vidya Kshetram and has been the Dean of the Faculty of Theology and the Head of the Department of Theology, Christ University. At present he is the President of Dharmaram Vidya Kshetram, Pontifical Athenaeum of Theology, Philosophy, and Canon Law, Bangalore.
Along with other academic responsibilities, he serves as the Director of Globethics.net India. paulachan.kochappilly@cmi.in

---

N. BAIJNATH, South Africa
Ethical Leadership in Higher Education in "the Era of Complexity."

Prof Narend Baijnath is CEO of the Council on Higher Education, since assuming duties in October 2015, and shortly thereafter appointed Research Fellow in the Department of Curriculum and Instructional Studies at the University of South Africa. Before joining the CHE, he was Pro Vice Chancellor of the University of South Africa. Prior to that he was Vice Principal: Strategy, Planning and Partnerships at the same institution. He holds a Master's Degree from Durham University, and a Doctorate from the University of the Western Cape. He is a member of the Academy of Science of South Africa. In 2008 he was appointed a Fellow at St Edmunds College, Cambridge University and simultaneously a research professor at OUUK. He currently serves on the following boards: CoL, SAQA, UMALUSI, QCTO.
Baijnath.n@che.ac.za

.

E. LEMMER, South Africa
"Infusing ethics into everyday practice in higher education"

Professor Eleanor Lemmer is a research fellow in College of Education at the University of South Africa having recently retired after 30 years' service at the university. During her career she held the position of Vice Dean, former Faculty of Education (1996-1999) and research professor (2011-2016) among others. Her areas of specialisation are academic habitus, autoethnography and parent involvement in schooling. She has been twice rated as researcher by the National Research Foundation of South Africa.

H. DAVIS & L. GOEDEGEBUURE, Australia
"Governance for sustainability in higher education"

Dr Heather Davis is the Postgraduate Program Director - LH Martin Institute for Tertiary Education Leadership and Management. The University of Melbourne. Her research interests include university leadership and management, shared leadership approaches, qualitative inquiry, social complexity theories and e-learning. She co-ordinates the Master of Tertiary Education Management and is subject co-ordinator for the elective in Sustainable Tertiary Education Leadership and Governance. Her background is in research management, knowledge work, adult education and professional development. heather.davis@unimelb.edu.au

Professor Leo Goedegebuure is the Director, LH Martin Institute for Tertiary Education Leadership and Management, The University of Melbourne. He has published 15 books and over 100 articles, book chapters and papers on higher education policy, mergers, quality assessment, evaluation research, differentiation, system dynamics, engineering education and institutional management. His current research interests are in higher education governance and management, both at the systems and institutional level, system dynamics including large scale restructuring policies, university-industry relationships, and institutional mergers. Most of his work has a comparative focus which has resulted in a strong international network.

director-mi@unimelb.edu.au

A. SINGH, South Africa
"The Relationship between the Sustainable Development Goals and the Role of Higher Education Institutions"

Avani Singh has a B.Comm (Law), LL.B and is currently practising as an attorney in the Constitutional Litigation Unit at the Legal Resources Centre in Johannesburg, South Africa. She completed her articles of clerkship at Webber Wentzel (in association with Linklaters), and was subsequently appointed as an associate in the Dispute Resolution: Media Law team at Webber Wentzel. Avani has also clerked for Justice Skweyiya at the Constitutional Court South Africa, and for Judge Eboe-Osuji at the International Criminal Court in The Hague. She worked as a research assistant to Professor Christof Heyns.

avani409@gmail.com

M.S. MAKHANYA, South Africa

"Getting down to business: The ethics of preparing graduates for global citizenship"

Professor Mandla Stanley Makhanya is the Principal and Vice Chancellor of the University of South Africa. He is also Treasurer of the African Council for Distance Education and President of the International Council for Distance Education. Professor Makhanya is also the Vice President of the Higher Education Teaching and Learning Association. Professor Makhanya is a sociologist with a DPhil from the University of Pretoria and a DTE from Unisa. He received a PhD (Honoris Causa) from Athabascar University in recognition of his outstanding leadership at Unisa and his contribution as a distinguished scholar in distance education. He maintains active scholarship through regular publications.

M. PROZESKY, South Africa

"Universities, cultural diversity and global ethics: opportunities for moral leadership"

Professor Martin Prozesky is an ethics trainer and writer operating under the banner of Compass Ethics. He is a Professor Extraordinaire of the University of the Free State, an Emeritus Professor of the University of KwaZulu-Natal, and from 1997 to 2007 directed the Unilever Ethics Centre at the University of KwaZulu-Natal (1997-2007). He studied at Rhodes, Oxford and in Cambridge, Massachusetts, with a doctorate from the former University of Rhodesia. His book Conscience: Ethical Intelligence for Global Well-Being appeared in 2007 from the UKZN Press. marproz@mweb.co.za

M. JEAN-LOUIS, Canada

"Change leadership, ethics and the future of higher education"

Maxim Jean-Louis is President – Chief Executive Officer of Contact North | Contact Nord, Ontario's Distance & Education Network. Since 1986 Contact North I Contact Nord helps 4 million residents in 600 small, rural, remote, Indigenous and Francophone communities in the province of Ontario, Canada access post-secondary and training opportunities from Ontario's 24 public colleges, 22 public universities, and more than 250 literacy and other training providers. Maxim Jean-Louis serves on the Board of Directors of the Ontario Trillium Foundation, Renewed Computer Technology and People for Education.

N.B. PITYANA, South Africa

"Leadership and ethics in higher education: Some perspectives from experience"

Professor Nyameko Barney Pityana is the retired Principal and Vice Chancellor of the University of South Africa. He is Professor Emeritus of Law at Unisa, and an Honorary Professor in Philosophy, Allan Gray Centre for Leadership Ethics, at Rhodes University, Grahamstown. He also served as Rector of the College of the Transfiguration, Grahamstown, an Anglican theological seminary. He holds degrees in Law and a PhD in Religious Studies and fellowships from King's College, London and the Stellenbosch Institute for Advanced Study. He is currently Secretary General of the Network of African Academies of Science, and Vice President of the Academy of Science of South Africa.

C.O. HOPPERS, South Africa

"Leadership and epistemological responsibility in African universities in the 21st Century"

Professor Catharine Odora-Hoppers is a UNESCO expert in basic education, lifelong learning, information systems and on Science and Society; an expert in disarmament at the UN Department of Disarmament Affairs; an expert to the World Economic Forum on benefit sharing and value addition protocols; and the World Intellectual Property Organisation on traditional knowledge and community intellectual property rights. She holds a South African Research Chair in Development Education at the University of South Africa, a National Chair set up by the Department of Science and Technology. She is a Member of the Academy of Science of South Africa, and a Fellow of the African Academy of Sciences (AAS).

E. ARCHER & P. PRINSLOO, South Africa

"Some exploratory thoughts on openness and an ethics of care"

Dr Liz Archer is a qualified Educational Psychologist with a PhD in Assessment and Quality Assurance. She started her career at the University of Pretoria. In 2011 she joined the University of South Africa. She has spent 17 years in training and consulting in education and research. She is a rated researcher with the South African National Research Foundation (NRF). She has been the recipient of a number of prestigious scholarships and awards including the SKYE fellowship. She has also presented conferences and guest lectures all over the world in countries such as New Zealand, Malaysia, Ethiopia, Austria, the Netherlands, Ethiopia and Zimbabwe.

Prof Paul Prinsloo is a Research Professor in Open and Distance Learning at the University of South Africa (Unisa). His academic background includes fields as diverse as theology, art history, business management, online learning, and religious studies. Paul is an established researcher and has published numerous articles in the fields of teaching and learning, student success in distance education contexts, learning analytics, and curriculum development. His current research focuses on the collection, analysis and use of student data in learning analytics, graduate supervision and digital identity. Paul was born curious and in trouble - nothing has changed since then. He blogs at https://opendistanceteachingandlearning.wordpress.com/ and his Twitter alias is @14prinsp

---

S. NAIDU, Australia

"Open educational practice: Caveat Emptor"

Dr Som Naidu spent most of his professional life in the higher education sector in various roles to do with enhancing learning and teaching practices in open, flexible, distance, and online learning, as well as education more generally. Currently at Monash University, most recently he served as Associate Professor (Learning Transformations) at Swinburne University of Technology in Melbourne. His undergraduate and postgraduate qualifications are in Education and Educational Technology. Dr. Naidu is Principal Associate of Technology, Education and Design Solutions (a consultancy and advisory service), current president of the Open and Distance Learning Association of Australia, and executive editor of its journal Distance Education. sommnaidu@gmail.com

DARYONO & SRI SEDYAININGSIH, Indonesia
"Universitas Terbuka Indonesia Open Policy: Securing the rights to knowledge and higher education"

Dr Daryono completed his PhD in law from Law School, the Australia National University in 2007. He is currently active in advocating open movement for educational purposes. In 2010 he was a member of international collaborative research on Open Education Resources (OER) funded by International Development Research Center (IDRC). The outcome of the research was the establishment of OERAsia. Following the research on OER Asia, he is currently engaged in the ongoing research on OER for development (ROER4D) funded by the IDRC. Since 2012 he is a member of Open Education Consortium (OEC) to advocate open education policy in Indonesia. daryono@ecampus.ut.ac.id

Sri Sediyaningsih is a senior lecturer in Communication Studies at Faculty of Social and Political Sciences, Universitas Terbuka (UT), Indonesia. Completing undergraduate studies in Communication from Gadjah Mada University, Yogyakarta, Indonesia; a Master of Science and Doctor of Communication from University of Indonesia, Jakarta. Her research interests are in communication technology for distance learning purposes. She has long careers in various communication fields as a newscaster in public television TVRI in this 90's era (1988-2001), a facilitator and a Board of Experts in various professional associations. Her latest book was entitled "net generation" published in 2015. dianb@ecampus.ut.ac.id

L.K. CHEONG, B.T. WONG, Hong Kong
"Building up a research ethics system: Experience of a teaching university"

Dr Kam Cheong Li, Director of Research at the Open University of Hong Kong, has involved in open education for more than two decades. He oversees research at the University and has served as a course developer, strand/programme leader, and course coordinator for distance-learning programmes. For the Asian Association of Open Universities, he is currently the Secretary-General. Dr Li has earned three bachelor's degrees, four master's degrees and a PhD. He is a productive author of over 100 publications, including refereed journal papers, book chapters, monographs and textbooks. His research interests lie in open education and pedagogical innovations. kcli@ouhk.edu.hk

Dr Billy Tak-ming Wong, Research Coordinator at the University Research Centre, the Open University of Hong Kong, has participated in processing hundreds of research applications, many of them for research ethical clearance purposes. He has obtained a BA, an MA and a PhD from the City University of Hong Kong. He has published many journal papers, book chapters and conference papers in areas of open education and research capacity development, besides having obtained paper awards in various academic conferences. His research areas include open and flexible education, mobile learning, blended learning, open-educational resources, and academic analytics.
Email: tamiwong@ouhk.edu.hk

D. SINGH, South Africa

"Responding to the challenges of gendered career aspirations: Responsible academic leadership in support of the golden triad of access, equity and justice"

Professor Divya Singh holds an LL.D, a Masters in Tertiary Education Management (UniMelb) and is an admitted Advocate of the High Court of South Africa. She is the Vice Principal Advisory and Assurance Service at the University of South Africa, where she introduced the institutional Ethics Office (responsible for promoting an ethical and values-informed culture at the university) and Social and Ethics Committee of Council. She is a Certified Ethics Officer from the Ethics Institute and the Executive Director: Globethics.net Southern Africa. Divya spent 26 years in higher education and has a slew of publications in law, gender violence, and governance. dsingh@unisa.ac.za

J.C. BOTHA, South Africa

"Nowhere to hide? Ethical social media use in higher education institutions"

Jeanette Botha is the Director in the Office of the Principal and Vice Chancellor at the University of South Africa where she is responsible amongst others, for higher education research, global trending and writing. She also fulfils a liaison and advisory function. Jeanette has had 18 years' experience at top management level, having worked with four Vice Chancellors. She obtained a D.Ed. in Higher Education Management in 2011, with a focus on higher education policy.

B. HUDDLESTON, United States of America
"Contributing to digital addiction in a distance education environment –
the ethical conundrum"

Brad Huddleston is an internationally respected speaker, consultant, teacher and author. He has worked with universities, schools, churches and law enforcement, and speaks on both the advantages of technology tools and dangers of technology addiction. Brad has an ongoing collaboration with the Bureau of Market Research (BMR) and its Neuroscience Division at the University of South Africa. He has a degree in Computer Science and a Diploma of Biblical Studies and is a frequent guest on radio and television and author of Digital Cocaine: A Journey Toward iBalance and The Dark Side of Technology: Restoring Balance in the Digital Age.

Globethics.net

Globethics.net is a worldwide ethics network based in Geneva, with an international Board of Foundation of eminent persons, 176,000 participants from 200 countries and regional and national programmes. Globethics.net provides services especially for people in Africa, Asia and Latin-America in order to contribute to more equal access to knowledge resources in the field of applied ethics and to make the voices from the Global South more visible and audible in the global discourse. It provides an electronic platform for dialogue, reflection and action. Its central instrument is the internet site *www.globethics.net*.

Globethics.net has four objectives:

Library: Free Access to Online Documents
In order to ensure access to knowledge resources in applied ethics, Globethics.net offers its *Globethics.net Library,* the leading global digital library on ethics with over 4.4 million full text documents for free download.

Network: Global Online Community
The registered participants form a global community of people interested in or specialists in ethics. It offers participants on its website the opportunity to contribute to forum, to upload articles and to join or form electronic working groups for purposes of networking or collaborative international research.

Research: Online Workgroups
Globethics.net registered participants can join or build online research groups on all topics of their interest whereas Globethics.net Head Office in Geneva concentrates on six research topics: *Business/Economic Ethics, Interreligious Ethics, Responsible Leadership, Environmental Ethics, Health Ethics and Ethics of Science and Technology.* The results produced through the working groups and research finds their way *into online collections* and *publications* in four series (see publications list) which can also be downloaded for free.

Services: Conferences, Certification, Consultancy
Globethics.net offers services such as the Global Ethics Forum, an international conference on business ethics, customized certification and educational projects, and consultancy on request in a multicultural and multilingual context.

www.globethics.net ∎

Globethics.net Publications

The list below is only a selection of our publications. To view the full collection, please visit our website.

All volumes can be downloaded for free in PDF form from the Globethics.net library and at www.globethics.net/publications. Bulk print copies can be ordered from *publications@globethics.net* at special rates from the Global South.

The Editor of the different Series of Globethics.net Publications Prof. Dr Obiora Francis Ike, Executive Director of Globethics.net in Geneva and Professor of Ethics at the Godfrey Okoye University Enugu/Nigeria.

Contact for manuscripts and suggestions: *publications@globethics.net*

Global Series

Christoph Stückelberger / Jesse N.K. Mugambi (eds.), *Responsible Leadership. Global and Contextual Perspectives*, 2007, 376pp. ISBN: 978-2-8254-1516-0

Heidi Hadsell / Christoph Stückelberger (eds.), *Overcoming Fundamentalism. Ethical Responses from Five Continents*, 2009, 212pp.
ISBN: 978-2-940428-00-7

Christoph Stückelberger / Reinhold Bernhardt (eds.): *Calvin Global. How Faith Influences Societies*, 2009, 258pp. ISBN: 978-2-940428-05-2.

Ariane Hentsch Cisneros / Shanta Premawardhana (eds.), *Sharing Values. A Hermeneutics for Global Ethics*, 2010, 418pp.
ISBN: 978-2-940428-25-0.

Deon Rossouw / Christoph Stückelberger (eds.), *Global Survey of Business Ethics in Training, Teaching and Research*, 2012, 404pp.
ISBN: 978-2-940428-39-7

Carol Cosgrove Sacks/ Paul H. Dembinski (eds.), *Trust and Ethics in Finance. Innovative Ideas from the Robin Cosgrove Prize*, 2012, 380pp.
ISBN: 978-2-940428-41-0

Jean-Claude Bastos de Morais / Christoph Stückelberger (eds.), *Innovation Ethics. African and Global Perspectives*, 2014, 233pp.
ISBN: 978-2-88931-003-6

Nicolae Irina / Christoph Stückelberger (eds.), *Mining, Ethics and Sustainability*, 2014, 198pp.ISBN : 978-2-88931-020-3

Philip Lee and Dafne Sabanes Plou (eds), *More or Less Equal: How Digital Platforms Can Help Advance Communication Rights*, 2014, 158pp. ISBN 978-2-88931-009-8

Sanjoy Mukherjee and Christoph Stückelberger (eds.) *Sustainability Ethics. Ecology, Economy, Ethics. International Conference SusCon III, Shillong/India*, 2015, 353pp. ISBN: 978-2-88931-068-5

Amélie Vallotton Preisig / Hermann Rösch / Christoph Stückelberger (eds.) *Ethical Dilemmas in the Information Society. Codes of Ethics for Librarians and Archivists*, 2014, 224pp. ISBN: 978-288931-024-1.

Prospects and Challenges for the Ecumenical Movement in the 21st Century. Insights from the Global Ecumenical Theological Institute, David Field / Jutta Koslowski, 256pp. 2016, ISBN 978-2-88931-097-5

Christoph Stückelberger, Walter Fust, Obiora Ike (eds.), *Global Ethics for Leadership. Values and Virtues for Life*, 2016, 444pp. ISBN 978-2-88931-123-1

Dietrich Werner / Elisabeth Jeglitzka (eds.), *Eco-Theology, Climate Justice and Food Security: Theological Education and Christian Leadership Development*, 316pp. 2016, ISBN 978-2-88931-145-3

Theses Series

Kitoka Moke Mutondo, *Église, protection des droits de l'homme et refondation de l'État en République Démocratique du Congo: Essai d'une éthique politique engagée*, 2012, 412pp. ISBN: 978-2-940428-31-1

Ange Sankieme Lusanga, *Éthique de la migration. La valeur de la justice comme base pour une migration dans l'Union Européenne et la Suisse*, 2012, 358pp. ISBN: 978-2-940428-49-6

Nyembo Imbanga, *Parler en langues ou parler d'autres langues. Approche exégétique des Actes des Apôtres*, 2012, 356pp. ISBN: 978-2-940428-51-9

Kahwa Njojo, *Éthique de la non-violence*, 2013, 596pp. ISBN: 978-2-940428-61-8

Ibiladé Nicodème Alagbada, *Le Prophète Michée face à la corruption des classes dirigeantes*, 2013,298pp. ISBN: 978-2-940428-89-2

Carlos Alberto Sintado, *Social Ecology, Ecojustice and the New Testament: Liberating Readings*, 2015, 379pp. ISBN: 978 -2-940428-99-1

Symphorien Ntibagirirwa, *Philosophical Premises for African Economic Development: Sen's Capability Approach*, 2014, 384pp. ISBN: 978-2-88931-001-2

Jude Likori Omukaga, *Right to Food Ethics: Theological Approaches of Asbjørn Eide*, 2015, 609pp. ISBN: 978-2-88931-047-0

Jörg F. W. Bürgi, *Improving Sustainable Performance of SME's , The Dynamic Interplay of Morality and Management Systems*, 2014, 528pp. ISBN: 978-2-88931-015-9

Jun Yan, *Local Culture and Early Parenting in China: A Case Study on Chinese Christian Mothers' Childrearing Experiences*, 2015, 190pp. ISBN 978-2-88931-065-4

Frédéric-Paul Piguet, *Justice climatique et interdiction de nuire*, 2014, 559 pp. ISBN 978-2-88931-005-0

Mulolwa Kashindi, *Appellations johanniques de Jésus dans l'Apocalypse: une lecture Bafuliiru des titres christologiques*, 2015, 577pp. ISBN 978-2-88931-040-1

Naupess K. Kibiswa, *Ethnonationalism and Conflict Resolution: The Armed Group Bany2 in DR Congo*. 2015, 528pp. ISBN : 978-2-88931-032-6

Kilongo Fatuma Ngongo, *Les héroïnes sans couronne. Leadership des femmes dans les Églises de Pentecôte en Afrique Centrale*, 2015, 489pp. ISBN 978-2-88931-038-8

Alexis Lékpéa Dea, *Évangélisation et pratique holistique de conversion en Afrique. L'Union des Églises Évangéliques Services et Œuvres de Côte d'Ivoire 1927-1982*, 2015, 588 pp. ISBN 978-2-88931-058-6

Bosela E. Eale, *Justice and Poverty as Challenges for Churches : with a Case Study of the Democratic Republic of Congo*, 2015, 335pp, ISBN: 978-2-88931-078-4

Andrea Grieder, *Collines des mille souvenirs. Vivre après et avec le génocide perpétré contre les Tutsi du Rwanda*, 2016, 403pp. ISBN 978-2-88931-101-9

Monica Emmanuel, *Federalism in Nigeria: Between Divisions in Conflict and Stability in Diversity*, 2016, 522pp. ISBN: 978-2-88931-106-4

John Kasuku, *Intelligence Reform in the Post-Dictatorial Democratic Republic of Congo*, 2016, 355pp. ISBN 978-2-88931-121-7

Fifamè Fidèle Houssou Gandonour, *Les fondements éthiques du féminisme. Réflexions à partir du contexte africain*, 2016, 430pp. ISBN 978-2-88931-138-5

Nicoleta Acatrinei, *Work Motivation and Pro-Social Behavior in the Delivery of Public Services Theoretical and Empirical Insights*, 2016, 387pp. ISBN 978-2-88931-150-7

Texts Series

Principles on Sharing Values across Cultures and Religions, 2012, 20pp. Available in English, French, Spanish, German and Chinese. Other languages in preparation. ISBN: 978-2-940428-09-0

Ethics in Politics. Why it Matters More than Ever and How it Can Make a Difference. A Declaration, 8pp, 2012. Available in English and French. ISBN:978-2-940428-35-9

Religions for Climate Justice: International Interfaith Statements 2008-2014, 2014, 45pp. Available in English. ISBN 978-2-88931-006-7

Ethics in the Information Society: the Nine 'P's. A Discussion Paper for the WSIS+10 Process 2013-2015, 2013, 32pp. ISBN: 978-2-940428-063-2

Principles on Equality and Inequality for a Sustainable Economy. Endorsed by the Global Ethics Forum 2014 with Results from Ben Africa Conference 2014, 2015, 41pp. ISBN: 978-2-88931-025-8

Focus Series

Christoph Stückelberger, *Das Menschenrecht auf Nahrung und Wasser. Eine ethische Priorität*, 2009, 80pp. ISBN: 978-2-940428-06-9

Christoph Stückelberger, *Corruption-Free Churches are Possible. Experiences, Values, Solutions*, 2010, 278pp. ISBN: 978-2-940428-07-6

— , *Des Églises sans corruption sont possibles: Expériences, valeurs, solutions*, 2013, 228pp. ISBN: 978-2-940428-73-1

Vincent Mbavu Muhindo, *La République Démocratique du Congo en panne. Bilan 50 ans après l'indépendance*, 2011, 380pp. ISBN: 978-2-940428-29-8

Benoît Girardin, *Ethics in Politics: Why it matters more than ever and how it can make a difference*, 2012, 172pp. ISBN: 978-2-940428-21-2

— , *L'éthique: un défi pour la politique. Pourquoi l'éthique importe plus que jamais en politique et comment elle peut faire la différence*, 2014, 220pp. ISBN 978-2-940428-91-5

Willem A Landman, *End-of-Life Decisions, Ethics and the Law*, 2012, 136pp. ISBN: 978-2-940428-53-3

Corneille Ntamwenge, *Éthique des affaires au Congo. Tisser une culture d'intégrité par le Code de Conduite des Affaires en RD Congo*, 2013, 132pp. ISBN: 978-2-940428-57-1

Kitoka Moke Mutondo / Bosco Muchukiwa, *Montée de l'Islam au Sud-Kivu: opportunité ou menace à la paix sociale. Perspectives du dialogue islamo-chrétien en RD Congo*, 2012, 48pp.ISBN: 978-2-940428-59-5

Elisabeth Nduku / John Tenamwenye (eds.), *Corruption in Africa: A Threat to Justice and Sustainable Peace*, 2014, 510pp. ISBN: 978-2-88931-017-3

Dicky Sofjan (with Mega Hidayati), *Religion and Television in Indonesia: Ethics Surrounding Dakwahtainment*, 2013, 112pp. ISBN: 978-2-940428-81-6

Yahya Wijaya / Nina Mariani Noor (eds.), *Etika Ekonomi dan Bisnis: Perspektif Agama-Agama di Indonesia*, 2014, 293pp. ISBN: 978-2-940428-67-0

Bernard Adeney-Risakotta (ed.), *Dealing with Diversity. Religion, Globalization, Violence, Gender and Disaster in Indonesia.* 2014, 372pp. ISBN: 978-2-940428-69-4

Sofie Geerts, Namhla Xinwa and Deon Rossouw, EthicsSA (eds.), *Africans' Perceptions of Chinese Business in Africa A Survey.* 2014, 62pp. ISBN: 978-2-940428-93-9

Nina Mariani Noor/ Ferry Muhammadsyah Siregar (eds.), *Etika Sosial dalam Interaksi Lintas Agama* 2014, 208pp. ISBN 978-2-940428-83-0

B. Muchukiwa Rukakiza, A. Bishweka Cimenesa et C. Kapapa Masonga (éds.), *L'État africain et les mécanismes culturels traditionnels de transformation des conflits.* 2015, 95pp. ISBN: 978-2-88931- 042-5

Célestin Nsengimana, *Peacebuilding Initiatives of the Presbyterian Church in Post-Genocide Rwandan Society: An Impact Assessment.* 2015, 154pp. ISBN: 978-2-88931-044-9

Bosco Muchukiwa, *Identité territoriales et conflits dans la province du Sud-Kivu, R.D. Congo*, 53pp. 2016, ISBN: 978-2-88931-113-2

Dickey Sofian (ed.), Religion, *Public Policy and Social Transformation in Southeast Asia*, 2016, 288pp. ISBN: 978-2-88931-115-6

Symphorien Ntibagirirwa, *Local Cultural Values and Projects of Economic Development: An Interpretation in the Light of the Capability Approach*, 2016, 88pp. ISBN: 978-2-88931-111-8

Karl Wilhelm Rennstich, *Gerechtigkeit für Alle. Religiöser Sozialismus in*

Mission und Entwicklung, 2016, 500pp. ISBN 978-2-88931-140-8.

African Law Series

D. Brian Dennison/ Pamela Tibihikirra-Kalyegira (eds.), *Legal Ethics and Professionalism. A Handbook for Uganda*, 2014, 400pp. ISBN 978-2-88931-011-1

Pascale Mukonde Musulay, *Droit des affaires en Afrique subsaharienne et économie planétaire*, 2015, 164pp. ISBN : 978-2-88931-044-9

Pascal Mukonde Musulay, *Démocratie électorale en Afrique subsaharienne: Entre droit, pouvoir et argent*, 2016, 209pp. ISBN 978-2-88931-156-9

China Christian Series

Yahya Wijaya; Christoph Stückelberger; Cui Wantian, *Christian Faith and Values: An Introduction for Entrepreneurs in China*, 2014, 76pp. ISBN: 978-2-940428-87-8

Yahya Wijaya; Christoph Stückelberger; Cui Wantian, *Christian Faith and Values: An Introduction for Entrepreneurs in China*, 2014, 73pp. ISBN: 978-2-88931-013-5 (in Chinese)

Christoph Stückelberger, *We are all Guests on Earth. A Global Christian Vision for Climate Justice*, 2015, 52pp. ISBN: 978-2-88931-034-0 (in Chinese, Engl. version in GE Library)

Christoph Stückelberger, Cui Wantian, Teodorina Lessidrenska, Wang Dan, Liu Yang, Zhang Yu, *Entrepreneurs with Christian Values: Training Handbook for 12 Modules*, 2016, 270pp. ISBN 978-2-88931-142-2

China Ethics Series

Liu Baocheng / Dorothy Gao (eds.), 中国的企业社会责任 *Corporate Social Responsibility in China*, 459pp. 2015, Available only in Chinese, ISBN 978-2-88931-050-0

Bao Ziran, 影响中国环境政策执行效果的因素分析 *China's Environmental Policy, Factor Analysis of its Implementation*, 2015, 431pp. Available only in Chinese, ISBN 978-2-88931-051-7

Yuan Wang and Yating Luo, *China Business Perception Index: Survey on Chinese Companies' Perception of Doing Business in Kenya*, 99pp. 2015, Available in English, ISBN 978-2-88931-062-3.

王淑芹 (Wang Shuqin) (编辑) (Ed.), *Research on Chinese Business Ethics [Volume 1]*, 2016, 413pp. ISBN: 978-2-88931-104-0

王淑芹 (Wang Shuqin) (编辑) (Ed.), *Research on Chinese Business Ethics [Volume 2]*, 2016, 400pp. ISBN: 978-2-88931-108-8

Liu Baocheng, *Chinese Civil Society*, 2016, 177pp. ISBN 978-2-88931-168-2

Readers Series

Christoph Stückelberger, *Global Ethics Applied: vol. 4, Bioethics, Religion, Leadership*, 2016, 426. ISBN 978-2-88931-130-9

Education Ethics Series

Divya Singh / Christoph Stückelberger (Eds.), *Ethics in Higher Education Values-driven Leaders for the Future*, 2017, 367pp. ISBN: 978-2-88931-165-1

Copublications & Other

Patrice Meyer-Bisch, Stefania Gandolfi, Greta Balliu (eds.), *Souveraineté et coopérations : Guide pour fonder toute gouvernance démocratique sur l'interdépendance des droits de l'homme*, 2016, 99pp. ISBN 978-2-88931-119-4

Patrice Meyer-Bisch, Stefania Gandolfi, Greta Balliu (a cura di), *Sovranità e cooperazioni: Guida per fondare ogni governance democratica sull' interdipendenza dei diritti dell'uomo*, 2016, 100pp. ISBN 978-2-88931-132-3

Reports

Global Ethics Forum 2016 Report, Higher Education – Ethics in Action: The Value of Values across Sectors, 2016, 184pp. ISBN : 978-2-88931-159-0

African Church Assets Programme ACAP: Report on Workshop March 2016, 2016, 75pp. ISBN 978-2-88931-161-3

This is only selection of our latest publications, to view our full collection please visit:

www.globethics.net/publications

Made in the USA
Columbia, SC
19 May 2017